Jack & Michael Whitehall

Him & Me

Jack & Michael Whitehall

Him & Me

With illustrations by Jack Whitehall

PENGUIN

MICHAEL
JOSEPH

MICHAEL JOSEPH

Published by the Penguin Group
Penguin Books Ltd, 80 Strand, London WC2R oRL, England
Penguin Group (USA) Inc., 375 Hudson Street, New York, New York 10014, USA
Penguin Group (Canada), 90 Eglinton Avenue East, Suite 700, Toronto, Ontario, Canada M4P 2Y3
(a division of Pearson Penguin Canada Inc.)
Penguin Ireland, 25 St Stephen's Green, Dublin 2, Ireland (a division of Penguin Books Ltd)
Penguin Group (Australia), 250 Camberwell Road,
Camberwell, Victoria 3124, Australia (a division of Pearson Australia Group Pty Ltd)
Penguin Books India Pvt Ltd, 11 Community Centre,
Panchsheel Park, New Delhi – 110 017, India
Penguin Group (NZ), 67 Apollo Drive, Rosedale, Auckland 0632, New Zealand
(a division of Pearson New Zealand Ltd)
Penguin Books (South Africa) (Pty) Ltd, Block D, Rosebank Office Park,
181 Jan Smuts Avenue, Parktown North, Gauteng, Johannesburg 2193, South Africa

Penguin Books Ltd, Registered Offices: 80 Strand, London WC2R oRL, England

www.penguin.com

First published 2013
001

Colour Reproduction by Altaimage Ltd
Printed in Italy by Printer Trento

A CIP catalogue record for this book is available from the British Library

HARDBACK
ISBN: 978-1-405-91090-3
TRADE PAPERBACK
ISBN: 978-1-405-91644-8

www.greenpenguin.co.uk

Penguin Books is committed to a sustainable
future for our business, our readers and our
planet. This book is made from paper certified
by the Forest Stewardship Council.

MIX
Paper from
responsible sources
FSC
www.fsc.org FSC™ C018179

For Hilary

Contents

Prologue

I was pleased to hear from Michael Whitehall on that Thursday morning. He had been a guest at a successful Good Companions lunch at the Reform Club two days previously and here was his call to thank me.

'Lovely lunch. By the way, I've written a book, of course. Now are you listening because we don't have much time? Jack and I think that we need an outsider who knows us well to write an introduction to our book *Him & Me*. And we've alighted on you. The problem is that we've run out of time. I'll email the book to you and if you could craft a 750-word masterpiece – warm and insightful – by the weekend, that would be just dandy. Talk later. Bye.'

I switched on my computer and with a sickening thud realized that, following the removal of a cataract the previous Saturday and the insertion of a long-range lens, I was unable to focus on anything under forty-six point. Distance – perfect. Everything close-up – pea soup.

This infirmity, added to my inexperience of literary criticism, was going to make for a tricky day.

I first ran into Jack on the set of *Would I Lie to You?*, where we were both guest panelists. He was fast becoming nationally known as a wit, performer and actor; it was easy to see why.

A charming young man, taught from time to time at Marlborough College, as it happens, by my no-nonsense daughter-in-law, Liz. Later, I mentioned having met him and she remarked, 'A very naughty boy – spent a good deal of time doodling in the margins.'

So whilst I met Jack on the set of *WILTY*, I was introduced to Father Whitehall, his *éminence grise*, in the Green Room after the show.

'Daddy, this is Nick. You'll have a lot in common. You can talk about the Blitz.'

As soon as I heard the first long, drawling vowel from Michael, I knew I was in good company. And when I turned to confront the voice, and Daddy's twinkling eye, I knew Jack came from good comic genes.

I half closed my eyes. Was I listening to Rex Harrison? I decided not. It was an edgy George Sanders, whose urbane suicide note, 'Dear World, I am leaving because I am bored', would please Michael in the unlikely event that he ever feels low.

So the septuagenarian Daddy and the not yet mid-twenties darling of the girls' upper sixth have set about a book together. And what a joy it is. Stories from their joint lives, told from their own viewpoints, each writing as well as the other. Daddy, with the driest of wits, ironic with nuggets of cruelty tossed in, to Jack's more urban vocab.

The stories pile one on top of the other, peopled by wonderful characters – the theatrical brigade from Michael's days as the most successful agent in London, and Jack's collection of increasingly bizarre pals as he enters his teenage years. Up pops Nigel Havers in a dinner jacket right at the start of the book, calling in to the Portland Hospital within minutes of Jack's birth to claim a role as a godfather with the exclusive right to be the boy's moral guardian, while Richard Griffiths would immediately start a running-away fund.

We travel through Jack's childhood and his prep school days, starting with his bravura performance to be refused admission to the Dragon School; the sports fields at Marlborough; his short-lived career as a nude life model there, part of a plan concocted to lure a dishy girl pupil to disrobe too.

So the names and anecdotes from both come pouring in, each writing lengthily on the same events, fiercely contesting the other's version. A nineteen-year tour of the Whitehall family, including the beautiful Hilary, mother to Molly and Barnaby, as well as naughty Jack.

What captivated me, apart from the arch humour and scintillating wit, was the deep affection that ran from page one between father and son. However hard they try to send one another up, it's clear that Michael and Jack have a special and unbreakable filial bond.

Oh, Michael, why couldst thou not have been my father, and if I had had a second son, Jack, would you have . . . ?

Nick Hewer

Introduction

January 2011, my good friend and long-time producer Ben Cavey suggests to me that it might be 'fun' to do a chat show complete with guests at the Edinburgh Fringe Festival with my father, Michael Whitehall. My father is a very amusing man. He was an agent to some of the country's finest actors but has never appeared on stage himself, but in a moment of weakness I mention the idea to him and he says as long as he can stay in a hotel that's separate from whatever 'squalid bedsit' I'm renting for the month, he will do it. Oh, and then sends a very long email to Ben about the terms of the deal he'd be getting. Agents, eh?

In the run-up to the Festival, booking the show becomes a nightmare. Every guest I suggest is vetoed by my father on account of them being either 'low grade' or too 'downmarket'. When I mention Jimmy Carr he simply roars with laughter, then says no.

He eventually insists that he will only travel up to the Festival if we book Simon Cowell. I tell him that I think it's highly unlikely that we'd get him as he's busy doing *The X Factor*. A lengthy rant about the death of culture in this country follows and I am asked whether I have even heard of the RSC. I realize that I have misheard him and that he actually said Simon Callow, who is up at the Fringe doing some random play. Simon Callow agrees to do it, so the show goes ahead. (Basically, if you think this book's shit you can blame Simon Callow.)

Backchat opens and is pretty well received although it is not quite as 'fun' for me as my producer made out. A long two weeks of my father telling me off for being unprofessional, accusing me every day of having a hangover and constantly reminding me that no matter how hard I tried, I would never be as good an interviewer as Michael Aspel. He also spends a lot of the show trying to flog a memoir he has written (I'm not going to mention the title here as it will only give him the publicity he so desperately craved). When I ask him to stop promoting it, he claims I am jealous as I'm 'illiterate and wouldn't have been able to write a book as good as his'.

One night I let slip that I've actually been asked to write a book myself. It is a revelation that is met with utter derision. Penguin are accused of having let their standards slip and I am told that it is my duty to literature to turn the offer down. By the way, we're still on stage when all of this is going on, the poor audience stuck in what is fast becoming a sort of middle-class *Jeremy Kyle Show*. Even our guest Miranda Hart was a little perplexed, but that was mainly because my father had spent most of the interview prior to this asking her if she was related to Tony Hart.

I must make clear the sole purpose of writing this book was not to show my father that all the money he'd, quote, 'wasted on my education to travel up and down the country telling jokes about my penis' was not frittered away and that I could achieve something, but it certainly was a factor.

I then had to decide what type of book to write. A novel seemed way beyond my abilities and the notion of anything autobiographical was ridiculous at twenty-four years old. All great writers wait till they're at least twenty-six: Ashley Cole, Jordan, Tila Tequila . . .

I racked my brains for what I could write about. Was there a subject or person who interested me? A prevalent theme in all of my work? A key figure in my stand-up shows, the inspiration for everything I do? I made the call. It turned out Kriss Akabusi already had a biography. So I decided I'd write about my father.

So how did he manage to worm his way on to this ticket? Was I pushed or did I jump? He is a very persuasive man, and he is married to an even more persuasive woman, my mother, who made it very clear that if I was going to write about him, he would have to have a right of reply. She applied a lot of pressure and towards the end of last year I called him up and said, 'Dad, do you want to write a book with me?'

His response: 'Yes, but only if my name appears above yours on the title. I am, after all, the only published author.'

'But (title of book withheld) was really just a bit of fun,' I replied. 'What I want to write is a proper in-depth insight into a relationship between a father and son, so much more than just a collection of funny stories,' and we have ended up with a book that I am proud to say . . . is just a collection of funny stories.

Writing this book has been totes amazeballs (I will be using the odd young-person phrase like this throughout the book because I know how much it annoys my dad); we've both in a sense become each other's biographer. I've been able to find out more about the man I love the most in the world than I ever thought I would; in some cases too much. To this end, I must apologize for the number of stories which end up with either my father or me without any clothes on. It seems nudity is a pretty prevalent theme in both our lives.

I also want to point out that although what you are about to read is written half and half, it is typed a hundred per cent by me, as my father hates computers, refuses to let me teach him how to use Word and struggles with the 'Interweb'. It means I have had to transcribe every word of his as he dictates it from a notepad. This included early on in the process an attempt to read to me the story of my own conception, which he thought would be a fitting way to start the book. He didn't tell me where the story was going, so I unwittingly started typing away and then, about five minutes in, was horrified to realize what he was talking about. They are images that will haunt me for the rest of my days and I'm pleased to say it is a story that will not be appearing in this book. Or hopefully any book ever.

I ended up doing what I do because of my father. He is the funniest man I know and throughout my life has been the source and, from time to time, subject of much amusement. People say they have dads that are their best friends. I've never thought of mine like that, as even my best friends I don't want to hang out with all the time. Whereas I will never tire of my dad's company even when he's getting on my tits.

As you'll see in this book, he is not a man who minces his words. In fact mincing in general is something that I would never associate with Michael Whitehall. He is certainly a product of a different generation and has some questionable views about the world (especially towards Germans), but is a loving father and devoted friend to me. Take everything he says with a pinch of salt and everything I say with a pinch of grammar. That's the main thing I've learnt from writing this; my father was right, I am basically illiterate.

One final thing. The real force behind this book is not me or my father, it is my mother. She has been our referee, our editor, administrator, tea maker, the one who's told us which family members we can and cannot make jokes about, and she also types all those bits of my father's stories I can't bear to listen to. She is a saint and by the end of this book you'll understand why – she's put up with us for over two decades. This book should really be called *Him, Her & Me.*

Jack Whitehall

P.S. Throughout the book you'll find annotations in blue that have been added in by my father and others in black that have been added in by me. Also, my father was a theatrical agent and over the years he picked up some rather annoying industry habits. To be exact, he is a massive name-dropper. A lot of the names he drops are people you will never have heard of (especially you younger readers). So I have taken the liberty of providing a brief glossary of names. My dad said this was totally unnecessary and an insult to the illustrious individuals who crop up in his anecdotes, but you'll find it at the end of the book anyway.

Part I

First
Memories

CHAPTER 1

A Black-Tie Affair

– MICHAEL WHITEHALL –

JACK'S BIRTH DAY, 7 JULY 1988, was a particularly auspicious date for me. Late fatherhood had been on my mind for most of my life. When I entered the wrong end of my forties, my mother, Nora, was forever reminding me that I would make a wonderful father but not if I left it too late.

'I know you're an agent and that all those actors you look after, or whatever you call it, are like your children – they certainly behave like children, and spoilt ones at that – but it isn't the same. You should think of yourself for once. I still don't understand why you muck about with them anyway; they're only interested in themselves. If only you could get yourself a proper job!'

I wasn't quite sure what I was doing having this conversation at this point in my life with my eighty-year-old mother. I was beginning to feel like Anthony Perkins in *Psycho*, by coincidence a client of mine at the time.*

'Picasso fathered a child when he was eighty-two,' said Nora. 'So there's no reason why you shouldn't.'

Nora liked quoting Picasso at me endlessly, drawing comparisons between the Spanish artist and myself despite the fact that in this anecdote he was twice my age.

I had always dreamt of having children some day and I couldn't quite believe it when it finally happened. I was hugely proud of Hilary

*CLUNK The first of many name-drops you will see in this book. Older readers, you might recognize a few; younger readers, you'll have heard of hardly any of them. Maybe to make it fun you could play a name-drop drinking game, one measure for every time he does it, two measures if you've heard of the person, and if it's Peter Bowles finish your drink.

for giving me such an amazing baby boy and so proud of him too. I quickly became an older father bore, and have remained one ever since!

Peter Saunders, the obstetrician, delivered Jack at the Portland Hospital wearing a dinner jacket, not at our insistence but because he was on his way to a gynaecological dinner.

'Do you want to put on some gloves and help?' he asked me.

For the money I was paying him, I thought he could do it on his own so I declined his invitation. A face peered round the door of Hilary's room.

'Any news?' asked Nigel.

It was my client the actor Nigel Havers.* I'd called him earlier and mentioned Hilary was coming to the boil, though to be honest I hadn't expected him to appear quite so quickly. The nurse on the front desk was in such a flutter at seeing Nigel, of *A Passage to India* fame, that she ushered him straight to the delivery room. By coincidence he was also wearing a dinner jacket. Looking back, the whole scene had suddenly become very *Downton Abbey*.

*CLUNK I'll stop it now, it's a waste of ink.

Aka 'the posh man' from Coronation Street and I'm a Celebrity Get Me Out of Here!

'Are you on your way somewhere?' I asked him.

'No, actually. When you rang I was trying on an old dinner jacket I bought from Piero de Monzi in Chelsea years ago to see if it still fitted, so I thought I'd come straight over.'

'Loved you in *Chariots of Fire* by the way,' said Peter Saunders, mid-delivery. 'Did you do all your own hurdling? Care to help?'

Peter offered Nigel some gloves as Jack's head started to protrude from Hilary's nether regions.*

'No, I'm fine, thanks, old boy,' said Nigel. 'As far as I can see you seem to be doing jolly well.'

And he was; producing a very handsome baby weighing seven pounds and fourteen-and-a-half ounces.

'My wife's going to kill me,' said Peter as he was clearing up the debris. 'I've got blood all over my dress shirt and it was brand new. I should have worn an apron but I always think I look like a pathologist in those things.'

As Peter departed, Hilary handed Jack to me. Nigel and I headed off on a lap of honour and left Hilary to be tidied up. While I went to the loo Nigel struck up a conversation with a dowager and her expectant daughter who were standing outside their room. We were back in *Downton Abbey* again.

'What a beautiful baby, Mr Havers,' she said. 'He looks so like you.'

'Thank you so much, but he's not actually my baby,' said Nigel. 'I'm just holding him while my friend goes to the loo.'

'Left holding the baby, eh?' gushed the toothy daughter.

'Quite,' said Nigel as I returned to join the party.

It is true the baby Jack did bare a striking resemblance to Nigel, and what with my friend's reputation as a bit of a ladies' man, I made a mental note to double check with him later just in case there was anything he wanted to tell me.

'Have you seen that poor baby over there?' said the dowager.

'Why, what's wrong with it?' asked the daughter.

'Oh, the poor little mite's got the most terrible dark rash across its face and over its tiny little hands too.'

'Mummy, don't be ridiculous, there's nothing wrong with it. It's a black baby!' she replied.

'What!' shrieked the dowager. 'At the Portland?'**

*Is that within BMA guidelines? That you're allowed to offer anyone that just happens to walk into the room a go at delivering a baby?

**Wow!

While Nigel and I had been showing Jack off, another two of my clients, Richard Griffiths and Leslie Phillips,* had phoned the hospital and been put through to Hilary. Leslie had called reverse charges, saying that he was in someone else's house, but Hilary was sure she'd heard his wife in the background, muttering and banging pots and pans around while she was cooking. Leslie always found a way to ring me reverse charges. It was business, so he thought the office, that is me, should pay for the call.

*CLUNK X 3, triple drop!

'Have we heard back from the BBC yet?' Leslie asked Hilary. 'They promised they'd have a decision by today.'

'Actually I've been rather tied up today having a baby and things, but I'll get Michael to call you back.'

Ignoring Hilary's reference to a baby, Leslie said, 'Will you tell Michael I really need this job? Maybe we should meet up and discuss what other things there are in the pipeline. Why don't I take him to lunch tomorrow?'

I'd had several experiences of Leslie Phillips 'taking me to lunch', all resulting in me paying the bill. On more than one occasion he'd pulled the dodgy credit card trick on me. This involved snatching the bill as soon as it hit the table and producing a card which the waiter would quickly return as it was out of date, in some cases by several years. I didn't hurry to call him back.

A rare picture of me and Jack where I've got all the hair.

"Ere, you're that guy from Chariots of Fire, aren't ya?'

Godmother Jo – a rose amongst thorns.

'Please Uncle Vernon, don't lock me in a cupboard under the stairs.'

We returned Richard's call and asked if he would like to be Jack's godfather.

'Delighted,' he said. 'I'll start putting money aside for a running-away fund for him, which he can use when he's eighteen. Fast cars, loose women, Las Vegas, whatever.'

Forward planning was always one of Richard's strong suits. As Nigel had heard me offering Richard a godfather role, and bearing in mind the competitiveness of actors, I thought it would be churlish not to ask Nigel as well.

'Of course, I'd love to,' he replied. 'Richard can look after Jack's finances and I'll take care of his morals.'

I didn't think Nigel was the perfect casting to oversee Jack's moral welfare but I knew he would provide him with plenty of entertainment over the years.

'Isn't it a bit early to be arranging godparents?' asked Hilary sleepily. The exertion of the last few hours was beginning to take its toll and Jack was looking pretty snoozy too.

'Well, we've had nine months to think about it,' I replied.

'I noticed you didn't suggest Leslie Phillips,' she mumbled. 'I'd like Jo Williams as well, to keep an eye on them.' I agreed, as Jo Williams was an old schoolfriend of Hilary's and one of the few I hadn't fallen out with.*

With that decision made Hilary and Jack fell asleep.

'Let's go and wet the baby's head somewhere, shall we?' said Jack's newly appointed moral compass.

By the time I got home I was extremely drunk and very hungry. There was nothing appropriate in the fridge for immediate consumption, so I opted for a tin of corned beef from the larder.**

As they do whenever I open any kind of tin, the key snapped off and I had to finish the job with a screwdriver. Drunk and desperate for food, I began scooping bits of meat out of the tin with my fingers until one of them attached itself to a razor-sharp piece of metal. Blood started spurting everywhere; it was like being back at the Portland. It was too late to call our local friendly doctor and, anyway, I was slurring too much to be able to explain what had happened, so I decided to call Hilary.

'Sorry, darling, did I wake you up?'

*Correction:
The only one
you hadn't
fallen out with.

**He's not really a
late-night-kebab-
on-the-way-home kind of
guy. Our larder is often
stocked with things like
corned beef, Spam and
other foodstuffs that
evoke wartime rationing
and allow my father
to fondly remember
the Blitz.

Hilary drowsily told me to put my finger under the cold tap and get some plasters from the bathroom.

'I'm feeling faint. Loss of blood probably,' I said.

'Too many vodka and tonics probably,' she replied. 'I'm sure you'll live.'

'How's my beautiful Jack?' I asked.

'Asleep, just like I was,' came the reply.

'I think I'll go to bed now,' I said. 'To be honest, I'm feeling pretty drained. It's been quite an emotional day for me, sitting in the hospital waiting for Jack to be born, ringing all these people, having to talk to endless doctors and nurses, keeping Nigel entertained and, of course, having my first baby at the age of forty-eight, and all the stress that that entails. I think it's been pretty amazing for me, don't you?

'Hello. . .? Hello?'

Silence on the other end of the phone and then a gentle snore. Still on a high, I tried to bore several of my friends about the momentous arrival, but fortunately for them they'd all gone to bed, so I headed off there too.

The following morning I was woken up by our cleaning lady, Mrs James. Mrs James was a native of Antigua* but more lately of West Kensington. She was an active member of the local Evangelist community, a brand of religion that I have given a wide berth during my life. I was raised a Catholic and for me church is about incense and guilt, not singing and holding hands. To my mind, a very small amount of happy clappiness goes a long way.

*Oh God, this could be dodgy territory.

Mrs James loved a bit of melodrama and this was a big moment for her. 'Where is Miss Hilary?' she asked nervously.

'She's in the hospital, Mrs James,' I replied.

'They have taken her, Mr Michael?'

'Well, I took her actually.'

Hilary had gone into hospital a few days early, as Peter Saunders was about to go off on holiday and thought it was best to get the baby induced before he went. Peter, as you may have realized, was never one to let something like a birth get in the way of his social arrangements.

'But they took her before her time, Mr Michael. You shouldn't have allowed it! You must ask the Lord to watch over her and protect her from evil spirits!' she wailed.

A BLACK-TIE AFFAIR

23

'Just calm down, Mrs James. She's fine and so is the baby.'

'The baby has been born before its time. Have they taken it from her? Don't let them take it from her, Mr Michael. The Lord will not forgive you.' Mrs James then started telling me about prematurely delivered 'devil babies' in Dominica, where her aunt lived, and the dangers of brain damage if mothers were forced into hospital to have their babies too early.

'Nobody forced Hilary to go to hospital,' I said. 'I took her there in the back of the Mercedes and a nice nurse showed us up to her room when we arrived.'

'And is the baby a boy or a girl?' she asked.

When I told her it was a boy she said that God had sent me a boy so that he could take over the family when I died. It was important at my age to have a son, she told me. Little did I know what was in store for me!

On my return home that evening her worries about Jack seemed to have subsided and she had transferred her concerns to the world of domestic appliances. She had left a note on the kitchen table saying: *Somethin' bad with hover it dont pik nuffin.**

I replaced the Hoover bag, probably for the first time. Perhaps fatherhood was changing me.

Two days later I was heading back to the Portland to collect mother and son. Hilary asked me to pick up a Moses basket at Peter Jones on the way. I hailed a cab in Sloane Square, carrying the basket and a couple of other packages.

'Portland Hospital please,' I said to the cabby.

I was rather breathless as the parcels were heavier than I'd thought. 'Presents for the grandchild, guv?' asked the driver.

'My son actually,' I snapped.

'They'll change your life, guv. I've got three grandchildren, Harley, Dean and little Tiffany.** They're all right little scamps but they keep you young. I bet your daughter's as pleased as punch.'

'My wife actually,' I replied.

He completely ignored me as only a cab driver can and spent the rest of the journey giving me unwanted advice from 'one granddad to another'. We finally arrived at the Portland and I told the bossy-looking receptionist that I'd come to collect Hilary and Jack Whitehall.

*I really hope those were Mrs James's actual words. The prospect of my father inventing Afro-Caribbean patois is too painful (and potentially offensive) to imagine.

I still have the note if you'd like to check it out, Jack

**He's definitely made these names up.

'Are you the father?' she asked in an accusatory way.

'Well, I hope so,' I replied. 'I've just spent eighty-five pounds on a bloody Moses basket.'

1. I simply do not believe that you changed the Hoover bag.

2. How and why was Nigel Havers just allowed to wander into a delivery room? I know this was the eighties but it's a bit suspect. Also, why was he so desperate to be there in the first place? Isn't the birth meant to be a kind of 'family only' affair?

3. Is Nigel Havers my real dad?

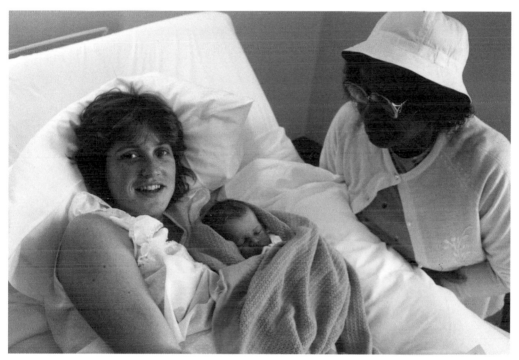

Mrs James looks over the sleeping devil child.

CHAPTER 2

The Curse of Timmy Twinkle

— JACK WHITEHALL —

Timmy Twinkle is a name that will forever strike fear into my heart. When I was growing up Timmy Twinkle was my father's favourite children's entertainer. A favourite children's entertainer is an odd thing for a grown man to have, but there we go. No matter how much we protested, he was gonna saddle us with him.

'gonna' — please write properly

Twinkle did not have the big, warm, cuddly grin of a Mr Tumble, nor the cheeky, infectious energy of Dick and/or Dom. In fact, he didn't look like a children's entertainer at all. With his old grey face, strands of straggly hair clinging to his slippery pate and thick glasses masking a pair of cold, dead eyes, Timmy Twinkle resembled more than anything else a 1990s Tory MP. Perhaps that's why my dad liked him. His appearance was made all the more sinister by the bright blue magic cape and 'wacky' patchwork adult pyjamas. Imagine John Gummer in fancy dress.*

*Nothing wrong with resembling John Selwyn Gummer. He was an excellent Chairman of the Conservative Party during the Thatcher government.

He was, in short, not the kind of man you'd want anywhere near your children. Even the photograph he chose for his website looked like a mug shot you'd see printed in the *Sun* under a story about a woman who's gone missing. Everything about him was creepy.

How, you might think, did a truly terrifying man like this ever get any bookings? Well, this very flaw was the reason my father had such fondness for Timmy Twinkle. There was no carrot in his act, just stick, and a lot of stick at that.[*] He presided over his young audience with all the joy and cuddliness of a guard in a Russian Gulag. I recently watched a home video of Timmy Twinkle in his pomp at my sixth birthday. It was almost as creepy as an episode of *Top of the Pops* from the seventies.

*Discipline is essential in the child entertainment business and this was Twinkle's strong suit.

Twinkle started his 'act' by warming up the crowd of obstreperous six-year-olds with a bit of cheery banter with the front row. It's a technique I've deployed many times in my own stand-up shows, although when I do it I like to think I have a little more warmth than Twinkle.

'Hello, what's your name?' Timmy asked my friend Natalya, a sweet, shy blue-eyed little girl who was sucking her thumb. She didn't answer and instead just tugged on his cape with a snotty hand.

'Is someone a little shy?' Timmy asked. I don't doubt he was trying to sound friendly, but he sounded so menacing those words still wake me from nightmares. I'm convinced that they may yet be the last words I ever hear.

'She's called Natalya!' her brother William[**] said with such enthu-siasm that he flecked Timmy's glasses with spit. 'Why are you wearing pyjamas? It's not bedtime, stupid,' William continued, oblivious to the danger. 'You're silly.'

**A very difficult child

As a heckle, it's not up there with the best, but it annoyed Timmy Twinkle. Twinkle, though, was a pro. He'd done the Putney/Barnes suburban circuit for years. He could handle this shit.

'Thank you, William. If you'd just quieten down now,' Timmy said, just about resisting the urge to make his first magic trick sawing William in half for the crime of questioning his bizarre dress sense.

By this time, the lack of content in Timmy's act meant that his easily distracted crowd were on their feet, wandering around the hall, talking among themselves and generally not paying much attention to Mr Twinkle.

'Sit down, children,' he said firmly, trying to assert some control. This had no effect on the more boisterous children, which included

William and myself. I was the birthday boy – I wasn't going to be told what to do on my special day, especially by a man in pyjamas. We decided that we'd ignore Mr Twinkle and carry on our game of who could spin round the quickest.

Had he lost control this early on? The parents looked concerned. 'Would you please sit down?' said Timmy slightly louder, but not loud enough to have an effect.

'SIT DOWN!' he bellowed suddenly at the top of his voice, hurling his wand down on to the floor and narrowly missing Natalya's head. He'd shouted so loudly that his face had done that thing Alex Ferguson's did when he'd berated an official. Twinkle was bright red, swelling with rage, he looked as though he was somewhere between having a stroke and doing a massive poo.*

Oh Jack, please.

Every child in the hall shot to the floor, where we remained rooted throughout the rest of the show. Twinkle's performance consisted of a few balloon tricks and a little puppet show, both of which seemed very out of place in a party that now had all the atmosphere of a non-alcoholic wake. Any audience interaction had to be asked for several times, so scared were we children of speaking out of turn. For all we knew, an errant 'He's behind you!' could have resulted in Timmy Twinkle locking you up in his magic box before slinging you into the back of his van, never to be seen again except in grainy images under the headline 'Tragic Tot'.

One trick of his involved him smashing a watch to bits with a hammer. This is when he looked most at home, crashing the hammer down on to the table, showing more fervour with every blow, possibly substituting the watch in his imagination for the dreams he'd once had, or William's hand perhaps.

'Who wants to help me out with my next trick?' he asked, re-arranging his comb-over across his sweaty forehead and holding the hammer in a clenched fist. Bizarrely there were no takers. In the home video, if you look beyond the sea of scared six-year-old faces, you can just make out my father in the background turning to a friend of his, no doubt to remark how much he admired Mr Twinkle's technique.

'Twinkle's always had bloody good discipline. You won't hear a word out of them.'

And so our parents were able to enjoy a pleasant hour in the garden drinking, while we were held hostage in the hall by a hammer-wielding master of the Dark Arts. This is probably why my parties as a child were so well attended. Kids that I barely even knew came; their parents had heard about Twinkle. I don't know where the Pied Piper of Putney is now, and I daren't find out, but I still worry that if I were to say his name in the mirror three times he might burst through it and choke me to death with a balloon poodle.

My father's grip over my birthday celebrations didn't loosen with age. Throughout my early teens, my birthdays would always have to be dinner parties or drinks held at the house so he could make sure no funny business occurred. On my sixteenth birthday, a cigarette butt was found in the flower bed and he reacted like he'd found a used needle. A witch-hunt ensued and Toby Roper was given a two-year ban from our house. I was loath to tell anyone that it was, in fact, my cigarette, as I knew I too would have been out on the street. Anyway, it didn't matter that much (cos) didn't really get on that well with Toby anyway, so I was happy for him to be the fall guy.

How much did I spend on your education?

Me organizing my first ever game of spin the bottle.

Do not approach this man.

But as we approached my eighteenth I wanted something a bit more exciting than dinner at my mum and dad's house. All my friends were having cool eighteenths at nightclubs or bars, and one of my mates had even hired a boat that went up the Thames. I didn't want to be the loser stuck at home still smoking cigarettes behind the shed.

'I'm not having my eighteenth at home,' I told my parents.

'Well, where then?' asked my father defensively, as though he couldn't even conceive of a birthday venue anywhere other than his garden.

'I want to have it at Cuba Club,' I told him. Cuba Club was a favourite of mine at that time, a seedy bar in Fulham that was the only place in London you could get into without ID and then get absolutely obliterated for under a tenner. It was a pretty skanky venue, full of seedy Latino gents who danced very crotchily in the direction of middle-aged Eastern European women as a DJ played Chumbawamba and spoke over every track as though we were all at a wedding or a rural fair.

*What the hell are those?

Cuba Club is the kind of bar that does deals like 'buy two Jägerbombs* and get the morning-after pill free'. If the walls of its seedy little hidden booths could talk, they would do so on a premium line. Cuba Club was sticky with DNA. I reckon if you took that light they have in *CSI* and flashed it over the floor, it would blow the bulb. For horny teenage boys, though, it was nirvana.

'That brothel on the Fulham Road that's full of those tarty slags?' said my father.

'Yeah. I don't think that's the *Time Out* description, though.' My protests were in vain, his foot was being put firmly down.

'It's my birthday, I'm not having it at home and that's final,' I said. I was standing my ground on this one and, after much argument, we eventually came to an agreement. I would not have it at Cuba Club, but my parents would have to find a club for me to host my party. Deal.

A week later my dad told me to come into his study to draw up a guest list for the club. Guest list? I thought Dad had pulled it out of the bag with one of the more exclusive West End clubs. Maybe he'd called the people at Chinawhite or Whisky Mist? We'd be partying with celebs, seducing heiresses with urbane conversation over expensive champagne cocktails. Nice!

'We need five people,' said my dad. Five was a small number, but, hey, it's probably because Dad's got us VIP passes. People would be talking about this party for months!

'OK, well, girls-wise,' I said, 'I want Natalya and Molly.'

— My beautiful daughter.

Dad sighed. 'There are no women allowed into the club, Jack.'

This was odd. I thought most clubs insist on a girl–boy ratio of about 7:1. I mean, that's why I invited Natalya and Molly in the first place. Then it suddenly struck me. My dad *hadn't*, had he? It would make sense – small group, no women, an eighteenth. It would be amazing, but it just seemed so un-him.

'Dad, are you taking us to a strip club?'

'Don't be ridiculous. Of course we're not going to a bloody lap club. What do you take me for?' he replied.

Well, I took him for a lot of things, but not the kind of man who takes his son to Stringfellows.

'I was going to try to keep it as a surprise but, if you must know, we're going to one of the most exclusive members' clubs in London.'

'Right . . . Groucho? Soho House?'

'My club,' said my dad. 'The Garrick Club.'

'What the fuck?!'

The Garrick was founded in 1831. Its patron is the Duke of Edinburgh, a man my father admires above all others. My father himself has been a member since 1979. The club is situated in Garrick Street, in a large Georgian building, and it boasts a member-ship largely drawn from politicians, literary types and theatricals.

— Early Victorian, actually.

There's a pretty broad range of ages, running from a handful of young Turks knocking on the door of fifty to anywhere around the hundred mark.*

The girl-to-boy ratio – the all-important factor at an eighteenth – was less broad. Not that women were banned. I assume there are some female chefs, for instance, and maybe a lady cleaner or two. But for any other woman to cross the threshold used to require a very special occasion indeed, and even then they were made to walk up the back staircase. And the Garrick made no excep-tions. My father once bumped into the Queen Mother, someone he

*This is ridiculous. The Garrick has a huge number of young members – Hugh Bonneville, Robert Lindsay and Simon Russell Beale to name but three.

admired almost as much as the Duke of Edinburgh, coming up the back stairs, presumably on her way to rendezvous with her bookie. The rules have relaxed somewhat in recent years, but even now it is certainly not a club you'd visit to pick up girls. I think the phrase is 'sausage-fest'.

What on earth is a sausage-fest? The Garrick Club's pork and Stilton sausages are some of the finest I have ever tasted, and they do a very mean toad-in-the-hole.

My father once told me a story regarding the membership book at the Garrick, which is kept in a members-only *salon privé*. When someone applies to become a member their name is put in the book and other members have to sign their names next to them and five or so years later they get elected. Although from time to time a name can be 'blackballed': on one occasion the politician Quentin Davies, who was notorious for having crossed the floor of the House of Commons from the Conservative to the Labour benches, wanted to join the Garrick.*

* *I have never been a fan of MPs who do this. Sir Hartley Shawcross changed parties and was appropriately nicknamed Sir Shortly Floorcross.*

Didn't Winston Churchill change parties? That's different. Twice.

***Categorically.*

Shortly after Quentin Davies's name appeared in the members' book someone wrote in thick black pen across the entire page: *You must be joking.* His application was withdrawn a day later. My godfather Nigel, also a member, told me that 'You must be joking' was written in italic handwriting that looked suspiciously like my father's. He denies it.**

Don't get me wrong. The Garrick is a beautiful place. It houses an impressive collection of fine paintings and boasts the best wine cellar in London. In the loos there are combs floating in jars of greenish pomade like rare preserved fish or Napoleon Bonaparte's penis. But if you shone that light from *CSI* around it the worst you'd discover is the corpse of one of its older members. It is, therefore, less than ideal for an eighteenth birthday party. Especially if, like me, you had been hoping for some birthday sex. The best I'd get in the Garrick was a bit of birthday sexism.

As the four of my friends whom my father had deemed worthy to come to the Garrick arrived, they were surprised to discover that there was no queue outside, no young girls in minidresses, no roped-off smoking area, no viciously slow-witted, knuckle-dragging bouncer, not even a sexy door-whore with a clipboard. Just the hall porter in his green suit and tie.

'We're meeting my father, Michael Whitehall,' I said.

'Not dressed like that, you aren't!' he replied.

We were all in smart shirts and proper shoes, but as he pointed out, no one is allowed into the Garrick without a jacket and tie. Lucky for us he had some in the cloakroom.

'I'll go down and see what we've got. You lads wait here.'

My impeccably coordinated birthday outfit was ruined somewhat by the jacket he returned with: a thick dark corduroy number that was far too big for me and still had dandruff on the shoulders from its previous occupier (who'd possibly been that corpse the *CSI* guys discovered). I looked ridiculous.

We went into the club to meet my father, who was already drinking with two other members at the bar. If I remember correctly they were discussing the Crimean War as we arrived, one of my dad's drinking buddies being the last surviving participant.*

My mates looked very unimpressed. I'd told them that as we were going out to a West End club we'd probably bump into a celebrity or two. But at least this was the only element of the evening that, technically, I didn't let them down on. Sure, the celebrity in question may not have been the footballer or glamour model my mates were expecting, but he was a celebrity nonetheless.

'Chaps, meet Peter Sallis,' my father said, indicating the younger man next to the war vet. 'Though obviously a few of you might already have realized who he is.'

The look of 'Who the fuck is this guy?' on my mates' faces was crystal clear, but my father misinterpreted it as star-struck awe, assuming that my eighteen-year-old friends were *Last of the Summer Wine* aficionados and that when he said good evening to them they would surely recognize him as the voice of Wallace of *Wallace and Gromit* fame.

Leaving Peter at the bar, we sat down in the main dining room and were treated to a set menu my father had arranged. The Garrick Club kitchen is very much aimed at pleasing the older palate. It's a red meat and red wine affair, with no piri-piri chicken in sight. Our main course, for instance, was liver and bacon; offal is not a very popular dish among the youth of today.**

My friend Freddie had prepared a short toast to make for me. He stood up, but, just as he clinked his glass and cleared his throat, a white-haired member (as though there were any other) looked over

*If this were true he would be at least 175. Very likely!

**Their loss. Offal is delicious.

from the main table in the middle of the room and barked at him to 'Sit down and be quiet please.' And thus, in that moment, my birthday parties had come full circle. Even aged eighteen my father had found a way of taking us to the only place where he could find the spirit of Timmy Twinkle. For all I know, the old man in the Garrick Club that day *was* Timmy Twinkle. Although I suspect Timmy is now in prison, or alternatively on the run in Argentina, wanted for lashing out at a child for snotting on his cape.

Most people end up having some sort of story from their eighteenth. Maybe they got off with the girl they'd always fancied at school but were too afraid to talk to. Others maybe got so drunk that they had to have their stomachs pumped. But, for me, the most exciting thing that happened on the night I turned eighteen was that when I went to the loo I took a piss next to the Bishop of London.

'Well, you can tick that off your bucket list,' my father said when I told him.

Hmm.

1. Your failure to recognize Peter Sallis is a failure on your part and certainly not Peter's. Peter is not only a very recognizable actor but also a very distinguished one. If you want to learn about real television acting, watch Peter in The Flaxborough Chronicles or The Pallisers, two stand-out programmes of the mid 70s. In short, if you were to have half the career that Peter Sallis has had (and I have yet to see any evidence that you will) your mother and I would be very proud.

2. Jack is being rude about the Garrick Club because he's jealous that he's not a member. The Garrick is a warm and friendly place where its members can enjoy fine food, wine and good company. Jack has repeatedly shunned my suggestions that he apply, even though I suspect he would be blackballed. He would probably rather frequent a dive like the Groucho Club (named after that deeply unfunny American comedian, a far cry from David Garrick, one of our greatest classical actors), where he can cackle and preen at the tittle-tattle of whatever dregs they let in there, while drinking Jaguar Bombs.

3. I don't believe you know what 'obstreperous' means.

The Master of the Dark Arts at work.

Part II

School's Out

CHAPTER 3

Fathers' Race

- MICHAEL WHITEHALL -

WHEN JACK WENT TO HIS FIRST PREP SCHOOL, Tower House in East Sheen, there was much discussion as to whether or not I should compete in the fathers' race at the annual sports day.

'Please don't, Michael,' said Hilary, 'you're bound to twist something.'

'Or get your gout back,' added Jack. At the time I was afflicted with a hereditary gout problem.

As I lurched into my fifties it might have helped my wife and children to view me in a more youthful light had I not been so totally inept at playing any kind of sport. John McEnroe's children must have been so proud of their older father's achievements on the tennis court, I thought, and what about all those American veteran golfers with trophy wives and adoring children running into their arms at the end of a gruelling tournament?

I'd avoided teaching sport to the children, leaving that to Hilary. When it comes to sport she is Wonder Woman. She was head of games at her school, played county-level tennis and held just about every school athletics record there was. She swam like a fish too. She still plays hockey on a regular basis, a lethal game which seems to largely involve one group of robust young women inflicting serious bodily harm upon another group, as their partners look on worriedly from the touchline. There is seldom a Saturday my wife does not come home with some kind of bruising on her legs and arms, but no matter how much I try to persuade her that it might be time to pack it in, she refuses to hang up her . . . racket? bat? mallet? ⟵————————— Stick!

Eventually, after years of avoiding instruction of my children in these matters, I decided to rack my brains for at least one skill that I could pass on to prevent my total emasculation. I came up with the idea of teaching them to drive.

'Don't be ridiculous.' said Hilary, 'There is no way you could possibly teach anyone to drive, and certainly not any of our children. You lost your temper after five minutes of trying to teach Jack to ride a bike and, if you remember, had Molly in floods of tears after her first lesson when you told her that bikes weren't really designed for girls to ride.'

'What I actually said was that girls weren't designed to ride bikes,* but anyway driving a car is a very different kind of skill,' I replied.   *Oh well, that's so much better.

'Please don't let Daddy teach me to drive, Mummy,' said Molly. 'The only thing I'll learn from him is how to swear or maybe to make obscene hand gestures at cyclists.'

When my dear mother, Nora, took her driving test for the tenth time, at the age of fifty-two, she managed to hit someone on a zebra crossing. She claimed at the time she'd been blinded by the flashing orange lights, or Belisha beacons as they were called in those days, and hadn't seen the elderly pensioner until he had shot across the bonnet and was staring in horror at her through the windscreen of her Hillman Imp. Fortunately he wasn't seriously hurt. When Nora returned to the test centre she asked the instructor if she had passed.

'Unfortunately not,' said the instructor. 'If you hit a pedestrian on a zebra crossing, Mrs Whitehall, it's an automatic fail. But better luck next time!'

She did, in fact, pass on her twelfth attempt, and drove really badly for the next thirty years.

Jack never took me up on my offer of lessons, which with hindsight is probably a good thing as the relationship between driver and instructor is fraught with danger.

But back in his prep school days, and after much discussion, Jack had a sudden change of heart regarding my running in the fathers' race. 'But of course you should run, Daddy. All the other fathers will be and if Trevor McDonald is taking part and can cope, surely you can?' Trevor's son, also called Jack, was at the school; he was one of the few fathers who made me feel slightly less geriatric.

So it was decided: I was running. I would make Jack proud even if it killed me, and I would have an opportunity to see if there was a father older than me at his school, a quest that I was on constantly throughout Jack's schooldays.

I was meeting Superman, Christopher Reeve, for lunch later that day at the Ivy, so had arrived at the sports field in shirt, tie and suit and a very nice new pair of Church's brogues that I'd recently bought in their summer sale.

'I told you to wear shorts, Daddy.'

I was then, and am now, a firm believer that only a certain type of man can get away with a short. I am not one of them.*

*I concur.

'Next thing you'll be telling me you want me to wear spikes.'

'Don't be silly, Daddy. It's a fathers' race not the Olympics, but did you have to wear a suit?'

To appease him I lost the jacket.

Sports day always attracted a good turnout of parents and Hilary was in her element, catching up with all the school gossip as a fringe member of a coven of mothers who always seemed to be in the know on a range of new school developments, often well before the school was aware of them. Mrs Pollock, known to her friends as Fishy, was quietly confident that her husband, Quentin, would win, having come second last year.

'Quentin felt that he'd been seriously interfered with at the start last year,' said Fishy. 'He's going to be more physical this year.'

Fishy had asked Hilary if I was running and when she said I was, she'd told Hilary that her father had been in a fathers' race when she was at St Mary's, Ascot, and he had ruptured his anterior cruciate ligament and had had to give up sport as a result. Hilary told her that I had never been involved in any sport anyway, apart from the odd game of clock golf,** so that wouldn't be a problem for me. Hilary told another mother, Mrs Chen, that I was having lunch with Christopher Reeve at the Ivy later and Mrs Chen asked her if I could get a table for them the following week, as whenever she rang they were fully booked for months in advance.

**What the hell is clock golf? Is it an app? What's an app?

'Fathers' invitation: one hundred metre sprint,' announced the

HIM & ME

sports master, Mr Townsend, through his antique loudhailer.*

As I began to walk towards the starting line Hilary and Jack ran after me.

'Please, Michael, you really don't have to. Why don't you let me run for you?' said Hilary.

'Don't be ridiculous, it's the fathers' race and, anyway, you're running in the mothers' sack race,' I said. 'Don't worry, I'll be fine.'

'But please be careful,' said Jack. 'It will be so embarrassing if you fall over.' In fact, I nearly fell over in the melee of fathers jockeying for position on the starting line.

'Inside lane for me,' shouted an aggressive young father to his wife as he jogged off in the direction of the headmaster, Mr Beale, who was brandishing a lethal-looking starting pistol.** I was beginning to feel like I was in Evelyn Waugh's *Decline and Fall*.

'Good luck,' said Jack, slapping me on the back and slightly winding me.*** 'I'm sure you'll be fine, just remember to dip your head at the finishing line in case it's close.'

'And don't try to show off,' said Hilary.

On your marks, get set...

As I jostled for a good starting position I was baulked by a small athletic-looking Hong Kong banker type, whom I recognized as Mr Chen. His son Harvey was in Jack's year and one of his most competitive friends, always beating him at everything. I saw this as an opportunity of getting even with the Chen family.

Mr Chen, looking patronizingly at my footwear, asked, 'Don't you have any other shoes?'

'No, actually,' I replied, wondering whether I should tell him that they were new and that I was 'running them in', but I remembered that he had absolutely no sense of humour.

I then noticed his footwear. He was wearing running shoes complete with spikes.

'I'm more of a four hundred metres man myself,' he said, chugging from a bottle of isotonic Lucozade before slinging it to the ground behind him, 'but I'm going to do my best.'

Mr Beale gave a short speech to the assembled fathers, thanking us for coming and reminding us that it was the 'taking part' that mattered and warning us not to be too competitive.

'It's important that the children don't think that we are taking this too seriously, otherwise they will be very upset if their fathers end up at the rear of the field.' For some reason, Mr Beale seemed to be staring at me when he said this.

The fathers began to take their starting positions as Mr Beale called

There was no need
for a photo finish.

Consoling Jack and Molly
after my defeat.

HIM & ME

them in. They all looked half my age and, typically, Trevor McDonald had had to take an urgent call on his mobile and had withdrawn. I could have beaten him, I thought.*

'On your marks!'

All the other fathers knelt down and put their hands against the line. Quentin Pollock flexed his elbows. I opted for a standing start, a little concerned that if I went down to a crouching sprinter's start, I might never get up from it.

'Get set!'

I got off to a flying start, having massively jumped the gun. I was a full three metres in front of an irate Mr Chen, but unfortunately within seconds the Church's brogues began to even things up. They may have had a one hundred per cent leather sole and heel but they were certainly no good on one hundred metres' worth of slightly damp and very uneven turf. As I slithered my way to the back of the field, puffing like a traction engine, I felt a shooting pain across my chest. My God, I thought, I'm having a heart attack. Now that would really embarrass Jack and Hilary. I could see the finishing tape in the near distance as I began to lose my balance. If only Superman were here and not waiting for me at the Ivy, he'd know what to do. And then I ran into the geography teacher, Mr Wright, who was standing at the finish with a clipboard.

'I'm afraid you were last,' he said helpfully, 'by about thirty metres.'**

I'd never been a fan of Wright but seeing as I'd lost most of the feeling in my legs I was grateful for his supportive shoulder. Mr Chen, to no one's surprise, won, followed by six foot five inches of Quentin Pollock, whose dipped head took a lot longer to hit the tape than Mr Chen's. Quentin, having picked up the silver medal for the second year running, looked far from pleased. The only consolation I could take from the race was that at least I didn't fall over.

'Well, at least you didn't fall over,' Jack said, death-staring a rather smug-looking Harvey.

'Perhaps you shouldn't have worn those new shoes,' said Hilary perceptively.

'Get your father a glass of water, Jack,' said Mr Beale, 'he looks a bit flushed.' I declined the water but had a sit-down on a bench by the side of the track. The pain across my chest had diffused.

'It was probably wind,' said Hilary, who by this point was beginning to limber up for her race, which was next. Mr Beale came and sat down next to me.

'Well done, sir,' he said. 'I stopped taking any kind of exercise myself after my sixtieth birthday. I'd take it easy if I were you.'

As I was only in my early fifties at the time I wasn't that keen on being put into the over-sixties category by the headmaster. Surely I didn't look as old as him?

'We had an older father like you here a couple of years ago who insisted on taking part in the fathers' race,' he said. 'He over ran the finishing line and broke his ankle falling into a pile of deckchairs. He was devastated and so were his children. He came last, just like you, poor bugger. Forgive me, I've got to go and start the sack race.'

I got to the Ivy, didn't book a table for the Chens, but arrived just in time to buy Christopher Reeve a pre-lunch drink.

'I could have done with some help from the "man of steel" this morning,' I said, and explained.

'Let me know if I can help in the future,' he said, grinning. 'Great shoes, incidentally.'

Hilary won the mothers' sack race in a school-record time.

1. Firstly gout is not, as my father suggests in this chapter, 'hereditary'. It occurs when there are high levels of uric acid in the bloodstream. This can be caused by, amongst other things, excessive alcohol consumption. (My father knows all this already, as it's exactly what his doctor told him when he was diagnosed with it.)

2. My father's threat to instruct me is the reason why I have never learnt to drive. I've always had an innate fear I'd end up like him behind the wheel. It's fitting that he mentions 'emasculation' in this chapter, as it is linked to the reason why he was banned by my mother from doing the school run. It was only the second time he'd undertaken the short, early-morning trip from Putney to Sheen when, in front of someone else's children, he said that a man who had cut him up on the Upper Richmond Road should be 'ripped out of his car and neutered'!

3. I find it hard to believe that even at my most desperate I would have actively encouraged you to wear shorts in public.

CHAPTER 4

The Reluctant Dragon

– MICHAEL WHITEHALL –

JACK DIDN'T WANT TO GO TO BOARDING SCHOOL. He had been propping up the bottom of his classes at Tower House School and had had an extremely difficult time with one particular teacher. Rosie Sweetman was waiting for Jack on his first day at the school. A charmless gawky giraffe with what my mother-in-law would have called 'an unfortunate manner',* Miss Sweetman was a bizarre choice to teach a reception class of four-year-olds. Halfway through his first year Hilary and I were called in to see her for a meeting.

'Jack is doing mirror writing,' said Miss Sweetman as she peered down at us from her desk, having strategically placed us on two of the mini chairs used by her pupils.

'That being what exactly?' I asked her.

'Well, he writes backwards, so you can only read his writing if you hold it up to a mirror,' she explained rather patronizingly.

'The boy's a genius. How amazingly clever of him,' Hilary replied.

Having not a shred of a sense of humour (she was a huge fan of the Chen family) she snapped back to Hilary that mirror writing was a sign of deep anxiety and distress.

'I have to ask you: is there anything going on at home that I should know about? Anything that might be worrying him?'

I was losing patience with this dreadful woman. 'I beg your pardon, madam?' I replied.

*Terrifying – the kind of lady who every time she orgasms a fairy dies.

'Is everything all right between you two?' she ploughed on, failing to pick up my tone. I noticed at this point that she was peering down at my wife's arms. Two days previously Hilary's hockey team had come through a fiesty encounter with the Leatherhead Ladies' 2nd XI that had left her sporting a vicious-looking bruise on her arm and AstroTurf grazes on both elbows.

'I can assure you that everything is and I can't see how this can possibly be any of your business,' I said. 'If there is anything upsetting him, it's clearly happening in your classroom. Do you have any thoughts?'

'Well, let's see if it sorts itself out,' she said, 'but if it continues you might have to consider some counselling for him.'

'Counselling?' I shouted. 'You're the one who needs counselling.'

As I tried to make a dramatic exit from her classroom, I realized that I was attached to the small plastic chair I had been sitting on. Undeterred, I waddled towards the door in the hope that it would drop off, but all decorum was lost when Hilary had to start tugging at it to remove it from my backside.

Fortunately Jack did manage to sort himself out and the C-word was never mentioned again, but this just underlined our view that Miss Sweetman may have been sweet by name but she certainly wasn't by nature.

Four years later, as Jack was about to transfer to the senior school, we had a letter from the new headmaster telling us that following discussions with Miss Sweetman they had decided that her talents would be put to better use with an older year group. They had decided to move her to take charge of the Upper School's reception class, where Jack was bound.

This was the last straw. It was bad enough that Jack's interest in art and drama at Tower House had been squashed, due in part to the emergence of a young boy two years above him by the name of Robert Pattinson, who seemed to get all the juicy roles that Jack aspired to in school plays – Peter Pan, Joseph, Bugsy Malone,* a pleasant enough young man, who came to me for professional advice some years later.

Did I think that Robert had any future in the world of acting? I strongly advised him to avoid it at all costs and told him sagely, 'It's a very crowded profession, Robert, and I think it's highly unlikely that there will be room for you in it.'

*Yeah, but who was better with the laydeez? . . . Umm, him. He was better with the ladies. He was better at everything.

R-Patz (bottom right) in a Tower House school photo with J-Whitz (top left).

Although I have not followed his career in any detail, I gather he has had a modicum of success, in which I can only wish him well.

I knew that Jack was a bright and interesting boy and that his artistic talents needed nurturing. Sadly the headmaster thought differently.

'Where were you thinking of sending him next?' he asked us.

'Well, we had hoped to get him into Marlborough College,' I replied.

'I don't think so,' he guffawed. 'Not a hope.'

So it was goodbye, Tower House.

* * *

Way back in the mists of the early 1960s I was, unbelievably, a prep school teacher myself. I remember an interview with the educational agency Gabbitas-Thring, which had a number of teaching vacancies on its books, none of which suited me as they were either for subjects that I was hopeless at, i.e. the vast majority, and usually involved games coaching, a subject I certainly wouldn't have known where to start with. At my own school I was forced to play rugby; the only skill I acquired was how to convincingly bend down and do up my shoelaces, as a six-foot brick shithouse from the opposition charged towards me in search of a try.* On one occasion in a school match I was even

*Like father, like son.

suspected of having fixed the result for the opposition, such was the number of flunked tackles I managed to complete, and this in the days well before the match-rigging scandals involving betting syndicates in the Far East.

'It doesn't do to be too modest,' said Mr Levy of Gabbitas-Thring. 'It's amazing what one can teach if one tries.'

I queried the games at a particular school which he had selected out of his file of vacancies.

'Don't worry,' he assured me, 'as long as you can keep them quiet, the headmaster will be happy. Just stand around in a tracksuit and make sure you have a loud whistle. Oh, and don't worry too much about teaching anything at this stage, just make sure you stay at least one lesson ahead of them.'

And when I asked him about an interview he said, 'Not really necessary for this one. To be honest, he's pretty desperate. He's actually got two vacancies, as the head of maths has run off with the young French teacher and the term starts next week. He'll probably just want a quick chat over the phone.'

I was able to pass on to these boys all of my vast sporting knowledge. They didn't win a game all season.

My letter of engagement from the school was a work of fiction. It mentioned my Oxford Geography degree and the fact that I had been a 'member' of the Ampleforth College 1st XI cricket team, but not that I was in fact the 1st XI scorer because of my neat italic handwriting. Unfortunately this resulted in me taking over all the games coaching.

Having successfully managed to stay ahead of my twelve-year-old charges (batting away awkward questions like 'Where is Addis Ababa, sir?' with 'Very good question, Bailey. The first boy to show me where it is in his atlas will get a house point.')* I left the teaching profession for pastures new.

*Kenya?

For some inexplicable reason I was approached some years later by *The Sunday Times* to write a series of pieces about prep schools. So, with a former teaching friend, Peter Nash, I was sent around the country, visiting schools and putting together a very partial top twenty, which was mostly based on the quality of the entertainment offered to us by the various headmasters – a yardstick which would definitely not be appropriate in these more league-table and results-driven times. In the end, Peter and I ended up visiting over eighty schools in order to end up with a top ten and the Dragon School came first. The headmaster was a wonderful, charismatic eccentric and the children were full of energy and spirit – mostly out of control but in a nice way, and everyone, pupils and staff alike, seemed to be very happy. And not a cane in sight.

So, when it came to moving Jack, there was only one destination. I had always been a great admirer of the Dragon School in Oxford. It had an impressive list of artistically inclined alumni – Sir John Mortimer, Lady Antonia Fraser, Sir John Betjeman – and was the kind of hothouse in which Jack's creative talents could thrive.

— And Dom Joly.

Another advantage of the Dragon was that it was over an hour's drive from our house and a boarding school. Jack was at a tricky age to have permanently under our roof, and I thought a boarding education might help to straighten him out. Additionally I was in the process of relocating my offices in Gloucester Road to our home in Putney and his bedroom had been secretly earmarked as a perfect space to house a considerable number of filing cabinets and assorted office paraphernalia.**

**That was the real reason – cold-hearted bastard!

It was indicated to me that, subject to a meeting with the

headmaster, Roger Trafford, and the director of studies and the satisfactory outcome of a short test, a place could be made available to Jack.

A couple of weeks later we drove up to Oxford with the usually hyperactive Jack very sulky in the back of our car. He gave us the silent treatment all the way there, as I waxed lyrical about his potential new school that had produced so many talented individuals.

'... and the composer Sir Lennox Berkley, Jack, who was renowned for the beauty of his *Variations on an Elizabethan Theme*, Neville Shute, author of *A Town Like Alice*, and Leonard Cheshire who founded the Cheshire Homes for disabled servicemen and was awarded the VC during the Second World War.'*

*All probably current members of the Garrick Club.

But even these illustrious names left the ten-year-old Jack cold.

On arrival at the school we were ushered into the headmaster's study overlooking the impressive playing fields. Jack sat on a window seat, Hilary and I on a sofa in front of Mr Trafford's desk. We drank coffee, Jack declined a soft drink. While we exchanged pleasantries with Mr Trafford about the traffic on the M40, the weather and other matters of huge relevance, I noticed that Jack, over on the window seat, seemed to have developed a physical strain of Tourette's. His legs hung loosely in front of him, his arms likewise, and he kept jerking his head in the direction of Roger Trafford and swivelling his tongue around in his mouth, a performance that looked to me as though it could have been modelled on Damien in *The Omen*. I checked Jack with a glance that he deliberately ignored. I saw right through his ploy.

'So, Jack, why do you want to come to the Dragon?' asked Mr Trafford. Before Jack had time to ignore the question Hilary filled in the expected silence, going into full flattery mode.

'Well, of course, Mr Trafford the school has such a wonderful reputation, particularly since you became headmaster, and with Jack's talents in art and drama I'm sure he would make a real contribution.'

I looked over at my son, who was now perilously dangling a globule of saliva from his mouth over Roger Trafford's rather expensive-looking carpet.

'I've arranged for Richard Gordon, our director of studies, to come over and take Jack through a few simple tests,' said Roger as the door opened and Mr Gordon came into the room.

'*Ah, Jacques. Comment allez-vous?*' said Mr Gordon with a welcoming smile.

'Wot?' said Jack.

Well, four years of learning French at Tower House had obviously paid off, I thought, but at least he had spoken, even though it was not the response Mr Gordon had been looking for. He didn't get up from his seat, nor did he shake Mr Gordon's proffered hand. And now with an increased audience he decided to up his twitch, which began moving down his legs.

'So, I've heard a lot about what a lively and amusing character you are, Jack.'

Jack ignored Mr Gordon, too busy pressing his tongue against the window beside him.

Jack trailed off with Mr Gordon and Hilary took the opportunity to up the charm offensive with Mr Trafford, asking him about his family and even feigning an interest in golf. Half an hour later, with Hilary's very limited golfing knowledge exhausted, Jack returned.

'Well, Mr and Mrs Whitehall, Jack and I had a very interesting chat, didn't we Jack?'

Jack remained mute but shook his head.

'I'll discuss the results of the test with Mr Trafford,' said Mr Gordon, 'and we'll come back to you.'

With twenty years of agenting behind me, I recognized the tone of his voice only too well. It's the same tone casting directors adopt when you attempt to foist a client on them who's totally wrong for a part: 'Would Nigel Havers be an idea for John McClane in *Die Hard*?' 'We'll come back to you, Mr Whitehall.' As we left his study, Mr Trafford made to shake Jack's hand but Jack shied away from him like the village idiot.

'Say goodbye to Mr Trafford,' I said to Jack, digging a hand into his shoulder.

Jack mumbled.

As we drove out of the school gates Jack ignored the waving registrar, Mr Devitt, too busy chewing the sleeve of his jumper, but then, as suddenly as it had started, his Tourette's disappeared and he began to speak in a normal voice.

'What the hell was that all about?' I asked him.

'I want to stay at Tower House with my friends. I don't want to go to boarding school,' Jack replied.

'I don't think there is much likelihood of them wanting you there anyway.'

And they didn't.

Mr Devitt rang the following day to let us know that Jack's test results were very disappointing. His IQ test came out at sixty.

'That's only a couple of points above mentally retarded,' I said down the phone.

'Well, we don't actually use that definition as a yardstick, Mr Whitehall, but, yes, it's in that ballpark. Looking at some of the answers he gave on his test paper, it would appear that Jack has severe learning difficulties. To be candid, I'm afraid we don't think that the Dragon is the right school for him. A lot of the children here are big personalities. Jack wouldn't be able to cope. He seems to be a very shy boy. I think a day school would be more suitable for him.'

I got Jack into my study and reported my conversation with Mr Devitt to him.

'So he agrees with me that a day school would be more suitable?' said Jack.

'How dare you make a fool of Mummy and me in public!' I replied.

'It wasn't public,' he said, 'and sixty sounds quite high to me.'

'I know exactly what your game is and you're not going to get away with it.'

Mr Devitt spoke to Mr Gordon, Mr Gordon spoke to Mr Trafford and it was finally agreed that Jack would be allowed a second interview, having clearly sabotaged the first. But before that happened we made a deal. I took Jack for a walk in Richmond Park and, while we were feeding the ducks, I told him that if he agreed to go to the Dragon and give it a try, he could leave at half-term if he really didn't like it there.

'Do you promise?' asked Jack.

'Yes, I promise,' I replied.

We hugged.

As I'd hoped, he loved it there, got into the odd school play and made lots of friends for life and I was very proud of the way he quickly and enthusiastically embraced the life of a Dragon.

Would I have agreed to let him leave if he hadn't liked it there? What do you think?

1. No.

2. The 'office paraphernalia' I was forced to house in my bedroom had been moved in the moment I stepped out the door. I'd wanted my room to be my own little *pied a terre*: lava lamps, mini basketball hoop, bean bags to chill out on with my mates. Instead, when I came home for the holidays, I had to lie in bed staring at three of the biggest filing cabinets you've ever seen. 'Hey guys, come over to mine for a sleepover?' 'Have you got a PlayStation, Jack?' 'No, but I do have several copies of Tim Pigott-Smith's *The Jewel in the Crown* contract or John Le Mesurier's residual statements for *Dad's Army*.

3. Nigel Havers as John McClane would have been amazing! Hans Gruber definitely would have stolen the money and got away with it, though. 'Where's John McClane?' 'Don't worry, Hans, he's probably flirting with the hostages.'

4. I did not lick the window.

CHAPTER 5

Touchline Tantrums

- JACK WHITEHALL -

NO!

As my father has already made clear, he ain't a gifted sportsman. The closest he gets to any cardiovascular activity is walking past an exercise bike in his bedroom, bought on a whim after a heart tremor and (having been used only once) quickly becoming an inanimate device from which to hang his Turnbull & Asser shirts.

He did also once play a game of cricket in the garden, but had to retire after the second delivery hit him square in the particulars, out PBW for a duck. But that was literally it in terms of him and sport. However, his own physical deficiencies in no way prevented him from being my greatest critic when it came to me playing sport. He was a fiercely competitive touchline parent whom you did not want to let down in a hurry – imagine a slightly more effeminate Judy Murray.

'I'm surprised you can even turn in the water with a rudder that small,' I remember him jokily telling me after I'd disappointed him at a school swimming gala. I was eleven.

He wasn't always purely negative. Sometimes he'd wade in with his own unique brand of advice. This was, if anything, worse than the abuse.

At Marlborough College, my secondary school, having failed to get picked by my coach for the 2nd XI football team for the third week running, my father suggested a ploy he'd picked up from the

*Fifties!

school he'd attended in the thirties.*

'Tell the headmaster that your coach Mr Brien has been touching you,' he said down the phone. 'It worked in my day.'

'What, and get him arrested?'

'Arrested? No, they'll just move him on without a fuss.'

'The problem is, Dad, you went to a Catholic school in the last century. That sort of thing doesn't happen any more.'

'Well, that's a damned shame. Particularly for the 2nd XI.'

It's safe to say that my father and Mr Brien didn't get on. Mr Brien was an eccentric teacher who'd been at the school for years. He had an intense manner, a wild mop of hair and a horrible grizzly beard. He and my father saw eye to eye on virtually nothing.

My dad, as a fee-paying father, was of the opinion that his son should have the divine right to play in any team he wanted. If I wanted to be in the girls' third XI hockey team, at five and a half grand a term, it was fucking happening.

Unfortunately Mr Brien, quite understandably, thought otherwise. I had been left out of the football squad altogether for the first three matches of the term.

'Has that ludicrous man picked you yet?'

'No, Dad. He doesn't think I work in the team's system.'

'System? What system? It's a school bloody football team, not the Champion's League. I'll tell you the system that does work – the direct debit that pays your school fees every month and that ridiculous man's salary!'

PBW.

As luck would have it, a couple of injuries halfway through the season and a change of heart from Mr Brien meant that I was selected to represent the school's 2nd XI for the first time ever. And in the starting line-up no less! I called my dad excitedly.

'Dad, I'm in the team!'

'Marvellous,' he replied. 'What did you tell them? Fumble in the showers, a cheeky hand down your tracksuit at the back of the coach?'

'No, Dad, I got in on my own merit,' I boasted, deciding to hold back the information that a large portion of the school (including half my team) had been hit by a mumps epidemic.

My parents insisted on coming to watch me play, even though the match was at a school in the deepest, darkest depths of Devon. A very long trip for them to make, but my starts were so rare that it was (apparently) well worth making the journey.

The match day arrived and I lined up on the touchline, really looking the part. I'd bought the most expensive football boots I could find, plus an Alice band for my hair so I'd look like one of those expensive Argentinian wingers. I crossed myself as I walked out on to the pitch. I was doing that nose-blowing thing where players block one nostril and messily exhale with the other well in advance of kick-off. The only things I was missing, in fact, were my parents, who still hadn't arrived.

A rare picture of me in a short!   Moments later I was subbed.

A word about wearing expensive clobber. Basically it's like wearing a 'Kick Me' sign on your back. All the people you play against take one look at you and think, quite justifiably, let's hospitalize the twat in the hairband.

I discovered this very soon after kick-off. Following a batch of aggressive slide tackles from my opposite number I decided that I'd spend the rest of the half standing as close to the touchline as I could, and avoid contact with the ball at all costs. It's a style of play that's more recently been developed by Emmanuel Adebayor, but I like to think I pioneered it.

The half dragged on, with Mr Brien shouting and making totally incomprehensible hand gestures at me. He was one of those teachers who – no sooner has he pulled his socks over the hems of his tracksuit bottoms and hung a shitty whistle from his neck – forgets that he's coaching fourteen-year-olds and honestly believes that he's José Mourinho. But still no parents.

Then, with about five minutes to go before half-time, I saw my mother bounding towards the field with my father, clearly in a mood, stomping along behind her. They'd obviously got lost and had an argument, but at least they were here now. That's what mattered.*

*My exact point to your mother.

The whistle blew. Thank God, it was half-time. I could sit in Mum and Dad's car with the heating on for fifteen minutes.

Although Mr Brien's hand gestures were incomprehensible, you could be pretty sure that they usually translated as, 'Jack, you're getting subbed.'

'Jack! Jack!' shouted Mr Brien, throwing his hands around as a boy took off his tracksuit next to him. It wasn't half-time, I was being subbed! After only twenty minutes. I got over to the touchline just in time for my father to arrive.

'What the hell is going on, Brien?' he said.

'Sorry, Mr Whitehall. I'm subbing Jack,' Brien explained. 'He's been totally out of the game.' Normally it's the manager giving the hairdryer treatment, but not on this occasion.

'What do you mean, out of the game? Jack was clearly conserving energy until we arrived.' *

'Sorry. I'm giving Bennett a runaround.'

'Bennett? Listen, Brien, do you see Bennett's parents on the touchline?' shouted my dad. 'No. They haven't made the effort, whereas we have driven halfway across the bloody country to this godforsaken dump of a school. Get my son back on immediately!'

Said calmly but with authority.

'Mr Whitehall, I'm afraid that's not how it works.'

By this point, the referee intervened and my father was (in footballing terms) issued with a touchline ban.

We spent the rest of the match sitting in the car with my father fuming as my mother insisted we stay and support the team.**

'Well, this is brilliant,' said my father. 'Spending my Saturday afternoon watching other people's ugly children kicking a ball around a field in the middle of a benighted, backward county populated by a load of inbred farmhands.'

It was a very tense drive back to London for the weekend exeat. Oh, and Marlborough lost four–nil. Bennett scored an own goal.

**One of Hilary's more annoying habits. When it comes to supporting school events, I have absolutely no interest in other people's children, which is why during Jack's thirteen years of education I never attended a single prize-giving.

The football season continued. My father served his ban and showed little interest in watching me play again. My performances, however, improved, and I'd managed to patch things up with Mr Brien after the incident in Devon. By the end of the season, I'd become a vital lynchpin of the 2nd XI midfield.

Our final game of the season was a tough home fixture against a Welsh school called Monmouth. I'd been begging my father to come and support me and, after some persuasion, he agreed on the proviso that, one, he wouldn't have to talk to Mr Brien and, two, if I got subbed he could leave.

He arrived very early so Mr Brien couldn't 'fuck him around' for a second time. As the match kicked off, the touchline was packed with parents from both schools, as well as the school's respective head-masters prowling along it. Mr Brien and my father stood on opposite sides of the field, a distance that my dad said wasn't far enough.

Monmouth was predominantly a rugby school, based in the middle of the Welsh valleys, so their team (as you might imagine) contained quite a few 'big units'. Monmouth certainly weren't afraid of the physical side of the beautiful game.*

Their tackles took no prisoners, but that was no excuse for my father to shout 'thugs!' at the top of his voice every time one of them made contact with me. The opposition may have been big units, but they were still only fourteen-year-olds.

My father's insistence on standing apart from Mr Brien also meant that he was very much at the Monmouth end of the field, sur-rounded by the boys' parents and by a now very pissed off Welsh headmaster. This did nothing to put him off his heckling.

'You bloody animal!' he shouted as one of the Monmouth def-enders barged me off the ball. It was becoming a little uncomfort-able; some of the offended fathers began tutting and shushing him, but this encouraged my father to become even more aggressive.

At half-time I dodged the team talk to give Dad one of my own. 'Can you please behave?' I begged him.

'Behave? I'm the only one shouting,' he replied.

'I know, Dad. That's why I want you to stop.'

The second half got under way and the chorus of abuse from the touchline continued. 'Thugs! Oiks!'

I think he even called their goalkeeper a donkey. Both headmas-ters were looking very uneasy.

With the game still poised at nil–nil, a trip in the box (or was it a dive?) prompted the referee to award a penalty to Monmouth.

'So you cheat as well!' bellowed my dad. 'It's a bloody disgrace!'

'Oh, give it a rest!' shouted one of the parents, no longer willing to remain silent.

'Can you tell your granddad to shut up?' the penalty-taker asked me at the top of his voice in a thick Welsh accent.

I don't know whether it was because my father heard this, or whether he was just incensed at the referee's decision, but I could

*Just as well you abandoned that camp hairband for this fixture. They would have murdered you.

see he had '*that*' look in his eyes, the 'Michael mist', the one he gets when he watches Fiona Bruce on the *Antiques Roadshow*, the one he gets when cyclists cut him up on the Kings Road or when he sees pictures in the *Daily Mail* of Peter Mandelson on holiday with his Brazilian boyfriend.

The Monmouth boy took a few steps back from the ball, ready to strike it and win the game. The crowd fell silent. All eyes on the spot. He ran up, swung his leg back and – just as he was about to make contact with the ball – there was a loud guttural sheep noise from the touchline.

'*Baaaaaaaaaaaaa!!*'

I didn't even need to look round to know where it came from. The boy completely scuffed his kick as a small pitch-side brawl broke out, with several angry parents having to be held back from hitting my dad. All you needed was* a few flares and it was like watching footage from the terraces of a local derby game in Belgrade . . . just with a few more Barbours.

To this day my father remains the only Marlborough parent to receive a lifetime touchline ban.

*Were!

1. My tenure as head of games at Great Ballard Preparatory School in the early 1960s resulted in unbeaten seasons for the school in rugby and football. So I think that I am more than qualified, Jack, to comment on all things relating to school sports coaching. Some people have said that this record was only due to a Persian boy called Parnian, lynchpin of my squads and indeed top scorer in all three sports. He was over six foot, shaved twice a day, and regularly beat me at arm wrestling. I would dispute this allegation. As indeed I disputed accusations from opposition teachers that Parnian was over age, the headmaster having assured me that he had had sight of his birth certificate.

2. You were clearly right to give up geography early. Monmouth is on the fringes of the Wye Valley, not part of the Welsh valleys.

3. I have no problem with Fiona Bruce per se. She's an attractive young woman and was a perfectly good newsreader. However, her knowledge of antiques is clearly non-existent and the ousting of television legend Michael Aspel to make way for her was an outrage.

CHAPTER 6

School Scandals

- JACK WHITEHALL -

I was not particularly rebellious during my years at Marlborough College. I didn't really smoke or do drugs, as some of my friends did, and was never caught having sex behind the cricket pavilion, largely because I never had sex.

The ways in which I got into trouble with the school authorities were far more unusual. One of the oddest situations came about thanks to my interest in art. I loved the subject and one of my best friends, Freddie, studied it with me.

A bit of a 'playa', Freddie was dating one of the 'fittest' girls in the school; a busty young temptress called Flo, who was very pretty but also very chaste. To date she'd quashed all of Freddie's eager attempts at amorousness. Their relationship amounted to little more than being awkward together in public and one occasion where Freddie had grasped a handful of breast that he'd timed at thirteen and a half seconds.

As well as being Freddie's best friend I was also his wingman. An unrewarding gig, it consisted of standing around at parties as he got off with the most attractive girl there, while I spoke to her wingwoman, who had no intention of killing time with anything more exciting than stilted conversation.

'I want to do a painting of Flo naked,' Freddie confided to me one lunchtime. 'You know, like in *Titanic*. Life-modelling.'

'Great idea, mate. Make sure you show it to me when you're

done,' I replied with the haste of a teenage boy who wouldn't let an opportunity to see nudity in any form pass him by.

'No, I need your help, Jack.'

Brilliant, I thought, here he is thinking of his best mate. Why should he get all the fun? He wants me to hold his palette or clean his brushes, allowing me to cop a cheeky glance or two at the fittest girl in the school. What a great friend!

'I want you to pose naked first,' Fred said.

Text-speak didn't really exist back in 2003, so I couldn't say 'WTF'. Instead, I just goggled at him.

'I'll draw you, then I'll draw her,' Fred explained, gathering from my expression that the idea struck me as a little left-field. 'That way I can convince her it's a legitimate art project.'

'You're not going to show her a picture of me, are you?' I stammered.

'I'll have to. I'll probably have to use it in the exhibition too, just to make sure.' The exhibition was an end-of-year thing, where teachers, parents and pupils milled around being polite about the art students' paintings on display. The very idea of my (ass) being critiqued by the headmaster was already making me sweat.

Bottom. We are not in America.

'No way, Fred.'

'But it's the only way I'm gonna get her kit off! You've got to help me, mate. Do you want me to die a virgin?'

'You're not a virgin.'

'Well, I feel like one. Posing for me, everyone'll be like, Jack, he's arty, he's edgy, he's –'

'Naked?'

There were so many holes in Freddie's logic. But he was very persuasive and he was my best friend.

The room he chose was a secluded one in the art block. We went there on a Saturday afternoon while everyone else was playing sports. It was deserted but worryingly cold.

'Fred, you know the way portrait painters throughout the ages have been expected to flatter their subjects? Well, please don't make my dick look small,'* I said as I took off my school uniform and got on to one of the tables, which didn't look like it had been cleaned in a while.

*This would have been beyond Freddie's artistic talents. As you well know, you have been fortunate in inheriting from me very generous proportions in that department, something for which you should be very grateful.
Yuk!!

HIM & ME

'Just hurry up, mate. I'll knock one out quickly. Flo's coming in an hour.'

'Two things, Fred. One, please don't use the phrase "knock one out" in this environment, and two, you promise I can stay to keep guard at the door when you do your picture of her?'

'Yes, mate, of course,' Fred said as he started sketching.

We spent ages in that room. Being a life model is one of those jobs where you have a lot of time to think, and think I did, mainly about how weird this situation was. Freddie found it awkward, too, but at least he had the drawing as a distraction.

Then I heard footsteps. Flo was coming down the corridor! Shit, I thought, is she going to come in here? I don't want her to see me naked. Fred is one thing, but not her. My clothes were on the other side of the room so it was too late to go for them. Trying to look my best, I puffed out my chest, sucked in my stomach, and slung the old boy over my thigh.

'Don't move, you idiot,' said Freddie.

The door swung open.

'Hello, Flo . . . oh.'

It was Mr Parling, the Head of Art! A small squat Damien Hirst lookalike with a passion for architecture, Parling surveyed the scene. I could understand his surprise. There was something very D. H. Lawrence about the whole thing.*

I tried to style it out, holding my ground. After all, what's unusual about a man sketching another man naked? It was 2005, after all. Sure, we didn't say 'WTF', but we were pretty advanced in other ways, right? YOLO.

No one spoke for a while. Mr Parling remained very calm.

'Put your clothes on, Whitehall,' he said without raising his voice. He glanced for the first time at the drawing. 'The proportions are all wrong. For a start, that's far too big.'**

Freddie told me he had pointed at my foot but, to this day, I have my suspicions. Also, feet are proportionate, so it amounts to the same thing.

Freddie never did get to see Flo naked. After the story of our homoerotic tryst got round, things dried up for a while. Unfortunately the story made it all the way back to Putney, because I had to field a

*I can't believe you have read any of D. H. Lawrence's books. To which one are you referring?
I'm referring to the film with Oliver Reed and Alan Bates.

**Parling clearly wasn't wearing his reading glasses.

rather tricky call from my parents a few days later.

'Naked, eh? With another boy?' said my father. 'Is there anything you want to tell me, Jack?'

'No.'

'It won't shock me, you know. I've met a lot of men who *bowl from the pavilion end* in theatreland.'

'Jesus, Dad.'

There was whispering at the other end of the phone.

'Your mother wants to ask you something.'

He handed the phone over. I tensed up, expecting to receive an earful.

'Where is this drawing?' she said. 'I thought it might look rather nice in the guest room.'

It's at moments like this when I see how my parents work as a couple. My father may sound eccentric, but I suspect my mother is actually the mad one.

The school's mock election was another incident where I had some explaining to do to my father. It was the first school election I'd been involved in at Marlborough and, never one to shy away from the opportunity to show off, I was desperate to get involved.

Each pupil taking part would have to do so under the banner of one of the parties running in the general election that year. I went to see the organizing committee to see what the deal was. They

This is Freddie's completed drawing of me. His art career failed to materialize.

informed me that all the major parties had been taken as I was late in applying. Patrick Stansbury – a bad-tempered pus-faced prefect who wore a double-breasted suit with shoulder pads covered in dandruff, a Timmy Twinkle in the making – had already bagged the Conservative Party candidacy. Of course he had. The Monster Raving Loony Party was also popular, and Lucy Pebble was going to represent the Green Party.

'All the parties have gone,' said one of the committee in a tone that suggested he was more than happy to see me sit this one out.

'Oh wait, no, there is one party left,' said a girl sitting next to him.

Brilliant. A lifeline, I thought.

'Who?' I asked

'Veritas.'

Who the fuck are Veritas? I thought to myself.

'Ah, of course, Veritas. My family have been voting Veritas for years,' I said, trying to impress the girl. It didn't work. 'I'll take them.'

The boy on the committee looked annoyed as he wrote my name down among the other candidates.

A quick search in the computer labs later told me that bronzed former daytime TV talk-show giant Robert Kilroy-Silk was in charge of the party. I took down what little information I needed and printed out some blurb. There was a hustings the following morning at break, where each candidate would get up in front of the school and explain why they should be voted in as the school's prime minister.

No actual power came with this post; it was more an exercise in debate. Nevertheless, it was a competitive event. I knew I had to get noticed at the hustings. I needed to make an impact. I needed inspiration. Where was I going to find it? I looked down at the printer. And, lo, it shat out a picture of Kilroy . . .

I came back from Boots with enough fake tan to drown half of Essex. In the bathroom of my boarding house, I dabbed some on but it didn't seem to be working. So I added some more and then some more, but I was still nowhere nearer to Kilroy's complexion.

Damn, maybe I'm immune to it, I thought to myself as I tried on some garish tie options and practised my best shit-eating, bigoted grin. A few hours later it had begun to take effect and by the time I went to bed I looked like Mark Wright.*

*Who the hell is Mark Wright?

* Who are these people?

I woke up looking like Ian Wright.* No one had informed me that if you don't wash fake tan off it develops. By the time I'd got to the hall where the hustings were being held it had got even darker. My friends tell me it noticeably deepened during my actual speech and, by this time, I wasn't the only one whose skin was changing colour. The headmaster's face had gone from pink to red. He was sitting next to Marlborough's MP, Michael Ancram,** who was also looking a little taken aback. After the speech I was marched off to the sanatorium to receive an industrial scrub-down. And once again my parents were informed. The email they received went as follows:

**Ah finally, I know Michael Ancram. A very fine and respected Old Amplefordian and indeed the Earl of Ancram.

> Dear Mr and Mrs Whitehall,
> We regret to inform you that disciplinary action has been taken against your son. During the school's recent mock elections, Jack took what was clearly intended as a bit of fun a step too far and appeared in the Memorial Hall hustings wearing so much 'fake tan' that it was racially offensive.

Like my father's touchline ban, it was yet another first: I am the only boy in Marlborough's illustrious history ever to have received a formal caution from the school for 'blacking up'. My mother was devastated, my father worryingly amused.

'A Veritas spokesman being racially offensive, eh?' he mused. 'I mean, it *feels* entirely appropriate.' This is one of the greatest things about having the father I do. He's always able to see the lighter side of any situation, even when I've fucked up majorly. I'd always get shouted at, but it wouldn't be long before he was able to have a laugh about it. The thing he seemed most annoyed about on this occasion wasn't the fake tan but the fact that I wasn't running as a Conservative.

The most trouble I ever got into at school, though, was also politically motivated. It was during my final year at Marlborough, and some friends and I had all developed into young firebrands. We hated the Establishment, read the (Guardian) and drank Fairtrade coffee while we discussed how ashamed we were of our privileged backgrounds. Even the posters on our dormitory walls had changed; the half-naked girls were torn down and replaced with slogans saying 'Free Tibet' and 'Tony Bliar'.

If I ever catch you reading that socialist propaganda again, I shall disinherit you.

We were no longer interested in frivolous things. We were grown-ups now. A year ago we were excited about being at the same school as James Blunt's sisters – fact. Now we were thrilled about being at the same school that Anthony Blunt, the Communist spy, attended – fact.

He's been at the thesaurus again!.

It was at the height of the Iraq War and we radical sixth-formers wanted to make a statement. We held a (clandestine) meeting in a common room to hatch a plan, a stunt that would stick two fingers up to The Man. We don't need no Marlborough education!*

*Oh Jesus and now we've got double negatives creeping in. I give up.

It had been a long journey to get to this point. I was never particularly politically active. In fact, the only time that I'd previously been involved in any kind of protest was when I attended the Countryside Alliance march in London during my second year at school. Marlborough had a lot of influential parents who were very pro-fox-hunting,** so the school granted a whole day off to anyone who wanted to take part in the march. I checked my diary, saw that I had a couple of science lessons in the morning and decided I'd go along for the ride.

**Not to mention their own pack of Beagles. A fine dog, the Beagle. Although the males can be very randy, as I discovered when I was involved with the Ampleforth pack.

The way I saw it, man landed on the moon almost half a century ago, so if some village idiot *still* can't make a hutch capable of keeping out what is essentially a fancy dog, then they deserve to find the mangled corpses of their chickens in the morning. However, I kept this to myself. I may not give much of a toss about foxes, but the kids on the coach were very passionate about hunting them.

'Did you know, Jack, there are more names on the pro-fox-hunting petition than there are on the one to ban it?' said a sixth-form boy who was so posh he sounded as if he was in pain.

'No, I didn't,' I replied politely, thinking to myself that there were more names on his petition because all of them were double or triple-barrelled.

Once in London, we plodded up and down the streets of Westminster, getting very odd looks from Londoners, who perhaps thought their city was being invaded by an army of gentleman farmers.

'Killing the fox is a sport!' blubbered an arse-faced man in corduroy trousers next to me.

Is it? Not really. I mean, the fox never wins. If at half-time they swapped round and the posh man on the horse was taken off it, stripped, given a bin liner full of old bits of food and then chased through the fields by a pack of hungry foxes, then, yes, it could be considered a sport. But fox-hunting in its current format is a little one-sided.

'What do we want?' the marchers chanted.

'To get off double physics,' I muttered. It was an awful day, after which I decided that protest wasn't for me.

But *the time it was a-changing,* to misquote Bob Dylan (something I did a lot at that time). Tony Blair had lied to us about WMDs and now our army was butchering innocent Iraqis. So, as my friend Giles Bouverat shared around the contents of a cafetière, we plotted how to get our voices heard.

We decided that our target should be the Combined Cadet Force (CCF), a risible bunch who dressed up like soldiers to practise marching in a car park every Wednesday afternoon. The army equivalent of the community support officer, they made the TA look like the SAS. We decided to attack them outside their barracks while they were on this weekly parade, and we plotted this attack down to the last minutiae in the style of seventeenth-century Catholics.

'Each of you must go back to your boarding house and gather more rebels for the attack,' said Giles as he laid out some dark chocolate ginger biscuits on to a bone china plate.

'We pounce covertly and then bombard them with water bombs, bags of flour, and anything else we can lay our hands on,' said another conspirator, adding some honey to his chai.

We'd get across our pacifist message through an act of un-provoked violence. It was brilliant. The brothers-in-arms I selected for the task were my friend Harry von Behr (a keen cricketer with a good arm) and Alex Lavarello, who was in the dormitory next to me. We made ourselves makeshift balaclavas out of beanie hats and, on the day of the attack, skived off games to go and meet the rest of the gang* behind the science block.

The assault itself was a blistering success. The CCF didn't know what had hit them. For boys with aspirations towards a military

*This is beginning to sound more Millwall than Marlborough.

future, they were utterly pants at defending themselves. We were in and out in five minutes, and none of our group was taken prisoner. A triumph, we thought.

That was until the next day. The CCF's parade ground had been fitted with CCTV cameras (the act of cowards, if you ask me) and Alex was called into the Second Master's office* to be shown the footage.

Now, I can't take responsibility for the reason our identities were rumbled, but I had certainly made one major error of judgement in the lead-up to the attack. Yes, our balaclavas covered our faces Yes, we were covert. Yes, the evidence was disposed of with all the efficiency of a tabloid journalist who's been tipped off about a police raid. There was no trail back to us, no smoking gun. However, there was one problem.

Alex Lavarello, whom I'd brought in, was eighteen stone and over six foot four tall. You could fit two of me and a Harry von Behr inside him. As he watched the footage back with the Second Master, he realized no balaclava could have hidden the fact that it was clearly him lurching around the CCF's parade ground like a rhinoceros in a burka.

'I know it's you, Alex,' he said bluntly. 'You will give me all of the names of the boys involved in this attack or I will expel you.'

Poor Alex.

*A very tricky customer who was in charge of discipline and certainly not one to pick a fight with.

The Dirty Half-Dozen.

Luckily for his sword, he did not fall on it. He gave all the names.

It was time to call my parents again, this time to explain that a suspension was heading my way for what was described as a 'premeditated act of terrorism'.

My father gave me an almighty bollocking, but then a few hours later called me back to tell me that he'd drafted a letter to send to the Second Master. In it he called him a 'petty little man' and claimed that of all the people who should have been able to cope with an attack it was the CCF. I told my dad it was probably best if he didn't send it; he reluctantly agreed. Though it was nice to know he had my back, as I gather Mr Lavarello was slightly less understanding.

1. Nudity is a recurring theme in your life. I seem to remember we had some other dealings with the Second Master, when his wife caught you completely naked in the middle of a field – allegedly making a film, of what type I can only imagine – when out walking their dog. I, on the other hand, have always been a man who does not display his body in public, or indeed in private either. As you know, I always wear pyjamas in bed, apart from, of course, when your mother and I are making the beast with two backs.
   I think I'm going to be sick!!

2. How dare you question your mother's sanity? There are very few people who would want a picture of you in the buff, let alone put it on display. You should be so bloody lucky.

3. I reluctantly decided not to send my stinging letter to the Second Master as I had a rare twinge of sympathy for him. This was due to the fact that the whole incident had been witnessed by a visiting conclave of prep school heads who were holding a conference at the college and had stumbled unwittingly right into the middle of the attack.

4. Although this chapter is a bit lefty for my liking, I am glad to see a fair bit of Blair-bashing.

5. Just to reiterate, I never want to see or hear of you reading the Guardian again.

Part III
Going Wild in the Country

CHAPTER 7

Invite at Your Peril

- MICHAEL WHITEHALL -

ALTHOUGH ONE OF THE ACTOR Martin Jarvis's main claims to fame* was being the voice of *Just William*, that was no excuse for Jack to behave like William when we were invited to lunch at the Eaton Terrace home of Martin and his wife, Ros. And not just any old lunch, but Christmas Day lunch. Hilary, who was pregnant with Barnaby at the time, and I were joined by several other guests, including the radio presenter Nigel Rees. The house was decorated to within an inch of its life, as was the Christmas lunch table, and the dress code was appropriately formal – even Jack was required to wear a bow tie. Nigel Rees was wearing an elegant grey suit and a pale yellow silk tie, which he announced had been a Christmas present from his wife that morning and had cost a fortune. Jack and Molly were the lone children in a party of seven adults and Jack was sitting between me and Nigel. After a smoked-salmon starter, which Jack managed to get not only all over his bib and hands but all over his face and up his nose, we proceeded to the dish of the day, an enormous turkey with all the trimmings. Jack was served first and tranched in to his gravy-covered lunch with great enthusiasm, quickly abandoning the children's knife and fork provided by Ros in favour of his hands. At this point Nigel made an attempt to engage the feral Jack in a little light social conversation while he waited to be served.

'Do you like Christmas?' asked Nigel.

Jack, who was playing with a very slippery Brussels sprout, ignored him and pushed the sprout into his mouth accompanied by a handful of mashed swede mixed with bread sauce.

'I bet you got some nice presents,' Nigel continued. 'This tie was a present from my wife. Do you like it?'

At which point Jack stopped eating and with two hands dripping with a mush of turkey, gravy and cranberry sauce, violently grabbed Nigel's tie and started pulling it.

'Tie, tie!' he giggled as the knot got smaller and smaller and tighter and tighter round Nigel's neck.

In an effort to avoid asphyxiation Nigel attempted to prise Jack's dripping, greasy hands off him, but in so doing managed to splash his immaculate jacket with the detritus from the tray on Jack's highchair.

Having removed his hands, Hilary manhandled Jack and his high-chair over to the other side of the table as he repeated 'tie, tie' at the top of his voice.

On the way home Hilary reminded me of a Sunday lunch a few months earlier when we had driven to north London to my lawyer Brook Land and his wife Anita's house. Jack was about ten months old and had turned into what Hilary's mother, Woose,* described as a 'happy puker'. He had picked up the rather mystifying habit of making himself vomit, sometimes by mistake as he was very intolerant of lumps in his food, or, more alarmingly, deliberately by shoving a finger down his throat and then roaring with laughter when he had achieved the desired effect. Worryingly these *Exorcist* moments seemed to have become a regular part of his repertoire and no doctor or priest could do anything about the 'happy puking' so, for a while, we were stuck with it.

On arrival at their house Hilary had asked Anita if she could feed Jack before we sat down for lunch, so as to chop out at least one potential type of vomiting that might be caused by a stray lump in his food. Jack having successfully finished, the rest of us sat down for our lunch. The party consisted of Hilary and me, Brook and Anita and their two children, then aged about six and eight. Anita had pulled out all the stops, crystal wine glasses, the best silver, the Villeroy and Boch, and all atop the whitest and crispest of linen tablecloths. As the last bottom hit its chair, Jack looked around the table, laughed, shoved his finger down

*My mother-in-law has always been known as Woose. No one is quite sure why.

his throat and projectile vomited right across the table, turning his head as he did so (although fortunately less than 360 degrees), thereby creating a travelling arc of vomit that covered the entire table. As he finished he roared with laughter, as did the Land children. For the first time, but certainly not the last, Hilary was speechless. Although Anita dealt with this crisis seamlessly, and indeed we have remained very good friends with them ever since, they have never invited us for lunch again, not even without the human sprinkler.

Happily he eventually grew out of this particular idiosyncrasy, but we were still left with another Jack gastroenterological-based oddity, in as much as he suffered from another complaint, which this time Woose diagnosed as 'toddler diarrhoea' (although perhaps 'happy shitter' might have been more appropriate). This meant that Jack produced nappies that were not only explosive but unpredictable and 'nuclear' in their power and aroma. Hilary was expecting again* (I was at my most potent,)** and, with Jack just eight months old, was unable to change his nappies as she suffered from bad morning sickness that seemed to last for most of the day. I, therefore, stepped into the breach and took on this particular duty. By the time he was a year old Jack had also perfected getting his nappy open before I was awake and spreading its contents over the bars of his cot. I believe a not dissimilar procedure was employed by disgruntled IRA inmates at the Maze Prison in Belfast. Our solution to Jack's dirty protest was to Sellotape him into his nappy several times round his waist before he went to bed. Therefore, the most important piece of equipment for the early-morning nappy was a pair of scissors to cut him free.

Scissors were not relevant when we had lunch at the Carlton Towers Hotel, Knightsbridge, with our friends Sid and Phoebe Goldstein, who were visiting from the USA. Sid was an eminent cardiologist on the London leg of a European lecture tour with his wife, who was scouring the West End art dealers for interesting additions to their modern-art collection. During lunch it became apparent that Jack had had some toxic activity in the nappy department and as Hilary was deep in conversation, catching up on all the family gossip, I decided swift action was required and headed off to the loo with Jack and the changing bag. Unfortunately, having removed the offending nappy and revealed the mayhem thereunder, I discovered that the changing bag had not been

*Why is Mummy always pregnant?

**Oh, God!

replenished from the previous day. My only option was to construct a temporary arrangement out of paper towels and as I was attempting to do this, two hooray men, who were clearly in the middle of a very liquid lunch, came into the loo.

'You've certainly got your hands full, haven't you, old boy?' said one of them.

'Actually, I wonder if you could do me a great favour? I'm not going to be able to cope with this on my own, and my wife is sitting at the table by the window with two other people – could you tell her to come in here and lend me a hand?'

'No problem, old boy,' said one of the men, clearly, unlike me, finding the whole thing a big laugh. Moments later the door slowly opened and I lifted Jack up and shoved him bottom first towards Hilary.

'I really can't cope with this. Over to you.'

'I beg your pardon?'

I peered around Jack. It was not Hilary but a middle-aged balding man in a pinstripe suit who looked far from pleased with being presented with the stinking backside of a baby. So much for the two men finding Hilary for me!

'I'm profusely sorry,' I said to the man, 'but I thought you were my wife.'

Which, not unsurprisingly, didn't totally put him at ease.

After he'd left, I rinsed through Jack's soiled dungarees and presented a pristine baby back at the table, albeit with a Heath Robinson nappy in place.

'You took your time!' said Hilary.

I could have killed her. I then spent the rest of my lunch trying to avoid eye contact with the balding man who was sitting directly opposite me giving me very shifty looks.

* * *

Seven years later Jack, now joined by his brother and sister, continued to be a deadly house guest, but the actors Richard Pasco and his wife, Barbara Leigh-Hunt, had asked us to spend the weekend with them and were insistent that we brought the children with us.

Dickie and Bar, as everyone called them, lived in an enchanting thatched cottage covered in honeysuckle and roses in a village near Stratford-upon-Avon. There was a pretty cottage garden with meandering crazy-paved paths, and it was a picture-postcard location. On arrival we quickly realized that a major drawback from our point of view was that it was in no way a child-friendly place.

At the time of our visit Jack, Molly and Barnaby ranged from the ages of four to eight so our house in Putney had been cleared of all *objets d'art* for the foreseeable future. The Meissen figurines were hibernating in the cellar and the fine bone china had been replaced by Thomas the Tank Engine and Disney Princess plastic mugs and plates. This was certainly not the case chez Pasco.

Bar was a collector, as was her husband, of things. Books, leather-bound first editions down to rare theatrical folios, fine china, bronzes, paintings large, small and very small, Victoriana, brass, glassware, jewellery, furniture, ornaments, clocks, walking sticks, silhouettes, silver boxes, decanters, dolls and doll's houses, pens and inkwells.* Empty surfaces were certainly not de rigueur at the Pasco residence. Bulls in china shops came quickly to mind.

*It was like we'd walked into one of David Dickinson's wet dreams.

We had been invited for the weekend, to arrive for tea on Friday and leave after breakfast on Sunday. It was a beautiful June afternoon as we squeezed past a precariously sited aspidistra sitting on an elegant black and gold plinth in the tiny hall. Bar showed us around. Delicately carved tables with chintz cloths piled high with books and other literary ephemera, a tiny desk complete with quill pen and inkwell, ominously filled with black ink, and delicate vases of fresh flowers from the garden sitting on tiny and hazardous-looking stands. An antique dealer's dream maybe, but for parents of young children, a total nightmare.

Jack's bedroom was a cosy little room with a substantial collection of rare hand-painted lead soldiers on a small oak sideboard. 'These are definitely not for playing with,' I warned Jack. The bedside table was made of walnut, on which sat some delicate lacework.

Jack had encountered fine lacework once before when we had week-ended with my ex-sister-in-law Fiona Armstrong and her husband, John. Fiona was a successful interior decorator who had been trained by David Hicks and her Arts and Crafts house in Hampshire was a homage to good, if slightly over the top, taste. Hilary** had packed lots of distracting entertainments in the hope of keeping the children occupied and away from any potential crises with regard to breakages and damage. Jack was passionate about drawing, so there were several

**Who was probably pregnant.

pads and lots of highly coloured felt pens in tow. He managed to leave the top off his black felt pen, which had left a large stain on the fine lacework in his bedroom. Fortunately Hilary's parents lived nearby and had also been asked for dinner. Hilary called her mother and asked her to bring some bleach with her, but in a disguised container. As Woose greeted Fiona with a kiss, she passed the small Diet Coke bottle that had been concealed in her handbag to me, like some dodgy drug dealer. I then smuggled it upstairs in order to carry out the repair and renewal, thereby avoiding any unpleasantness. Some weeks later I had a concerned Fiona on the phone asking if Hilary was all right. It turned out that she'd found the empty Coke bottle whilst cleaning out her guest room and given it a sniff. I assured Fiona that my wife had not been smuggling alcohol into the house, but was forced to come clean about the mishap with the lacework.

Back at the Pascos', sitting on the delicate lacework was an engraved cut-glass decanter filled with water, a matching glass by its side. Also on the table was a silk box filled with tissues. Next to it stood a scented candle and a box of matches. As we moved out of his room to continue the tour, I secretly pocketed the matches. Jack managed to attach himself to the box of tissues, but fortunately Hilary was in the slips ready to catch them.

'I need a tissue,' said Jack. 'They're my tissues.'

I checked him with a glance. 'Later, Jack,' I replied as I gently put him into an armlock.

Hilary's and my room was beautiful and sunny, with a large double bed and a small single for Barnaby tucked in the corner, under a leaded window with a shelf below it. On the shelf was a collection of Victorian china farm animals.

'We thought Barnaby would like those above his bed,' said Bar.

His bedside table was a replica of Jack's apart from his decanter, which was smaller and a lot more fragile-looking. Hilary earmarked it for subsequent resiting.

'Those farm animals are not like your Duplo farm set, Barnaby. Look but don't touch or you're out,' I cautioned him. I was beginning to sound like a bouncer in a strip club.*

Molly's bed was in a cramped corridor with a long trailing plant covering the wall and two enormous vases of roses. Molly thought it

*Urgh, how would you know?!

*Because of course at home Molly always goes to the loo in the garden?

looked like an indoor garden and I reminded her that if she wanted a wee during the night to remember that it wasn't.*

'Would everyone like some tea?' asked Dickie.

As we sat in the deep button-backed chairs and the children took over the long sofa, Bar wheeled in an antique brass trolley piled high with scones, jam, cream and a tall cake stand with an assortment of home-made pastries, a teapot in a woollen cosy, silver milk jug and sugar bowl and seven fine china cups and saucers. The centrepiece was a large plate of finger sandwiches that had been delicately piled high like a Jenga tower (a game that was very popular with the children at the time). It teetered dangerously as she wheeled it in and you could tell that if one wrong sandwich was taken out of the structure, the whole thing would come toppling down in a demolition disaster of cream cheese and cucumber. There then followed an angst-ridden hour with Hilary playing a hazardous version of musical chairs

Taking tea with the Whitehalls.

as she darted from child to child, preventing chunks of Bar's home-baked walnut cake being trodden into the Persian rugs underfoot. At one stage Molly's ponytail became entangled in a large dollop of Bar's home-made strawberry jam sitting precariously on a mound of double cream atop Jack's scone, which Hilary had to deal with quickly, utilizing a starched linen napkin before Molly spread it on to the back of the pale-coloured sofa.

'Jack's a lively boy,' said Bar as I scooped up a large Delft porcelain bowl filled with potpourri, which had inexplicably been put on the table next to the cake stand and which Jack hadn't noticed as he reached for his third chocolate éclair. 'But he's certainly got a good appetite.' I watched him intently as the cream and chocolate began to cover his hands and realized that, of all Bar's delicacies on offer, this was definitely the most lethal as the éclair contains materials of potential stainage both within and without.

Once the tea had been removed and Hilary had been able to breathe a sigh of relief, peace broke out as Dickie switched on the TV. Hilary then proudly produced her new Sony mini camcorder, which she had bought a couple of days earlier with the money that her mother had generously given her as a birthday present. It was the first time out of the box and Hilary studied the instruction manual with relish, while the children watched *The Chuckle Brothers*, one of Jack's special favourites then and, indeed, now.* For readers of my generation who are not familiar with their body of work, the Chuckle Brothers are, to my mind, a vastly inferior version of Laurel and Hardy.** In the particular episode Jack was watching the moustachioed duo were performing a sketch in which they clumsily attempted to carry a large antique mirror up a flight of stairs. I gave Jack a 'don't get any ideas' look.

The following day the much-admired camera was in constant use as we wandered around Stratford-upon-Avon, seeing the sights. It was a relief to spend some time in a child-friendly environment; although Anne Hathaway's Cottage was a bit of a struggle, feeding the ducks on the Avon was an easier task and very photogenic.

On Sunday morning Bar had laid on one of her special breakfasts. Fresh duck eggs from the farm opposite, locally dry-cured bacon from the butcher in the village, some of his award-winning organic sausages, tomatoes from her kitchen garden and even some home-grown

*Yeah, so what?

**How dare you?

There's two hours of my life I'll never get back.

mushrooms. 'I'll just have some tea and toast thanks, Bar. I don't really do breakfast,' I said, and added, as I saw Jack, Molly and Barnaby starting to salivate, 'and nor do the children.' For me, the very thought of Jack getting his hands on rashers of greasy bacon, runny eggs and bouncy sausages,* not to mention the squeezy ketchup container, was beyond the pale. Hilary, who was trying to keep on top of her diet, shot me a withering look, as she knew that she was now duty-bound to eat her way through every element of Bar's breakfast. The children unhappily munched their way through a couple of slices of toast.

*Are sausages 'bouncy'?

We started to pack up for our return to London and I gave the children a big hug. 'I'm very proud of you three – you've done really well.'

For 'hug' read 'firm handshake'.

Dickie and Bar were also travelling up to London that morning, so as we loaded up our car they began to close up the cottage. As I looked through into the kitchen I saw a small white terrier hovering by the Aga. 'I didn't know you had a dog,' I said.

'We don't,' said Bar. 'Dickie, that bloody dog from up the lane is in the kitchen.'

After much shouting and shooing, it hurtled out of the front door and ran up the lane. By now Hilary was walking the children to the car and carrying, amongst other things, the prized video camera.

'Let me carry that for you,' insisted Dickie.

I caught a waft of the unmistakable aroma of dog poo. The dog had left a large turd on the tiled kitchen floor and Dickie had managed to tread in it and walk it through the house.

'Dickie, there is dog poo everywhere now. Have you trodden in it?' Bar asked accusingly.

As he attempted to wipe the poo off the sole of his shoe, the camera slipped out of his hand and smashed on to the flagstone patio. And it didn't just smash; the whole front of the camera sheered off and, as Dickie picked it up, fragments detached themselves and pinged on to the dog poo-smeared ground.

Ashen-faced, Dickie burbled an apology as he handed Hilary what remained of the camera. 'I'm so, so sorry, Hilary. I can't believe what I've just done!'

Jack looked at him, clearly thinking that while he had avoided a single breakage over two days Dickie had managed to smash a camera that Hilary had only had out of the box for less than twenty-four hours.

'Don't worry, Dickie,' said Hilary, 'we can easily get it fixed. Accidents happen.'

'Bad enough having dog poo in your kitchen,' I said, in an attempt to put a positive spin on things, 'but even worse if it's someone else's dog.'

'No, I insist on paying, Hilary,' he said. 'Let me know how much it's going to cost to repair and I will send you a cheque.'

'I didn't think we'd get through the weekend without any breakages,' I said to Hilary as we drove off, waving our goodbyes. 'But I certainly didn't think the breakages would be on their side.'

By the time we got to the motorway, Hilary was looking decided peaky.

'You're not upset about the camera, are you?' I asked her.

'No, it's not the camera, but I think there was something dodgy about that duck egg. Can you pull into this service station?'*

*Probably morning sickness.

1. Have you ever stopped to think that the puking may have been a cry for help, that in fact it was not 'happy puking' but 'unhappy puking' or 'not doted upon enough as a baby puking'? Just saying.

2. Don't act like your shit don't stink. Yeah, I filled my nappies, but you should have cherished the opportunity to perform the task of changing me. It is a very good way to bond with a child and maybe if you'd done it a little more often we'd argue less. In fact, I shall look into seeing if there is some way we can make up for all the missed opportunities. I watched a documentary recently about 'adult babies' — maybe this is something we could explore.

3. In this chapter you admit to a) Sellotaping me into a nappy and b) putting me into an armlock. Is it too late to call ChildLine?

4. Mummy did have a drink problem.

5. My dad has been very dismissive of the Chuckle Brothers — 'inferior Laurel and Hardy'! More like Rochdale's answer to Morecambe & Wise. Barry and Paul are two of the finest comic actors of their generation and to my mind not just comic: I see ChuckleVision as more of a comedy drama. Paul in particular is an enigmatic screen presence; he can turn you from laughter to tears with one flick of that trademark moustache. My dad is probably just bitter because he tried to sign them once.

CHAPTER 8

High Jinks

– MICHAEL WHITEHALL –

DURING THE INTERVAL OF THE MARLBOROUGH COLLEGE production of Peter Weiss's *The Persecution and Assassination of Jean-Paul Marat as Performed by the Inmates of the Asylum of Charenton Under the Direction of the Marquis de Sade* – known for short (fortunately) as *Marat/Sade* – I had a chat with the headmaster. He clearly didn't feel it was an appropriate play for the school to be doing – nor indeed did I, especially as we were sitting in the front row watching Jack, then aged fourteen, and his chums, writhing around on the floor simulating sex.* He was playing one of the inmates, a part with no dialogue but a lot of rolling around.

*We were fighting.

At a supper party after the play I mentioned to the headmaster, Edward Gould, that I was producing Terence Rattigan's *The Winslow Boy*, with Edward Fox playing Arthur Winslow and Simon Ward as Sir Robert Morton, which was shortly to visit Bath before coming to London.

'Now that's much more my cup of tea than the dreadful rubbish we've had to endure for the last couple of hours,' said the headmaster.

Mr Gould was a stickler for good behaviour and up to this point in his time at Marlborough Jack had failed to impress on this front, indeed a recent stunt involving fake tan and a school election was still fresh in the memory.

I had been trying to get him onside for some time and as the *Marat/ Sade* supper party was drawing to a close I was handed a top trumps card by Mrs Gould.

'Edward tells me that you are producing *The Winslow Boy*. I love Terence Rattigan.'

'Well, we're playing Bath in a few weeks' time and I'd love to give you a couple of tickets for the show,' I replied.

'Oh, that would be wonderful. And you have Edward Fox in it too,' she said, 'another great favourite of mine. How exciting.'

A few weeks later we headed off to Bath, having arranged to stay the night with the parents of one of Jack's schoolfriends, Archie, en route. The Maynards, a trendy couple with a rambling Elizabethan manor house near Stroud, whom we had never met before, were keen for us to stay overnight with them and bring Jack with us. We had planned to stay at the Royal Crescent Hotel in Bath, as I was not a fan of sleeping in strange people's houses, but Jack wanted to be with Archie, so we accepted the invite to shut him up.

We arrived in time for dinner just as Hilary announced to me that she felt quite ill and thought she had a temperature – great timing, I thought. Our hosts, Jonny and Rosie, showed us into a very ethnic-looking guestroom, with an enormous double bed covered in cream-silk netting and a lot of smouldering scented candles and incense sticks littered around the beamed bedroom and bathroom.* *Much like my parents' bedroom at home!

Dinner was a vegetarian affair with all my least favourite things – curried aubergine, a lot of mushy spicy stuff in bowls – all washed down with a local West Country organic white wine, which was thoroughly unpleasant, as was the whole meal. The centrepiece was a hot suet-crust vegetable pie, a dish I had encountered only once before at a dinner party in London a year or so previously. · Hummus.

Our hosts on that occasion were the Hammonds, a deeply unattractive couple with six children (why do unattractive people always have so many children?**) whom we dined with just the once. Having been served a large portion of the dreaded and very dry vegetable pie, I quickly realized that I was not going to get it down. Help, however, was at hand in the form of their large Alsatian, which was neatly poised under the dining-room table, right in front of my feet. I was sitting next to Mrs Hammond and as she stood up to offer the other guests second helpings of her ghastly pie, I slipped mine under the table and pushed it into the dog's mouth. **Maybe they were trying to get a good-looking one and just gave up after six.

'Well, you certainly enjoyed that,' said Mrs Hammond as she cleared my plate.

'Delicious,' I replied.

At this point there was a retching sound under the table and there sitting at my feet was a wet, regurgitated lump of vegetable mess as the dog padded off to the next room. Avoiding Mrs Hammond's eye, I grabbed the remains and put them into my jacket pocket. By now it had a very foul smell emanating from it. (Why do people say vegetarian food is good for you? Visit the recently occupied lavatory of a vegetarian and savour the gassy aromas of lentils, legumes and brassicas and you'll realize it isn't.) As I left the house I reached into my pocket to get my car keys and discovered that they had lodged themselves into the middle of the now dissolved pie and I was unable to shake Mr Hammond's hand as mine was now covered in vegetarian mush. So I was forced to go for a very theatrical kiss and one-armed hug, which I think surprised him as we had only met that evening and I couldn't even remember his name.

I ate what I could of the Maynards' pie in Stroud. Hilary's flu was beginning to kick in and she had a violent sneezing attack. 'I think you're ready for bed, Hilary,' I said to her, standing up from the table.

'Who wants some more suet-crust pie?'

HIM & ME

I was keen that she had a good night's sleep and was on top form for the Goulds' suck-up evening the following night. I was then conscious of a lot of chopping happening on the sideboard, which I assumed was some kind of exotic dessert being prepared by our host.

'We know what you London media folk are like. I'm getting some post-dinner goodies ready for you,' said Jonny.

He appeared to be using his credit card as part of this process, which seemed strange to me, as indeed did the fact that he was doing the whole thing on a mirror.

'I'm just doing a couple of lines for us,' he said.

The penny dropped. My experience of drugs was extremely limited and, indeed, I had caused some embarrassment at the old *Evening News* Film Awards when a young actress handed me a badly rolled strange-smelling cigarette, which I put out in the ashtray in front of us and she didn't seem at all pleased.* And on another occasion a helpful friend told me that my orgasms would reach the summit of excitement if I inhaled something called amyl nitrate at the appropriate moment. He even gave me a small supply of phials of the stuff to get me started. It was all a total disaster. As I was attempting to grab the thing off the bedside table it slipped out of my hand, rolled under my bottom and I heard a crack.

*Wow, it's like reading Trainspotting.

'What is that disgusting smell?' asked my companion. No peaks of excitement there then. I was also bleeding as I hadn't realized the thing was glass and by the time the sheets had been changed and the bed put back to normal the passion had long since sapped away. However, the bleeding had continued, so I made a cautionary late-night visit to the Chelsea and Westminster A & E, and having admitted to using amyl nitrate, or more specifically not using it, I got some very strange looks from the duty nurse. 'Poppers', as the nurse referred to them, and an injured bottom seemed to cause a lot of eyebrows to be raised, for some reason.**

**That is the most disturbing passage of prose I've ever read.

'Actually, I'm going to have to leave it. We've got an early start in the morning, but thanks anyway,' I told Jonny.

'Overdid it last night, eh?' he said. As I headed upstairs, I heard our hosts trying to persuade Hilary to join them.

'I'll tell you what will clear up that flu of yours,' said Jonny, 'some shisha.' I don't like raw fish, so I continued up to bed. Unbeknownst

That's sushi, you idiot!

to me, with much reluctance and in the face of persistent persuasion, being a polite girl Hilary accepted his invitation in the hope that it would shut our host up and indeed make her feel better. Mrs Whitehall is very naïve in these matters, unlike myself. Little did she know exactly what she was letting herself in for, as it wasn't until she had been puffing away on the shisha pipe for twenty minutes, that Jonny started bragging that it contained the finest Nepalese stunk.

It's skunk not stunk . . . I'm told.

I went to the bedroom, hit my head on a low beam between the bedroom and the en-suite bathroom going in and coming out, and settled down in bed reading* a copy of Madonna's erotic coffee-table book *Sex*, which our hosts had thoughtfully left on the bedside table next to copies of *Country Life* and *House & Garden*.

*Rereading.

Having dozed off for half an hour or so, I was awoken by Hilary's sudden arrival back in the room.

'You're having a late one,' I said.

'Ssshhh,' she hissed. 'Get out of bed and look for bugs.' This seemed to me an odd suggestion in the middle of the night. It wasn't a particularly hot night and we were after all in Wiltshire, not Calcutta, despite what the décor might have implied.

'The room is bugged, they're listening to us. Close the windows,' she said as she disappeared under the bed.

Having been woken up so abruptly, I was now desperate for a wee, so I headed off to the bathroom, hitting my head on a beam again.

'Those fucking beams!'

'Yes, that's it, check the beams,' said Hilary, reappearing from under the bed. 'That's a very common hiding place for bugs.'

Hilary had suddenly become an authority on the location of surveillance equipment.

'What are you talking about? What's all this about?' I barked.

At which point there was a loud knocking on the door.

'Don't let them in!' whispered Hilary. 'They're coming for us. Get into bed and pretend we're asleep.'

Ignoring this advice, I opened the door and there stood Jack in his pyjamas and dressing gown. 'I can't sleep and Archie snores,' he said. 'Please can I come and sleep on your sofa?' I thought in the circumstances it would be better if Jack stayed in his own room. I didn't want him to see his mother in what appeared to be the advanced stages of a drugs overdose, not that I was a great expert in these matters.

I walked him back to his room and when I returned Hilary was looking even more frantic, scanning beneath the loo seat for concealed radio transmitters. I returned to the bed.

'I'm going downstairs to find something to eat, I'm starving,' she said.

'I'm not surprised,' I said, 'after that ghastly dinner.'

'I'll be back in a minute,' she replied. Ten minutes later she returned with quantities of foul smelling cold vegetable fritters, a handful of olives and a weird foreign-looking crisp.* She got into bed and started munching through them, dropping crumbs everywhere.

A poppadum.

'Why didn't you eat them in the kitchen?' I asked.

'I was frightened that they might have taken me,' she said.

'Taken you where, for fuck's sake?' I was beginning to lose it. And then she fell into a deep sleep and kept me awake by shivering, sneezing and sleep-talking for the rest of the night.

When I went down for breakfast the following morning without Hilary, who had opted to have a much-needed lie-in, Jonny and Rosie had disappeared and Jack and I were entertained by the elderly housekeeper. Over breakfast Jack's friend Archie apologized for his parents' absence. 'I'm so sorry they are not here to say goodbye to you. This always happens after my dad has been on a bender.'

Jack explained to me that the word 'bender' now meant an evening of excess and not what it had meant in my day, which was a relief as I was beginning to wonder about Jonny's activities the previous night and what Rosie would have made of it. I certainly didn't have him down as someone who *picked lilacs in the springtime*.

Hilary woke up at about midday and seemed a little worse for wear but assured me it was nothing that a shower and cup of coffee wouldn't sort out. By the time we set off for Bath at five o'clock she seemed to have pulled it together, notwithstanding the original flu symptoms, which were still present.

We met the Goulds in the foyer before the play.

'Hilary, Michael, how lovely to see you,' said Mr Gould.

Hilary went in for a kiss as I plonked one on his wife's cheek.**

**I beg your pardon?*

Drinks and programmes were awaiting our arrival and during the interval we shared a bottle of champagne. They were pleasantly surprised that Jack had joined us.

'Jack loves Rattigan,' I told Mr Gould. 'Don't you, darling?'

I gave Jack one of my *If you let me down on this one I'll kill you* looks. He didn't.

'Yes, I really do, sir,' he said to his headmaster, 'and a lot more than Peter Weiss.'

After the play had finished we took the Goulds backstage and bumped into Simon Ward on our way to Edward's dressing room, so we had a brief chat with him.

'What an extra treat to meet young Winston. It's one of my all-time favourite films,' said Jane excitedly.

Naturally we didn't tell a soul about what had taken place the previous night. But while we were in Bath we did buy a picture called 'Headcases' as a memento of our bizarre trip to Wiltshire, which now hangs in our kitchen next to Hilary's spice rack.

1. My mother's spice rack is something which is very rarely used in our house as she has to cater for a man who thinks 'hummus' is spicy.

2. Please never under any circumstances use the phrase 'plonked one on her cheek'.

3. I think this chapter serves to teach us a valuable lesson. Kids, don't do drugs. But more importantly, adults please don't do them either.

4. I have on occasion at a music festival or club night been known to enjoy the odd popper. I can safely say I will never touch them ever, ever again. Ever.

CHAPTER 9

Camping It Up

- JACK WHITEHALL -

My dad is not one for the great outdoors, and his reluctance to throw himself into the spirit of things made for a very fractious camping holiday.

A trip to Padstow started badly when my mum insisted we drive down via her Aunt Grace in Gloucester. As the more geographically minded reader might realize, my mother employed the term 'via' very loosely: Gloucester lay well over an hour out of our way. Undeterred, we hit the road and – after what seemed like days in the car – arrived at Aunt Grace's grubby-looking cottage, which was surrounded by an unkempt garden.

During the journey, we'd discovered that Grace was one of those 'aunts' who aren't actually a relative, just a single friend of my mother's parents. My grandparents had obviously decided Grace wasn't going to have much luck family-wise, so they tried to incorporate her into their own set-up. That's got to be a depressing moment in your life, when your friends start referring to you as 'Aunt Grace' or 'Uncle Jack'* to make you feel a little less completely and utterly alone.

None of us were close to Aunt Grace, other than my mother. None of us, in fact, were even quite sure who she was.

'Is she the barren aunt?' asked my father.

*Uncles Richard, Nigel and Neil (of whom a lot more later) excluded, of course.

My mother didn't respond. She hates it when he describes women as barren, and he uses this adjective for any married woman without children, no matter what their age.

The journey was hot and I felt pretty carsick. Matters were not helped by my mother refusing to stop off at a service station for food as, quote, we couldn't keep Grace waiting. This was an excuse I struggled to understand, because I suspected a 'barren' woman living with a cat in a cottage in the middle of nowhere probably isn't going to have the kind of jam-packed social calendar that would collapse like a house of cards if I spent twenty minutes in a McDonald's.

By the time we arrived we were all starving, but my mother had promised us tea at Grace's, so at least we had that on the immediate horizon. On the way up the path my father fantasized over what kind of tea Grace might have laid on for her guests. 'These country girls normally bake. Maybe she's knocked up a walnut layer cake or some nice warm scones.'

The eyes of my siblings lit up at the thought of such treats. Then my mother dropped her bombshell, a small piece of information she'd failed to disclose until this moment. 'I doubt she's been rushing around making you cakes all day, Michael,' said my mother. 'Grace has ME.'

'Oh, fuck. *Grace!* She's the one that never gets out of bloody bed.' Just as my father began to accuse my mother of deliberately deceiving him by failing to remind him of Aunt Grace's condition the front door opened. Grace (clad in a wan sort of nightgown) greeted us limply, forgetting my name and then asking my mother to make sure the children didn't touch anything as she hated cleaning.* All in all, she was very far from being the hostess with the mostess.

'Would you like tea?' she wheezed breathlessly. 'Oh, wait. I don't have any tea bags. You see, I haven't been to the shop this week.'

My face sank as my father rolled his eyes.

'A water maybe?' she offered instead.

'*A water*,' my father muttered to me. 'Like it's some kind of cocktail.'

'Perhaps she should have a Red Bull?' I whispered to my dad.

'Do you have anything we could eat, Grace?' my father asked her. She waved a Dickensian-widow hand at an empty larder, and

HIM & ME

* She also seemed to have a germ phobia, which was very tedious.

Is this a sex aid?

then at an equally empty fridge.

'Both barren,' my dad whispered a little too loudly. 'Typical.'

'I normally just eat takeaways.'

My father soon had us out of the cottage and back on the road in the frantic search for something to eat. 'If you're inviting someone for tea, surely the first thing you make sure you have is bloody tea bags!' said my dad. It didn't take him long, though, to move on to what was really on his chest.

'We didn't have ME in my day. It was known as bone idleness!' he said, now spitting out bits of a sorry-looking pasty he'd bought in a fit of desperation at Taunton services. 'Would a man like Sir Winston Churchill have had "ME"?' he asked, labouring the quotation marks around the two letters.

'People don't choose to have ME, Michael,' said my mother.

'Nonsense, Hilary. Do you think for a second that if Winston had "ME" when the bombs were raining down on St Paul's he'd have lain around in bed all day?'

'Yes,' said my mother. It took all my self-control not to add an 'Ohhhh yessss', but my father despises those adverts and it seemed like the wrong moment.*

'I'm sorry, Field Marshal Montgomery,' continued my father, 'Mr Churchill can't make it to the war rooms right now because he's not feeling well. Ridiculous.'

A pause as the car rolled on.

'"ME",' my father snorted. 'It's like bulimia or people who are allergic to nuts. The only treatment these modern conditions require is a good slap.'

We arrived at the campsite early that evening. My mother had discovered it online and the site appeared to be very popular as only a few pitches remained empty. As we pulled up, we saw a cluster of static caravans planted at the entrance and an idyllic stream at the end of the field with kids gambolling in it in the sunset. Our Mitsubishi Shogun careered into the campsite.

My father wound down the window and spoke to the thick-set guy manning the gate. He had bad teeth and was gumming a cigarette as he stood on the porch of his static home, a shirtless boy at his side.

*The Churchill car insurance adverts are a dog turd on the grave of our nation's greatest ever leader.

'Where do we check in?' my father asked as though this man was a concierge. He pointed at a small shed and then spat on the floor. The man spat, that is, not my father. He's not really the spitting type.

In the shed we found the owner of the site, an equally frosty customer who took an instant dislike to my father. I don't know whether it was the long interrogation my father gave him re the campsite's security arrangements,* or his joke that he'd like a *Daily Telegraph* with his wake-up call, or perhaps it was just the fact that, in the middle of a field in Cornwall, Michael Whitehall was still dressed in a three-piece linen suit.

*Which were not impressive.

'Why didn't you wear something more casual?' my mother asked him as he trudged back to the car, his brogues now covered in mud.

'This *is* casual, Hilary. What could be more casual than linen?'

'You could have worn something practical like some jeans and a fleece.'

'A "fleece"?' he said, doing his quotation-mark thing again. My father would sooner be seen in a onesie or the Borat mankini than a fleece.**

**No and no!

We found our plot and began to unpack the car. Molly and I were looking for the tent. Barnaby, meanwhile, was very helpfully pulling out one of the sleeping bags from its casing and on to the ground, getting it covered in mud. My father, who by now was extremely out of his comfort zone, decided to set off up the field to 'check out the facilities'. He returned five minutes later with a face of utter disgust.

'Right, that is it. I am not staying here,' he said, putting one brogue down in a cowpat. 'The state of those lavatories is revolting!'

'Oh, don't be silly,' my mother replied. 'It's a campsite, Michael, not the Savoy!'

'I know it's not the Savoy, Hilary. The Savoy does not have moss growing out of the cistern. The Savoy has lavatory paper. The Savoy has a lock on the door. These lavatories don't have a lock on the door, because there isn't a door to put one on in the first place! Oh, and the Savoy does not place some mute thumb-sucking gypsy boy directly opposite the cubicle in which its guests are trying to relieve themselves. I wouldn't force my worst enemy to use that hovel. I –' my father continued, reaching his crescendo – 'wouldn't even make Peter Mandelson take a dump in there.'

'Why can't you just embrace it, Michael? Try to be at one with nature. Most people when they go camping just go and squat in a bush,' said my mother.

The mere suggestion of him squatting in a bush was the final straw. 'That's it, I'm going to a hotel!'

My father is fussy about lavatories, to the point where he calls them 'lavatories' as opposed to dirty words like 'bog' or 'toilet'. Their cleanliness has always been of paramount importance to him. At home our lavatory is exquisitely kept and lavishly decorated. This obsession has a side-effect, though. My father gets toilet envy.

I've never seen him more upset than when he found out his favourite restaurant in London, the Wolseley on Piccadilly, has a secret loo that's only available to a select few. A sort of VIP shitter, if you will. We had lunch at the Wolseley last year and when he saw the maître d' unlocking it for the late Michael Winner, I thought my father was going to burst into tears.

The sight of the bathroom at this campsite was enough to have Daddy on the phone, looking for a way out. I might add that the speed with which he managed to find himself a hotel was suspiciously quick. I mean, at the height of summer and in a popular tourist destination, to find a room available with an hour's notice? It stank of premeditation.*

*I categorically deny this, Jack.

My father's mind was firmly made up. He would go and stay in the hotel in the nearby town and we would remain on the campsite, despite the poor security features for which he'd berated the campsite manager.

'Are you at least going to help us put up the tent?' my mother asked as my father tried to clamber back into the car and make a swift exit.

'Oh, God, if I have to,' he said grumpily.

We should have let him leave while we had the chance as his help came in very much a directorial capacity. Standing in this muddy field in his linen suit shouting out confusing instructions and gesturing with the handle of his umbrella was not the assistance my mother had hoped for when erecting a three-room tent.

An hour later our tent was finally up thanks to the help of our neighbours.

'I doubt even Aunt Grace could sleep in that thing,' my father said, before roaring off in a cab and leaving us to fend for ourselves. A mother and her children left shivering in a tent, using a bush as a loo with a solitary packet of wet wipes between us, while the so-called hunter-gatherer of the tribe sat in a plush hotel drinking his way through the minibar. My father can be a class act.*

The next couple of days of the family holiday went by. The set-up we had in place – although unconventional – seemed to work pretty well. Me, my mother, Molly and Barnaby would spend the day on the campsite, playing in the woods, running around and having fun. Then, in the evening, we would go and meet Daddy for dinner at the hotel.**

After dinner he would go up to his room and we would go back and sleep in the tent. We didn't get shouted at by him and he got to use a toilet with a seat. It was a win-win situation. Molly even suggested to Mummy that we adopt this system when we got home.

*This is a vicious lie. It was a beautiful warm summer evening, you had the best tent on the site, a top-of-the-range camping stove from Peter Jones, hampers full of food and I had left your mother with three-quarters of a bottle of Puligny-Montrachet, which I had only opened to make sure it wasn't corked.

**We certainly didn't get our money's worth out of that camping stove.

My mother insisted I put my T-shirt back on for this photo.

'We could all live in the garden and Daddy could stay in the house,' she said. My mum definitely seemed tempted.

By the final day we were heading for a completely argument-free holiday, with Grace's 'tealess' tea party a distant memory.

The campsite was amazing. I had all the essential camping experiences that a boy should have at that stage of his life. Prodding a dead bird with a stick, throwing stones in a stream to try to kill fish, and (most importantly) farting in Barnaby's sleeping bag just before he got in it. I even made a holiday friend.

Roy wasn't like other friends I'd made on holiday. Most of those were the kids of my parents' friends. I had originally met Peregrine Fellowes on holiday, for example, the son of my dad's old friend Julian.* We were different ages, and didn't necessarily have that much in common, but we'd been thrust together on a family holiday and we became firm friends.

Roy was very different to Peregrine. Peregrine lived in a country mansion and was rarely seen without a colourful corduroy jacket. Roy lived in one of the static caravans on the campsite and was never seen wearing a shirt. I thought Roy was so cool. He taught me how to fish, let me play on his Game Boy, and his dad even took us down to the beach in the back of his truck. Compared to my friends from Putney, Roy was like Mowgli.

Yet, despite the fact that I talked about Roy non-stop to my mother, I was instructed never to mention my new best friend to my father during dinner, as my mother was intuitive enough to know that my dad might not have been as big a fan.

One day, as Roy and I were taking a stick to the mangled corpse of a dead magpie, both now shirtless (that's right, I'd gone fucking rogue), he confided in me that he'd developed a bit of a crush on my sister, Molly. Weird, I thought. Molly? My sister? A girl? Come on, Roy, I wanted to say, you're meant to be badass.

'Roy, mate, you can do so much better. Trust me, Molly's annoying.'

Then I had a thought. If Molly and Roy were to start going out and eventually get married, then Roy would be my brother-in-law! I'd get to see him all the time and we'd be able to be best mates forever. We could live on the campsite as one big fat happy family. I'd never have to wear a shirt again!

An arrangement that would have suited me down to the ground. You were at your most bombastic.

Now who's the name-dropper?

*Another fine Old Amplefordian.

'I'll put in a good word for you, Roy,' I said sagely.

It turned out, however, that I needn't have bothered. Molly, too, was smitten by Roy's bare-chested charms. Within hours of my giving Roy the go-ahead, they were holding hands and playing kiss chase; no grabbing in a car park as Channel 4 might have you believe, Roy was more the gentleman traveller. Roy and Molly clicked so much, in fact, that by the following day Roy had practically forgotten his old pal. He spent all his time with Molly, taking her down to the stream to fish, prodding dead birds together. Whether or not she was topless too, I don't know.

I was heartbroken. Betrayed by my friend – Peregrine would never have done this – had the last three days meant nothing to Roy?

Evening drew near and, as was the routine now, Daddy arrived in the car to collect us and take us up to the hotel for dinner.

'Where's your mother?' he asked as she walked out of a bush, dragging a half-naked Barnaby and a handful of soiled dock leaves. He shuddered and then asked where Molly was.

'With her stupid boyfriend,' I replied without thinking, still raw from Roy's betrayal.

'Boyfriend?' snapped my father.

'Yeah, she's going out with Roy, my friend who lives in a caravan. They're kissing by the stream.'

'Hilaaarrrryyy!'

For a man who had no knowledge of how to put up a tent, the speed with which my father dismantled one was remarkable. He was like an SAS commando behind enemy lines whose position had been compromised. Barnaby barely had time to put his trousers back on before he and I were slung into the car, which was swiftly locked as the search party went out. Down from the stream came Mummy and Daddy clutching a bemused and slightly blush-cheeked Molly.

We sped out of the campsite, heading back to London via the hotel to pick up my dad's stuff.

'You're overreacting, Michael,' said my mum.

'But why do we have to leave, Daddy?' I added, feeling guilty for exposing my sister's tryst.

'To stop your sister eloping with a gypsy,' said my father. 'Unless you want her to end up running a bloody funfair?'

Now you have to remember that, at the time, I was twelve, Molly was nine and Barnaby seven. The idea of having a sister running an actual funfair was just about the coolest thing ever. Molly could get me infinite goes on the dodgems, free candyfloss every day! – she might even let me have a go at the shooting games with an air rifle that hadn't had its barrel bent. Heaven.

But even at that tender age, I knew my father well enough to realize this was probably not the response he was looking for. I kept my opinions to myself.

There was silence in the car. Then Barnaby piped up. 'Are we going to stop off at Aunt Grace's for tea on the way back, Daddy?'

1. I am still speechless about this whole episode and have nothing further to add, other than to say that thankfully we never clapped eyes on Roy again (unless of course Molly is still seeing him on the QT?).

2. Jack has me quoted as referring to Field Marshal Montgomery being present in Winston Churchill's cabinet war room during the Blitz. I would never have said this. As you all know, Montgomery did not reach the rank of Field Marshal until the 1st of September 1944, a full three years after the Blitz. It would have been Lieutenant General Montgomery but more likely than not, he's got him confused with Field Marshal Ironside. Alas, my son is not a geographer or a historian.

3. I have since received assurances from the owners of the Wolseley, Chris Corbin and Jeremy King, that if I were to need use of it, the VIP lavatory would be at my immediate disposal.

4. The reality is that I was extremely good at erecting tents. In the early 1950s I was in the Ampleforth scout troop, had loads of badges, loved the uniform, especially the woggle and learnt all the outdoor skills that a young boy needs – tying knots, lighting a fire with twigs, navigating by the stars and, a particularly essential skill in those days, keeping one step ahead of the errant hands of over-familiar scout masters. *

*I'll ask again, is it too late to call ChildLine?

My big fat gypsy bromance.

Part IV

A Matter
of Life
and Death

CHAPTER 10

Man and Beast

– JACK WHITEHALL –

'I shall pick them off one by one,' my father declared, perched on a wooden chair in the garden, an air rifle raised to his beady eye. Rats had infested our home and we'd tried everything to get rid of them. My mum had laid traps, but to no avail. Pest control had been equally unsuccessful.* So – in one last-ditch, desperate effort – my father had decided to take matters into his own hands. There he was, sat on the back porch like some gun-toting old sheriff in a rocking chair anticipating an Indian raid.

*We had a rat man round whose opening gambit was that he had a sneaky admiration for the rat and its ability to adapt and outwit its main predator – us. He was a man who should definitely have considered a career change, as he clearly didn't have his heart in it and failed to kill one single rat.

'It's just a waiting game now. Who blinks first. Me versus beast,' he muttered, getting into the role. Perhaps he imagined himself as a dashing nineteenth-century solider somewhere exotic, colonial India maybe, hunting tigers in a Rudyard Kipling sort of a way. To my eyes, though, the scene more closely resembled one from *Dad's Army*. The air rifle he was using was an antique and I suspect that – even if it did still function – the chances of my father being able to hit a moving target were extremely slim.

His hunting companion was Mabel, a terrier we all loved but who was very much on her last legs. Mabel was about twelve years old and completely knackered. She was used to spending the autumn of her life crumpled in a ball in the sitting room. But today was a reprieve, a last hurrah, a chance to show there was life in the old dog yet. The Mabzoider, as my dad called her, was perched by his side, acting as his gun dog, ready for action.

'And what I don't pick off, the Mabzoider will catch,' he claimed, though this scenario seemed a little unlikely. Mabel was hardly the Hound of the Baskervilles: riddled with cataracts, almost completely blind in both eyes, sporting a pronounced limp and with general all-round poor health it would have to be a pretty immobile rat for Mabel to catch it. Mabel couldn't catch worms. Actually, come to think of it, I think by that stage she might have had worms as well.

My dad, Mabel and a rifle – three antiques. All we needed was Sylvester Stallone and we had *The Expendables 3*. 'If I glance one of the rats, Jack, make sure you send the Mabzoider off in the right direction,' my father instructed me, ignoring the fact that – in the highly unlikely event of him hitting one of the rats, and the equally unlikely event of me being able to marshal Mabel – by the time Mabel got to the wounded body it would have had time to bleed out, die and possibly even decompose completely, or be eaten by its own ratty brethren.

Your classic hunter will hide in total silence for hours in order to catch their prey. In this, too, my father was a dead loss.

'Why do they have to be in our garden?' he bellowed, waving the gun in the direction of the beautiful gazebo he'd recently bought, but which was now strewn with a mess of rat excrement and uncon-sumed pellets of poison. 'Why can't they be in the Chambers' garden?' he added, indicating our neighbours. 'Mind you, even a rat wouldn't want to be in proximity to Vivienne Chambers!'

My father didn't see eye to eye with Vivienne, and not just on account of her diminutive height. She was an aggressive woman, involved in all sorts of action groups and residents associations who, by all accounts, had been going through the menopause for nearly a decade (his observation, not mine). She complained about everything and everyone. Unluckily for us, she also lived in the house at the bottom of our garden.* I mean the house that backed on to our garden, not literally a house 'at the bottom of our garden' – that makes it sound like she was a hobbit we kept in our own little grotto. Although, admittedly, it sometimes felt like that, not least because she was hobbit-sized.

We had many run-ins with Vivienne. My father once lost his temper and called her a 'weasel' when she'd threatened to report

*I certainly would never have bought the house had I known what was over the fence.

*One of the many ruses I deployed to try to drive her out. When I was having a burn-up and fanning the flames in the incinerator, I sometimes pondered on the tragic death of Joan of Arc and how good Mrs Chambers would be in the title role.

'I will be on to the Environmental Health Officer as soon as the yuletide season is over, Mr Whitehall!' she squealed in her shrill little voice over the fence. 'This directly contravenes the Clean Air Act. You are polluting my airspace, Mr Whitehall. You are violating my personal area!' The thought of violating Vivienne Chambers' 'personal area' was enough to make my father have what looked like a small stroke. I don't blame him. To judge from his haunted appearance, I doubt Mr Chambers had done any 'violating' for years.

Perish the thought!

'If you don't go away, Vivienne, I will throw you on to this fire,' my father shouted back. I have to assume she was livid, because I couldn't see her face over the five-foot fence.

The following summer there was another flashpoint that (thank God) I wasn't around to witness. My father opened his curtains one morning and – looking out of the bedroom window – received a nasty shock. There was Vivienne Chambers in her garden, basking like an emaciated seal in the early-morning sun. Topless. My father went straight round to our neighbour Edwin Mullins for moral support.

'I need a drink, Edwin.'

'What's happened, Michael?' asked Edwin in a concerned voice.

'I've just seen Vivienne Chambers disporting in the altogether,' my father said in what I imagine to have been a hoarse, hunted tone.

'Oh, God, join the club,' came the reply. 'I was subjected to that last year and it will be burned on to my retinas for the rest of my life. They look like two fried eggs on a plate – I couldn't eat breakfast for weeks,' Edwin went on as he poured out two large vodka and tonics, triple measures, one of which my father accepted with a shaking hand.**

**One of the only times in my life that I resorted to a short before midday!

After that particular incident, the fence at the end of our lawn was raised another three feet and a thick hedgerow of Leylandii was planted. Just to make sure.

So there was my dad, sat waving his gun, probably hoping that, if he did fire off a round at a passing rat, the bullet would sail through the animal, the fence and land somewhere painful in the slack-breasted hobbit.

The truth is we'd never had much luck with animals. When I was ten, after much nagging, my mum bought me a hamster, Doodle. My grandpa had been ill, and she thought that having a hamster I'd love, care for and then see die would help me come to terms with loss and grief. A wise bit of parenting by my mum, the only problem being that Doodle ran away within a week.*

'Well, as you said, Hilary, the boy must come to terms with loss,' said my dad coldly. But it was no use. I threw a tantrum, threatened to run away and was promptly bought a new hamster. This newer model, Highbury, was stronger, faster and cuter than Doodle had ever been. What lesson this taught a young boy about losing those you love is anyone's guess. But I remember spending a whole holiday thinking that if I lost my grandpa, I could throw a tantrum and get given a better grandpa in return.

Rabbits were bought, lost and died. One of the corpses was even found in Vivienne Chambers' garden. 'Maybe it saw her sunbathing like I did and just keeled over,' hypothesized my father to his unamused teary children. And after the departure of the Mabzoider to the Big Kennel in the Sky, Charlie, a long-haired, shaggy-looking terrier arrived from Battersea Dogs & Cats Home.

But maybe the most traumatic experience in relation to animals came on a trip to my granny Woose's house when I was about twelve. We travelled down to Kent for a weekend and, on our arrival in the village where they lived, drove past a deer that had been hit by a car. It was in a bad way — we couldn't tell if it was dying or dead, but either way it was pretty mangled. Me, my brother and sister were very into Disney films at the time and the sight made my sister particularly upset.

'Will Bambi be OK?' asked Molly.

'Yes, he'll be fine,' said my mum, turning from the bloody mess to my father with a look I was old enough to realize read as 'Bambi's fucked'.

Later, after dinner at my granny and grandpa's, with Molly and Barnaby still a little shaken up, my Uncle Billy arrived. Billy, like 'Aunt Grace', was an 'uncle' who wasn't actually an uncle. Still, at least he was technically related to the family, being a distant cousin of my mother. Uncle Billy had been orphaned at a youngish age and my grandmother had kindly taken him under her wing. Billy, to quote

*Through your own carelessness, I seem to remember. You went to bed, leaving him in a hamster ball running around your bedroom. Not surprisingly, in the morning, there was the hamster ball, open, and no sign of Doodle.

my father, 'never took on a wife' and instead chose to marry himself to the church. He was manically religious, but friendly enough, if a little bit odd. He lived in a camper van at the end of my grandparents' drive but viewed their house as an extension of his own living space, though he seldom troubled them for the use of their washing facilities, preferring the *au naturel* approach to personal hygiene. He always wore army boots and camouflage trousers, sported a big bushy white beard and looked like a homeless David Bellamy.*

David Bellamy looks like a homeless David Bellamy.

When he appeared in the kitchen that evening he was covered from head to toe in mud, having just played a football match for a local team; he had clearly decided to sidestep the post-match shower.

'All right, guys, peace be with you,' he said as he took some milk from the fridge, which he proceeded to glug straight from the carton, his bearded mouth engulfing the top of the receptacle. A bedtime Nesquik was firmly off the menu for anyone who liked, say, chocolate or strawberry flavour over that of sweaty mud-flecked beard.

'We saw Bambi, Billy. He had been hit by a car. I hope he's going to be OK,' said Molly.

'The sting of death is sin, and the power of sin is the law,' said Billy with his usual tact. A man of the world like Billy knows that emotionally fragile little girls just love being quoted Corinthians.

My mum explained the deer's predicament, and Billy was keen to know exactly where we'd seen the body. After she told him, Billy left, muttering something about the will of God.

Fuck knows what he's going to do, ran the unspoken general consensus. Knowing Billy, he probably thinks he can heal it.

'Tea or coffee?' asked Woose.

'I'll have a coffee please,' said my dad. 'Black.'

'You have it white, don't you?'

'I'm on a diet,' he replied, as Woose plonked the carton of milk down in front of him.

The following day was spent helping my grandparents pick vegetables from the garden: carrots, peas and cabbage. Growing up during the war had endowed my grandparents with certain characteristics, which they'd passed down to their four children. These characteristics include the determination to forage and hoard. No piece of home-grown fruit or vegetable would ever go to waste. No 'buy one get one free' offer was ever not taken up, however unnecessary the duplicate being bought. Every leftover was bagged, tagged and bunged into the fridge for future use.

Certainly no sell-by date was ever adhered to. Last Christmas I was given some cherry-brandy liqueurs by my granny (because obviously a boy in his twenties can't get enough cherry-brandy liqueurs). The box had a large shiny sticker with a sell-by date on it, and I noticed there'd been an attempt to peel this sticker off. When that hadn't worked Woose decided to just block it out with a thick black pen. My cherry-brandy liqueurs had been redacted on a need-to-know basis, like documents left over from the war in Iraq. Held under the right light, however, you could just about make out the year '1988' under the black ink. Maybe it was like when you give someone a CD of the hit singles from the year they were born. I'll give my granny the benefit of the doubt. She's the only member of our family who likes liqueurs, so she ate the whole box in a fit of waste not want not Blitz spirit.

My mother hoards a bit, but she's positively wasteful in comparison to my grandmother. Woose's pantry is always piled high with tins of food, dried fruits, pickled vegetables, potted meats and spreads, including some hideous-looking thing called Heinz Sandwich Spread. It looks like a bunker being prepared for a nuclear holocaust: walls of tinned goods on one side and endless industrial-sized sacks of potatoes on the other. Woose doesn't throw *anything* away. Her house is the only place you can still find Marathon bars and jars of jams adorned with gollywogs. I've never opened a can of Coke at my granny's house that still had all of its fizz. Every packet of Rice Krispies has long since lost its snap, crackle and pop. Her food is literally from 'a different time' – her Rice Krispies are so old that Snap, Crackle and Pop are also gollywogs. Going into her larder is like stepping out of the Tardis and into the 1940s.

My granny is also a big fan of swiping stuff from any restaurant that's stupid enough to lay anything out as complimentary. A free sachet of ketchup will not be out long if Woose is around. But she doesn't stop at ketchup. Salt and pepper (sachets or shakers), bar snacks, the little milk pots you get in hotels. On aeroplanes she will ask strangers sitting five seats away if they've finished with their teaspoons, which sit at the bottom of her capacious handbag for the rest of the holiday.

Literally anything that's free will end up in her bag. I think she might be the reason our economy's fucked – I'm amazed Heinz hasn't gone into administration. She also loves any 'all you can eat' or 'serve yourself' establishment. The Harvester salad buffet bar is her holy grail, the hoarder's Mecca. We take her there once a year on her birthday so she can fill up a couple of bin liners full of complimentary potato salad and coleslaw.

'Mum, do you need that much?' my mother will ask.

'Billy will have it for his supper. You know what his appetite's like,' Woose will reply as she shovels a good few kilos' worth of croutons into a carrier bag.

My mum recently had lunch with Woose at a Harvester. At the end of the meal my granny told my mum to put her leftover chips into a napkin, so that she could give them to Billy for his tea. My mother did as she was told. But when she tried to slip the chip-filled napkin into my granny's handbag, she snapped at her 'Don't put them in there, Hilary, they'll melt the butter.' My mother looked inside. It was already full with several mini packs of Anchor.

Although my mother is roped in to help from time to time, my granny's main accomplice is Billy. As well as being a volunteer at the church, Billy is a part-time caretaker at a local school. I know that's almost a cliché, but it's true.

One of Billy's roles there is to clean out the bins and he's developed a penchant for looting discarded items. This is why my granny's fridge will often be filled with half-drunk bottles of Coke, Dairylea Dunkers with only one dunker left, and slightly mouldy bits of old fruit that schoolchildren wantonly binned, but which Billy's magpie eye saw glinting from under old crisp wrappers and other bits of detritus. Billy's worst 'bin binge' actually happened on his way home from school, when he discovered a half-defrosted chicken in a bin on the high street. He casually fished it out and brought it back to my granny.

'It's only two days past the sell-by date,' he told her. No matter, it could have been two years past the sell-by date. For my granny a free chicken is a free chicken. It was served up that very night with a side of pilfered salad cream and a handful of two-week-old Harvester macaroni salad, a single dunker protruding from its cavity.

Our trip was drawing to a close, with just Sunday lunch to go. Billy had gone out on an early-morning mission to do something or other, but he was back now and my granny was slaving over the stove. Her Sunday lunches were always a highlight – the crown jewels of her cooking repertoire – and we were looking forward to roast beef accompanied by the vegetables we'd helped pick for her that morning and her usual choice of three different puddings, as she liked to make sure we didn't go away hungry.

As we tucked into our food that Sunday, though, we all seemed to be making slightly heavy work of chewing.

'This beef's a little on the tough side, isn't it?' my father said sheepishly. 'Did you go to a different butcher?'

'Butcher? Oh no. And it's not beef, Michael,' said Woose. 'Billy brought it home this morning. It's veni–'

'What's for pudding?' interjected my mum, quickly changing the topic of conversation.

My mum and dad went quiet, concentrating on their vegetables and giving their unidentified meat a pretty wide berth, while my brother, sister and I tucked in to second and third helpings.

'Thank God I stuffed up on all those nuts,' said my dad as we got into the car, nuts that had no doubt been swiped from the local pub. We pulled out of the drive and drove past the area of the road where the deer had been on our way down the previous day. The road was now empty, but for a lone skidmark of blood on the pavement and some muddy footprints next to it. These footprints clearly belonged to someone dragging the carcass in the direction from which we'd come.

'Look, Bambi made it! Yay!' said my sister.

'Yes, Molly. It looks like she did,' said my mum as her stomach gurgled.

Oh, and my father and Mabel never did pick off any of the rats by the way. I'm sure if they had, however, that Billy would have been more than happy to take the bodies off our hands and lug them back down to my granny's for her to whip into a tasty Sunday lunch. Rat casserole, anyone?

The Deer Hunter

1. I am a better marksman than you would ever give me credit for. I have been on many a shoot and very seldom returned empty handed.

2. Woose may be thrifty but she has always been extremely generous to us.

3. I am extremely fond of Heinz Sandwich Spread. Some say it looks and smells like sick, but I disagree. I think it has a very delicate aroma and is delicious with bread and butter. However, unlike Billy and Woose, I'm not sure that I would chance it past its use-by date.

4. On the waste not want not front, I gather Billy didn't let the pelt go to waste either. I shudder to think what he used it for. Presumably some kind of fur throw, for those cold nights in the camper van.

5. Having a slightly delicate constitution, I have never been able to face venison again after this episode. Thank God for your grandmother's three-puddings policy. I partook of all three home-made choices that day: Queen of Puddings, fruit jelly with cream and chocolate brownie.

CHAPTER 11

Clipper Rash

– MICHAEL WHITEHALL –

SOME YEARS AGO, IN A HOPELESS ATTEMPT at cutting the Whitehall family's running costs, I started doing things that, prior to that point, had been totally alien to me, some more random than others.

Going to the Garrick Club on the bus lasted a very short time and ended when I had an altercation with a very surly driver who wouldn't accept a fifty-pound note for my fare from Sloane Square to Putney Common.* Ditto sending my shirts to the local dry cleaners instead of to Burlingtons – a brief encounter with the Deluxe Dry Cleaners not only wrecked my shirts but gave me back a very nasty short-sleeved garment made by a company called G-star Raw, which was certainly not mine. There were other ludicrous non-starters, like switching off lights obsessively, driving slowly on motorways to conserve petrol (seventy miles per hour has always seemed pretty slow to me anyway), banning Hilary from using the tumble dryer (as a result finding wet laundry draped all over the radiators throughout the house) and buying reduced-price foodstuffs at Waitrose, although at least there was never any question of shopping elsewhere.**

And then there was the question of our terrier Charlie's grooming arrangements.

'How much?' I said to Hilary. 'You spent forty-five pounds getting the dog's hair cut? That's more than the bloody dog cost and more than double what I spend on my hair!'

*You're ridiculous.

**Well at least that's what you think. My mother has been known to shop around a bit, making sure to serve you any produce bought from other supermarkets under the pretence that it's Waitrose. Those 'Waitrose' hot cross buns you enjoyed last Easter, the finest and moistest you'd tasted for years – they were from Lidl! I shall never trust her again.

'Well, you haven't got much left,' Hilary replied. Perhaps realizing that she might have been ripped off at Perfect Pets, she added, 'OK, I'll buy some clippers and do it myself.'

'I'm not letting you loose on my hair,' I replied. 'You know Timothy Williams of Timothy Williams Hair Design, Barnes, is the only person I allow near my hair.'

'Not you,' said Hilary crossly, 'the dog.'

'What are you watching?' I asked her a couple of weeks later, as she was sitting in front of the TV in the kitchen.

'It's the DVD* that came with the dog clippers I've bought. It shows you how to "create a skirt" and do a graduated style. I can't believe I'm actually watching this, but I'm not going to let you win on this one. I've said I'll clip Charlie and save us forty-five pounds and clip him I will!'

*The director's cut.

Once Mrs Whitehall makes up her mind, woe betide anyone who tries to get her to change it.

I have to say that Charlie didn't look hugely pleased, as his mistress hacked away with her rasping whining clippers at his long curly locks, large clumps of which were now scattered across the kitchen floor. 'That's so gross, Mummy!' said Jack. 'Wouldn't you have been better off doing that in the garden?' he added helpfully.

Forty-five minutes later we managed to keep straight faces as Hilary brought Charlie into the sitting room. He looked a mess – a short-haired mess admittedly, but still a mess.

'Why has he got a stripe down half of his back?' I asked Hilary.

'Very observant, Michael,' she said through heavily gritted teeth. 'That's where I didn't have it on the right setting and it was cutting too short.'**

**Seriously the dog looked like one of Brian Harvey from E-17's eyebrows.

'Might it have been better to finish before you adjusted it?' asked Jack.

'You've suddenly become an authority on canine grooming, have you, Jack?' she said. 'He's done now and I've saved your father forty-five pounds.'

'Minus the cost of the clippers, of course,' I added.

A couple of days later, Charlie had developed a very nasty rash on his stomach, which, being a dog, he wouldn't leave alone and kept licking, until his whole undercarriage had turned bright red. ——

Bright red undercarriage, we've all been there. Speak for yourself.

The following morning, before she headed off to Kent to see her mother, Hilary handed me the name and phone number of our vet, with strict instructions to take Charlie there as soon as possible. I made an appointment for that afternoon and instructed Jack to accompany me.

'Can't you do it on your own?'

'No, Jack, you can bloody well come with me. I can't cope with vets and I might not be able to park, so you can just be helpful for once,' I replied.

'Charlie Whitehall!' called the dippy blonde on reception later that afternoon. I remarked to Jack that it was an extraordinary coincidence that there was someone at the vet with the same surname as us.*

*I thought he was joking!

'What's the problem?' asked the hatchet-faced lady vet in a clipped South African accent. She bore more than a passing resemblance to P. W. Botha.

'He's got some kind of complaint on his stomach area,' said Jack.

Mrs Botha** inspected it.

**Oh, we're calling her that now, are we?

'This dog has clipper rash,' she announced. 'Have you been clipping him?'

Jack and I exchanged looks.

'No, definitely not,' we replied, unfortunately in unison.

'Don't lie to me.' she said, 'Someone has given this dog a very nasty clipper rash.'

Jack and I exchanged looks again. How could Hilary have done this to us?

'It wasn't either of us,' said Jack.

Mrs Botha eyeballed me.

'I've no idea who did it. My wife looks after all this kind of stuff,' I said, trying not to look too shifty.

'Well, you must ask your wife who did this, as it has not been done properly. The dog now has an infection. He must be treated with antibiotics and I will prescribe cream which must be applied three times a day to his infected areas. And this must include around his genitalia.'

Looking straight at Jack, she added, 'And whilst he is here I shall empty his anal glands for you. Now, one of you must hold him while I administer the antibiotic injection.'

At this point Jack developed a problem with one of his shoelaces, much as I used to at those rugby-tackle moments, so the vet handed Charlie to me as Jack ducked out of sight.

'That will be one hundred and thirty-five pounds,' said the dippy blonde at the reception, 'and we'd like to see Charlie again in a week.

'We're certainly not going back in there again,' I said to Jack on the way home. 'We could have Charlie clipped three times for that. And as soon as we get home I'm going to chuck those bloody clippers before your mother gets her hands on them again. And, as I held the dog for his anal gland evacuation, you can bloody well rub the cream around his dick!'*

*There was no way that I did! Mum did it, of course!

1. No dogs were harmed in the making of this story. Having applied the cream to Charlie's undercarriage, he was back in perfect health within a couple of days.

2. We were both so traumatized by the experience that we ended up moving vets and now go to a nice man in Putney who has never gone anywhere near Charlie's anus.

3. You ended up looking really cool in that G-star Raw T-shirt.

CHAPTER 12

In Sickness and in Health

– MICHAEL WHITEHALL –

JACK ENDED UP IN HOSPITAL on a few occasions when he was a child as indeed did I. His early years were dominated by the fact that he was a mouth breather, due to a permanently blocked nose. He also had some speech delay and seemed to mispronounce words. What with this and the dribbling, he could soak the front of a T-shirt in minutes, and by the time he was two, Hilary didn't think it was appropriate for him to still be wearing a bib or the spotted handkerchief that she used to tie round his neck to catch the dribble. However, this needed looking into and, after consultation with an ENT specialist, Jack was found to be in need of having his adenoids removed and grommets fitted in his ears. The condition was known as glue ear.*

This procedure required an overnight stay in hospital. Hilary was otherwise engaged with a baby pending, so I found myself sharing a room with him at the Chelsea and Westminster. Having had a general anaesthetic, he looked very sorry for himself. Hilary had loaded me up with Jack's security blanket, known as Quilty, from which he was never parted, particularly not in moments of stress, as well as the contents of Jack's library – *Thomas the Tank Engine* (a great favourite of his then and now), *The Tiger Who Came for Tea*, and *Dogger*, which I hasten to add was a children's book about a boy and his dog.**
Jack eventually fell asleep in my arms, tightly cuddling Quilty.

*And thus the least pleasant paragraph ever written reaches its crescendo.

She's pregnant again!

**Not a man and his car.

The following morning he was as right as rain and started to hear things that he had never heard before. Whether hearing my nasal drawl with more clarity was deemed an advantage, I'm not so sure.*

* * *

With his hearing and nasal problems now sorted, we had to attend to his visual deficiencies. Glasses were bought and subsequently lost, bought again, then broken, and finally scrapped altogether as the appeal of contact lenses became irresistible. This left only his teeth to be fixed.

Before Jack started school Hilary wanted me to invest what was akin to the GDP of a medium-sized Pacific island in having his teeth fixed.

'They look fine to me,' I said to Hilary, inspecting Jack's mouth. 'He's only ten, they'll grow straighter and that gap between his two front teeth will close up in a couple of years. Kenneth More used to say that a gap in your teeth was very sexy.'

'I don't care what Kenneth More thought,' said Hilary. 'Jack's having them fixed. We're going to see Mr Flynn. Fiona says he's the best orthodontist in the country.'

'And probably the most expensive,' I mumbled.**

Part of my reluctance to put Jack through this was my own child-hood fear of dentists. I was terrified of my Aunty Winnie, who was my father's sister, but I was even more terrified of her husband, Uncle Charles, who was a dentist. Charles had a dental practice in Beauchamp Place, Knightsbridge, which, although miles away from where we lived, we were obliged to use as he didn't charge us. My vivid memory of Charles, in addition to the smell of his surgery – a mixture of disinfectant, cigarettes, alcohol and fear – was him peering over me in his white coat as I lay shaking in his chair. The fact that he was also a dead ringer for Clement Attlee didn't help, as we were an ardently Conservative family and Attlee was the enemy. The horror increased when he produced from behind his back a hypodermic needle that could have anaesthetized a horse and then reached for a piece of equipment that looked like a pneumatic drill. Uncle Charles was a man devoid of any bedside manner and would always prepare me for the needle and the drill with the words, 'This will hurt!'

It did.

*I'm like the man with the pea in his ear in Captain Corelli's Mandolin.
A literary reference from Jack – that's a rarity.
It's a film with Nicolas Cage.

An old British film star that my dad looked after.

**He also had the worst breath I've ever smelt, like a wet-fish trawler on a hot day.

Nightmares consisting of a veiny red nose, a hideous drill and a cigarette smouldering in an ashtray kept me well away from dentists for many years to come.

Graham Flynn, however, a warm, softly spoken and gentle man, struck fear into my heart in a different way, not with a drill but with his accounts department. It seemed to me that all orthodontists live on the Isle of Man, where they have tax-sheltered the millions of pounds paid to them by the doting parents of the buck-toothed. A legend in the world of child orthodontics, Flynn was based in Harley Street and operated upon a production line of preparatory-school-aged children. He would have six of them lined up in individual dentist's chairs at the same time, as he sat in a wheeled chair and travelled down the line at speed, attending to their every dental need.* He had the look of a man who, when taking a flight from Heathrow to Douglas on a 'golfing trip', might appear at the airport without any clubs in tow, merely a large black briefcase.

*Though you could smell him when he was about three chairs off.

Before: the teeth that had 'nothing wrong with them'.

After: the £4000-smile.

The first stage of Jack's treatment was to realign his jaw to correct his overbite with the use of twin 'blocks'. I told Mr Flynn that I was not remotely surprised that Jack's jaw needed realigning as he never stopped talking. The blocks were two large pieces of clear plastic that Jack was to leave in his mouth at all times except when he was eating.*

One day, as usual, Jack had placed his blocks in a napkin while he ate lunch in the school dining room. He then forgot to pick them up at the end of the meal and didn't realize that he had lost them until he was in class later that afternoon. Panic! Rather than face the wrath of his mother, who knew the precise cost of the blocks, he rang me up in tears. 'We have to find them, Daddy. You have to come up here and help me.'

Up to this point I had never had any contact with the contents of industrial-sized dustbins following a lunch service for 650 children. It was not a pretty sight. Having sifted through the first two bins to no avail we started on the last one. Fried noodles and overcooked vegetables on a second encounter are not something to linger over** and just as I was about to give up all hope Jack shouted, 'Daddy, we had Fruit Corners for lunch! I definitely think we're getting near now.'

I plunged my hand into a layer of yoghurt- and fruit-splattered cartons, which were mixed in with hundreds of screwed-up napkins.

'Foraging for food, Mr Whitehall?' said a voice behind me. 'Times that hard, eh?'

It was Desmond Devitt, Jack's housemaster. 'We don't like parents scavenging around in the school dustbins. Not good for our image.'

I explained.

'Good luck,' he said, walking off to his next class.

'Very helpful,' I said to Jack, 'but, to be honest, I draw the line at opening up all these napkins; I'm in a suit. If I flick them out, you'll have to do it.'

Half an hour later the bin was empty and still no blocks.

'You're going to have to tell Mummy. I can't,' Jack said. 'Will you ring her now?'

'Do you know how much they cost?' I asked.

'I've no idea.'

'Well, don't worry. I'm sure it won't be too expensive to replace them.' I was beginning to feel sorry for Jack; it was the sort of thing

*I believe they were called 'blocks' because they effectively blocked any chance you had of getting a girlfriend.

**It smelt like Mr Flynn had breathed into a bin liner.

I could easily have done myself and I felt he needed a bit of moral support. I made the call.

'How much? A thousand pounds for a couple of bits of plastic? You must be joking!' I shouted down the phone to Hilary.

'at' Hilary.

After Jack's second pair of blocks had done their realigning Mr Flynn announced that the next stage of treatment was called 'train tracks' and would cost us two thousand pounds.*

*The hope you had of getting a girlfriend when you stopped wearing the blocks was suddenly derailed, hence 'train tracks'.

'How do I know that these won't end up in a Fruit Corner?' I said.

'Because these are cemented to his face, Michael.'

'Bloody good thing too.'

People often remark on Jack's wonderful smile but all I can see is four thousand pounds and a wheelie bin full of Fruit Corners.

* * *

Jack showed how protective he was of me from a very young age. Our incinerator at the end of the garden was often a slow starter and early one January, in an attempt to get all the Christmas cards and round robins disposed of well ahead of Twelfth Night,** I made the fatal mistake of hurling a full can of petrol on them. As I applied a match there was an explosion of nuclear proportions, accompanied by an ominous smell of burning hair, which turned out to be coming from my head and eyebrows.

**Vivienne Chambers had been particularly annoying that Christmas.

'I can't believe you did that,' said Hilary helpfully as she inspected my now reddened and hairless face. 'We'd better get you off to A & E.'

As we got into the car a three-year-old Jack said, 'Why don't you take Quilty, Daddy? It'll make you feel better.'

'And it will keep you company while you're waiting,' said Hilary.

* * *

I have had the odd bout of 'tummy trouble' over the years and very soon after Jack had arrived at the Dragon for his first term as a boarder I was rushed off to hospital and ended up having emergency surgery. With impeccable timing Jack was due at Marlborough College for an introductory interview with his prospective new housemaster, Niall Hamilton. In retrospect we should have postponed it, but Hilary took the view that it was best to carry on as normal and so kept the appointment without me. When she called in to visit me that evening, having dropped Jack back at school, I asked her how it had gone.

'Not great to be honest. Jack was in a really odd mood. He looked very uninterested and clammed up whenever he was asked anything.'

'That's really strange,' I said. 'I know he wants to go to Marlborough.'

'Well, something was up,' said Hilary. 'And despite my best efforts, he wouldn't tell me what was bothering him.'

The following day the penny dropped. Roger Trafford called to say that he had had Marlborough on the phone and they were not at all sure that Jack was the sort of boy that they were looking for. He had been morose, silent, had snapped at his mother and seemed to have nothing to offer. As a result of this conversation Roger Trafford had called Jack into his office to see what he had to say for himself. At which point Jack had burst into tears and told Roger how upset and worried he was about me. He had calmed Jack down and said that he would sort things out with Marlborough. Hilary brought Jack into hospital to see me that weekend and I reassured him that I was on the mend and that he mustn't worry. Roger arranged for Jack, Hilary and me to have a second go with the housemaster later in the term. On this visit Jack was a boy transformed, to the point where Mr Hamilton could hardly get a word in edgeways, Jack was chatting and joking so much, something he continued to do for the five years that he was under Mr Hamilton's care. I often wonder, on reflection, if he would have preferred the silent version

* * *

There was one upside for Jack and me when we were ill and that was that as soon as the sainted Richard Griffiths got wind of it, he would be on the telephone and even the most routine of calls would turn into a collector's item. His 'get well soon calls' were far better than any medicine and usually had a much more lasting effect.

He would often ring me for a chat and, if Jack was around, talk to him too. But Richard and Jack (then in his early school days) on the phone would be a decidedly one-sided affair.

'How are you, Jack, dear boy?' Richard would ask him.

'I'm fine, thank you, Richard. And how are you?' Jack would reply.

And by and large that would be the end of Jack's contribution to the 'conversation', because Richard would systematically launch into a long and seemingly endless anecdote of the shaggy-dog variety, peppering the story with dialogue involving Jack, such as 'So the giant then poured himself a large Scotch and poured a second one for his friend Jack Whitehall, who was joining him later.' This would send Jack into fits of hysterical laughter, which would continue throughout the conversation. Jack never spoke much but he laughed a lot and had great fun listening to his 'Uncle Richard'.

I enjoyed thirty-five glorious years of being Richard's agent and friend and Jack twenty-four unforgettable years of being his godson. He was the best godfather a boy could ever wish for. Dear Richard died in 2013 and Jack and I will miss him forever.

When I rang him to talk business, he would swiftly veer off the topic of his career. 'Don't fret, my dear, I'm sure something will come along and if it doesn't then fuck it,' he would say and then expound on more important matters: his theories on the failure of the O-rings on the ill-fated space shuttle *Challenger*, or the current form of his beloved Middlesbrough FC, or the ever murkier corruption in the deep-sea fishing industry. He would somehow link these hypotheses with his views on John Eliot Gardiner's Bach cantatas or the dietary deficiencies of cabin boys in the days of Horatio Hornblower, which

Moments later Richard went into make-up.

would then turn into another shaggy-dog story. He knew something about everything.

However, when the boot was on the other foot and I called him and was droning on through a list of contracts to be signed, travel and accommodation arrangements to be agreed, and dates for medicals and costume fittings (costume fittings were definitely not a favourite part of Richard's professional life) he would, quite literally, fall fast asleep.

'So, is Tuesday the ninth at eleven a.m. good for you, Richard?'

Silence.

'Richard?'

Silence.

'Hello?'

A slight snuffling sound followed by deep and contented breathing would emanate down the phone.

But always the courteous gentleman, he would call back and apologize when he had woken up. 'I fell asleep, didn't I, Michael?' he'd say.

'Well, yes, Richard. But only slightly and what I was saying was terribly boring.'

Jack also experienced Richard's narcolepsy when I took him to visit the set of *Pie in the Sky*. We arrived at the studios just as the crew broke for lunch and Jack (then aged four) and I were taken to Richard's trailer. Being Richard, he had laid on a delicious lunch, with a cold bottle of champagne for him and me and plenty of treats for Jack, including a range of exotic fruit juices, cold chicken, pork pies, smoked salmon, a large strawberry jelly and lashings of double cream. Richard wasn't called for filming until mid-afternoon, so after lunch I left Jack and Richard drawing together, art being a common bond between them, while I went to chat to the producer. When I returned Richard was sitting in a chair on the grass outside his caravan, fast asleep, with Jack sitting on his lap wide awake.

'Are you OK, Jack?' I asked.

'Yes, I'm fine, Daddy,' he whispered. 'But Richard has been asleep for quite a long time and I didn't want to wake him, so I have been sitting here very still.'

The massed bands of the Royal Horse Guards in full flight wouldn't have disturbed Richard, I thought, as proved to be the case when the runner came to call him back to the set and couldn't wake him easily either.

Jack learnt some very good strategies from Richard when it came to jollying along the sick that he put to good use when I had another bout of tummy trouble eight years later, during Jack's gap year. It was the Christmas holiday from the Chelsea School of Art, where he was doing his foundation year and he was also doing evening shifts in our local pub, as well as fitting in stand-up gigs wherever he could. But every afternoon Jack would come and visit, bringing me the post, jollying me along with the latest gossip from the pub and keeping me amused with stories of mishaps on nights out with his mates in London or reports of the latest round of whichever comedy competition he was involved in. Jack has always been such good company and a joy to spend time with. He manages to find the funny in everything, a skill that he has put to such good use in his stand-up career.

Hilary and I used to worry about Jack when he first started on the comedy circuit, especially when he started to play the northern clubs.*

*'Northern' means anywhere north of King's Cross.

We used to think that a bunch of drunken Geordies would hear his dulcet middle-class tones ringing out across the room and make mincemeat of him. But he always managed to win them over with his charm and humour. If a posh boy can survive in a comedy club in Newcastle on a Saturday night, he can survive anything! Though I have to say the potential cost of the dental bills arising from a bad gig in Newcastle is enough to make my eyes water.

1. I cannot believe that you were going to let me go through my life with those ridiculous buck teeth because Kenneth More thought that a gap in your teeth was sexy — it isn't!

2. I hated wearing those blocks. Cynical readers might question whether my leaving them on that tray was indeed an 'accident' at all, but I'm afraid that, at this time, I couldn't possibly comment.

3. Richard Griffiths was a truly brilliant man and such a joy to talk to that he made getting ill something you almost looked forward to, as you knew he'd be on standby to cheer you up.*

*Hear, hear!

Part V

Stars in His Eyes

CHAPTER 13

Dressed To Kill

- MICHAEL WHITEHALL -

FROM A VERY EARLY AGE JACK ADORED, and I mean adored, dressing up: Captain Scarlet, Troy Tempest, Aladdin, Robin Hood, dinosaurs, Captain Hook, Peter Pan, Power Rangers, medieval kings, knights, wizards, vampires and, rather worryingly, the Little Mermaid.* The one thing that linked all these characters, at least when Jack was portraying them, was that they all wore tights.

'Fireman Sam is a fireman,' I told Jack one day, 'and I think it very unlikely that he would wear tights.'

It fell on deaf ears.

Worse still, Hilary often had to make these costumes. There was one Christmas when she spent weeks wrestling with metres of pink satin and gold lamé, running up a Power Ranger suit (why did it have to be the pink one!?).**

'Do you think this is wise, Hilary?' I asked her. 'You'll turn the boy into Liberace.'

When she wasn't at the sewing machine she would be on the phone, often in tears, to Woose, who at this stage was working as a social worker in a child guidance clinic, so was good for a bit of advice on Jack's foibles.

'How can I get him to stop wearing tights?' Hilary would ask.

'He'll grow out of it,' Woose would reassure her.

'Yes, but when?'

Little did we know how long it would take. ***

*Her name is Ariel.

**Because Kimberly was the coolest by far.

***Twenty-four years and counting.

Many a family occasion was ruined before we'd even left the house. There was a memorable pre-party crisis when Jack insisted that Hilary make his hair look 'just like Scott Tracy's from *Thunderbirds*'. After several fruitless attempts and gallons of hair product Hilary explained to a now inconsolable Jack that she was never going to be able to get it looking exactly like Scott Tracy's hair, as Scott Tracy was a puppet.*

Jack didn't only confine his penchant for dressing up to himself; frequently he would insist that all members of the family joined him.

On one occasion our friend Anne Mullins, Molly's godmother, was made to dress up as Darth Vader because he 'didn't have enough baddies to scare people'. Then there was the party when he insisted that his elderly grandparents don pirate outfits and I myself was once forced to 'dress up properly' as a clown before I was allowed through the doors of one of Barnaby's parties, which in retrospect was a bit of an error as the entertainer was running late and everyone looked to me to step into the breach. It wasn't going to happen. The children all seemed to find it very amusing. I didn't. Still, they weren't laughing for long as, moments later, Timmy Twinkle arrived and quickly knocked them into shape, with a 'trick' that involved him picking out a particularly

*Still not an excuse that I think holds up. Such a quitter.

Asked politely.

Wearing my first ever onesie.

Hilary assured me that this photograph had been destroyed.

*Seriously, that was the trick? The man was a monster.

**They were probably traumatized for the rest of their lives.

***Because that's the last thing they'd want in Buckingham Palace; someone with German ancestry.

annoying child from his young audience and putting him in a cupboard.* The children were subdued for the rest of the party. **

One of the first and most spectacular costumes Jack ever wore was courtesy of his cousin Graham. Graham worked as a footman at Buckingham Palace. Jack was very keen to meet the Queen, so he and his siblings joined Hilary and me on a backstairs visit that Graham had arranged for us. However, before our visit could be confirmed, we had to go through endless security checks to prove that we were fit and proper people. There was a ten-page questionnaire to complete and we had to send in copies of our passports. No problem for Hilary and the children but I was a little concerned for myself, as in all passport photographs for many years I've always resembled a Nazi war criminal who has chosen to settle in London rather than Buenos Aires.*** Once we had been given the green light, we arranged a date.

Graham met us at the staff entrance of Buckingham Palace. His tour started with a visit to the kitchens, on the basis that we would work our way up the building starting from the bottom. In the kitchen we met a Mrs Patmore lookalike, who showed us the system for letting the staff know which Royals were in and which were out for each meal. This seemed to consist of lots of little magnetic name tags. There were

I was the only boy willing to dress up as the woman on a school trip to Hampton Court.

My granny dressed as a pirate and my grandfather as one of those sailors from the Jean Paul Gaultier adverts.

two lifts outside the kitchen, with a sign on one saying: 'Not to be used between 12 noon and 2 p.m. and 7 p.m. and 9 p.m. when the Queen is in residence'. Graham explained that this lift was used to take up the Queen's lunch and dinner and bring it down again when she'd finished, so no one was allowed to use it in case they tampered with her food. I could see Jack trying to work out how he could get involved in this process.

Next we found ourselves in a sewing room, which had floor-to-ceiling shelves full of beautifully pressed linens. Another Mrs Patmore lookalike (is there an agency that supplies these kinds of people?) was sitting on a bentwood chair, darning a pair of socks that she told Jack belonged to Prince Philip.

'You never darn my socks,' I said to Hilary.

'If you want to get your socks darned, get yourself a housekeeper,' she replied.

There then followed a seminal moment when the children got as close to the Queen as they were going to get on this visit.* There on the table in the middle of the room was a silver tray containing a small teapot, one cup and saucer with a slight lipstick stain and a plate of biscuits. Jack asked Mrs Patmore if she had enjoyed her tea.

'Oh no, dear, that's not my tea. That was Her Majesty's four o'clock cuppa, and, look, she's left three of her biscuits for you.' I noted that they were not Duchy Originals, as presumably even the Queen couldn't afford those. Jack looked very reverential as he shyly munched through Her Majesty's biscuits.

Having confirmed that she was no longer there, Graham then showed us the Queen's sitting room. Jack said it reminded him of his granny's sitting room in Hampshire as it had a three-bar electric fire and was generously furnished in a style best described as 1950s suburban.

The granny to whom Jack was referring was Woose. On top of her hoarding habit, another eccentricity of Woose's was to be fiercely competitive when it came to members of her extended family. Her grandchildren's exam results were stacked into league tables, and there was no hiding place for underachievers. Sporting acumen was analysed like she was playing Moneyball, and she even kept a height chart in her kitchen to see if anyone wasn't growing quickly enough for her liking.

*She walked into the sewing room brandishing a broken bra strap saying, 'That Prince Philip will be the death of me!' You stupid boy.

If only the casting director of Twilight had seen this: Jack centre stage, with Molly and Barnaby.

Do you have this in a small?

'Did you know that your cousin Tom is a whole inch taller than you?' she asked Jack one day as she made a pencil mark on her wall above his head.

'My dad says that height is no indication of intellect,' he said. 'Albert Einstein was a short-arse and so is Henry Kissinger.'

But it didn't get through to her during Jack's pubescent years and we had to endure a constant battle of one-upmanship between him and his cousin Tom as to who was growing more quickly. Graham, being somewhat older than Jack and Tom, was not included in this competition.

On Graham went with his guided tour, through a myriad of passages and staircases until we finally reached his tiny room in the eaves, a large proportion of which was taken up by a clothes rail, on which hung several different versions of a footman's uniform. Graham explained that there were different outfits for different occasions and that they were all very heavy to wear, especially in the summer. There was one in particular that caught the eye, a spectacular red uniform with large amounts of gold braid. Graham had appeared in a photograph on the front page of *The Times* wearing this particular uniform, sitting atop a horse-drawn carriage, behind Prince Charles and Princess Diana. Jack was desperate to try this one on, even though he was only four, right down to the top hat. Graham helped Jack into it and Jack marched around the room as best he could with the heavy coat weighing him down.

'I'm hot,' said Jack.

'Get some fresh air,' I suggested.

The window in Graham's room overlooked the huge rear garden of the Palace. Hanging out to cool down, wearing Graham's uniform, Jack noticed a very large woman walking several yapping Corgis down a path.

'Is that the Queen?' he asked me excitedly.

I looked at her. She was wearing tracksuit bottoms and trainers.

'Yes, I think it is, Jack,' I lied, thinking it would be nice for him to believe that he had actually seen the Queen, even if the woman that he'd spotted was clearly not the type to leave three biscuits at tea.

1. Who's to say it wasn't the Queen? Behind closed doors maybe she rocks a tracksuit and trainers.

2. I didn't cry because my mum couldn't make me look like Scott Tracy from Thunderbirds, I probably just had something in my eye, or maybe it was an allergic reaction to all that hair product.

Her majesty walking the corgis.

CHAPTER 14

Running Away

− JACK WHITEHALL −

When I was young, running away was one of the many things I did that pissed my father off. I used to run away all the time as a means of solving any dispute we had. Whether it was him banning me from watching WWF wrestling (he disapproved of me watching 'a lot of half-naked oiled-up men grappling each other')* or replacing my Limp Bizkit album ('tuneless din') with the monks of Ampleforth singing plainchant. As soon as I felt like I was losing the argument I'd stamp my foot, pack my bag and be off out of the door.

I was very concerned.

I say 'pack my bag', of course, but really that task was beneath me, so I'd make my mother do it for me. I'd stand right beside her and check she was packing all the essentials that a homeless boy needs when living alone on the streets of London. And what were these 'essentials'? Sleeping bag? Hot-water bottle? An umbrella? Oh no, no, no.

'Have you packed my Frubes?'

'Yes, Jack. And your Cheestrings,' my mum replied, wedging them into my Thunderbirds backpack.

'Peperami?'

'Yes.'

'Monster Munch?'

'Yes.'

'What flavour?' I asked, suspicious of her taste.

'Pickled onion.'

'Hmmm,' I muttered as if unwilling to believe her. 'We'll see.' I started double-checking the contents of my rucksack.

'And here's your *Shoot Football Annual*,* Jack, so you have something to read while you're sleeping rough.'

*A rare engagement with the written word.

Reading? Like that was important when she'd made a much bigger mistake!

'Mother,' I said tartly, '*where* is my Tamagotchi?'

'I didn't think you needed your Tamagotchi.'

'Ha!' I gave a mirthless, withering laugh. The woman was so slow. 'Homeless people get more money if they have pets, Mother.'

After all these scrupulous preparations, though, the actual act of running away never involved me getting very far from home. I would storm out of the front door – smashing it as loudly as I could so that my evil father would hear it over his warbling monks – then walk down to the end of the road and wait there for as long as it took him to come and collect me.

It was very important to me that, despite the fact that I was standing no further than a hundred metres from the house, my father came to collect me in the car. I don't know why this was. Maybe I liked to think our relationship was worth the petrol money.

So there I would stand and wait for him to pull up in the car and tell me that he loved me. This was another crucial deal-breaker. I had to hear those words coming out of his mouth.

'I love you, Jack.'

A difficult sentence for a man of his generation to utter. But, if said like a proper loving father, it was the key to getting his small, flouncing refugee into the car and back home, everything forgiven and forgotten.

I'd say this running-away cycle happened about once a month.**

**Once a fortnight.

The reasons for me running away were varied, but some issues were a constant cause of friction between my father and me. Something that gave him particular displeasure was my obsession with dressing up.

As my father has already pointed out, I used to dress up all the time, mostly in costumes that my mother had made by hand. From Power Rangers and Thunderbirds to Captain Hook or Peter Pan, they would always have a slightly camp twist. This is because, at that age (and although it's hard to believe, given that I am now hewn from testosterone and granite), I was a little flamboyant.

In my mother's words: 'a creative child'.

In my father's: 'a nancy boy'.

Then, one summer, everything changed. The Mighty Morphin Power Rangers were all but forgotten. The Captain Scarlet costume proved not to be invincible. I had discovered the legend of Robin Hood.

All of a sudden, I had a new hero. My father was less keen on my obsession with Robin Hood, as I don't think he cared much for the character.

'What are you doing, Jack?' he'd ask as I fired arrows at him.

'I'm stealing from the rich and giving to the poor!' I'd cry.

'My God,' he'd moan. 'First a transsexualist and now a socialist. All this redistribution of wealth – he's nothing more than a Blairite with a quiver!'

Closer to home, my father felt my interpretation of the character was a little too effeminate. Robin Hood is a warrior. He rides horses, has swords, fights, has a babe – what could be manlier than that?

Well, certainly not *my* Robin Hood, that's for sure. My green tunic was one of my sister's dresses, my shoes were spray-painted ballet slippers and my tights . . . Well, they were tights.

As all you ladies will know, one gets through quite a lot of tights, especially if you're playing around with your Merry Men all the time. So I got through a lot of tights: nylon stockings, Lycra cycling tights, cotton leggings, long johns, even a pair of fishnets I stole from my parents' wardrobe.* I took a particular liking to the fishnets, much to my father's dismay.

*Hilary's, not mine.

'I'm sorry, Daddy, but they're just so well ventilated,' I'd tell him, putting my ballet pumps down.

I would dress as Robin Hood all the time and I mean all the time. On trips to the supermarket or restaurants, playing in the park, at the cinema, on holidays home and abroad, even at Auntie Vera's funeral. There was everyone in suits except for me, stood over the coffin in a tunic and tights. To be fair, they were black tights. You know, out of respect.**

**A particularly embarrassing incident.

***Very reluctantly.

My dad's right when he says that I even tried to get my family involved in my craze. My father made a perfect Sheriff of Nottingham*** and Barnaby a pretty good Will Scarlet. On one trip to the hairdresser's, I asked the man cutting our hair if he could give Molly a haircut like Friar Tuck, with a little bald bit on the top. My mother intervened and vetoed a tonsure, the spoilsport.

One birthday, though, my suspect tastes caused the biggest falling-out me and my dad ever had. The problem began with my birthday list, which contained some items of which my father strongly disapproved.

The first of these were Rollerblades. My sister had got some for her birthday and I didn't want to be left out. I had my eye on a nice garish set of Roces Rollerblades that had a sparkly purple bolt down each side. I nagged and nagged my mother to buy them for

This is what happens when you let me direct a photo shoot.

me and eventually ground her into submission. She even gave them to me a few weeks before my actual birthday, partly to shut me up, but also because I'd already found them hidden in the spare room.

My joy was short-lived, however. When my father saw me in bright glittery rollerblades, singing tunes from *Starlight Express*, he immediately confiscated them, firing off a warning that 'no son of mine would be seen gliding around like a woofter!'*

This meant that, come the morning of my birthday, tensions were already high. This brings me on to the second present I had requested that year. A Pocahontas doll.

'A doll! You're a boy! Boys don't play with dolls! Why can't you play with guns? Cops and Robbers? Cowboys and Indians?' my father asked desperately.

'Pocahontas is an Indian, Daddy,'** I replied. 'I have Action Man and Captain Scarlet, and several of the Thunderbirds. But none of them have any women, Daddy. You said men without women are not to be trusted.'

Here I rather masterfully turned one of his homophobic comments against him; he'd said it months ago when watching Peter Mandelson on *Question Time* and I bet he didn't think it would come back and bite him like it did.

*Don't believe a word of it. They were confiscated on grounds of health and safety. We lived near a main road and the idea of you whizzing round on those deathtraps terrified your mother. Also, I don't like anything in the house that reminds me of Andrew Lloyd Webber.

**Smartarse.

'Come and get me, Merry Men!'

'And Action Man is a soldier, Daddy. He needs a woman to look after him when he comes back from fighting in all those wars. She can cook for him and wash his uniform for him and sing in a choir to raise money for all those lost dolls.'

Help the heroes! That was my message. My father left my room defeated, and I felt pretty convinced that I'd done enough.

Come the 7th of July I was hoping (expecting, actually) to receive a brand-spanking-new Pocahontas doll. At six a.m. my parents were woken up by an over-excited Robin Hood jumping up and down on their bed. My presents were produced and I ripped open the smaller ones, barely even noticing what was inside them. I had my eyes on the prize, the main event: a long, slim-ish doll-like box.

I shook it. It felt very promising; I think I could faintly hear from within Pocahontas's thick luscious black locks of hair swishing in the box. I unwrapped it greedily.

A Leatherman. What the hell? How dare he? Why would I want a portable multi-tool!

'What is this?' I said, my bottom lip already heading north.

'This is a Leatherman, Jack. Every man should have one of these.'

'I want my Pocahontas! Give me my pocket money now!'

'No.'

'If you don't give me my pocket now, I'm running away. Forever!'

My father folded his arms.

'Give it to me!' I yelled, stamping my foot.

'Over my dead body,' came the reply.

'Fine. Mother, pack my bag!'

'Already done,' said my mum, lifting up a pre-prepared rucksack from next to her bed. She'd clearly seen this latest wobbly coming.

'Wait, Jack,' my father said to my departing back.

Had he changed his mind? Was this some kind of sick practical joke? Did he have Pocahontas with him right now? I turned.

'Don't you want to take your Leatherman?' Dad smirked. 'It could be useful, out there on the streets.'*

I only stopped once more before I stormed out of the front door, and that was to retrieve the forbidden rollerblades from my father's study. Admittedly, storming anywhere after I'd put them on was quite a hard task, a bit like when you try to angrily hang up an

*He'd need a lot more than a Leatherman to protect him the way he was dressed.

Or leave a classroom
with a tiny plastic
chair stuck to your arse.

iPhone or slam an automatic door. It didn't quite work, but I gave it a damn good go.

I glided down the street and started the stand-off, the Whitehall family dance as old as time. I didn't have to wait long; my dad knew the drill by now and I saw him in the distance, still in his dressing gown, getting into the car. He was also holding his wallet – a promising sign.

I remember feeling a lot of anger towards my father that morning. I thought he was a mean, miserable old bastard for treating me like this on my birthday. But now, with the benefit of hindsight, I actually feel slightly sorry for him.

Why? Let me tell you this. You get some odd looks from neighbours when they see you kerb-crawl an eight-year-old boy clad in bright purple rollerblades and green fishnet tights, like a child hooker in *Starlight Express*. And the looks get even odder when they see you – yourself only wearing a loose dressing gown – leaning out of your car, brandishing a twenty-pound note and shouting, 'I love you. Now get in the fucking car.'

Once I'd dried my eyes and arrangements had been made to purchase the doll, we could get on with the rest of the day. Next up, the small matter of my birthday party and an appearance from Timmy Twinkle. Well, at least I wouldn't be the only child in tears that day.

1. This is not a good example of parenting. Basically your mother and I indulged you far too much and I should have followed my initial instincts and put a Yale lock on your bedroom door and double-locked you in there whenever you kicked off.

2. I have nothing against the character of Robin Hood per se; I have very much enjoyed Hood when played by Douglas Fairbanks, Errol Flynn or Richard Greene. My issue was with Jack's extremely camp interpretation of the role, which was less Russell Crowe and more Russell Grant.

3. And don't exaggerate. It was not a twenty-pound note, it was only a fiver. You're over-pricing yourself.

Part VI

'Tis the Season to be Jolly

CHAPTER 15

His Christmas

– MICHAEL WHITEHALL –

CHRISTMAS EVE WAS THE TIME when the Whitehall family headed off to Westminster Abbey for their annual Christmas carol service. Our friend Stuart was the assistant registrar of the abbey and his duties included organizing events, such as the carol concert. Memorial services were also his thing and he would always give us advanced notice of ones that might be of interest to us and how the tickets were going.

'Would Thora Hird be of any interest?' he'd ask. 'Or Edward Heath? He's not going as quickly as we'd hoped.'

We'd always have embarrassingly good VIP seats for these events and on one occasion were even ushered into a family-only area after the service to meet Roy Jenkins's widow.

'I'm drawing the line here,' said Hilary. 'I'm not entirely sure who Roy Jenkins was*and I'm certainly not planning on having a chat with Lady Jenkins about what a wonderful man he was.'

*Join the club.

We had particularly good seats in the choir stalls for the carol service when Jack, Molly and Barnaby made their first appearance in 1994. After the service Stuart ushered us into a *salon privé*, where drinks and canapés were served. From my point of view the big attraction of this event was the abbey's wine cellar: good, well-constructed clarets, none of that ghastly spiced mulled wine that people often insist on serving up at Christmas. Also served up at the abbey's Christmas party was a very jolly friend of Stuart's who rejoiced in the name of Peter Dick-Peter.

'That's a funny name,' a six-year-old Jack said to him, and before

Mr Dick-Peter had a chance to reply, 'My daddy called someone a dick the other day.'*

'That's a very rude word, Jack,' replied Peter Dick-Peter.

'So why's it your name, then?' said Jack.

As well as being a very impressive location I liked this event because it started at four thirty, you were in the drinks room by six p.m. and home by seven thirty p.m., having completed all your Christmas church duties. No midnight mass consequently required, no cold Christmas-morning service at the local church, which would invariably lead to Hilary wittering on to every one of our neighbours individually about what their festive plans involved and just enough religion to purge my Catholic guilt.

My Uncle Peter and his wife Vera were waiting for us when we arrived home with our friend Neil Stacy. Neil was our annual Christmas house guest. He had studied medieval history at Oxford and had a double first and a D.Phil. to his credit, but had unwisely chosen a theatrical rather than an academic career. Although an actor of distinction, poor Neil has probably become best known for having been a regular character in ITV's comedy series *Duty Free*. For younger readers this was a more upmarket version of *Benidorm*, but only slightly. He was also a published author, having written, mostly in Latin, several books for the Oxford University Press with mouthwatering titles such as *Surveys of the Estates of Glastonbury Abbey, c.1135–1201* and *Charters and Custumals of Shaftesbury Abbey, 1089–1216*. No slouch in the world of academia, nor was Neil off the pace when it came to Christmas in the kitchen, but although he enjoyed cooking, it gave him little or no pleasure unless he had the right tools.

'I've never understood the phrase "bad workmen blame their tools". It's not a phrase I recognize,' he would say. Even if Neil was knocking up the simplest of snacks, there would always be endless discussion as to the precise accessibility and location of ladles, timers, graters, garlic crushers, paring knives, julienne slicers, sauté pans and steamers. Not to mention melon-ballers, lemon-reamers, citrus-zesters, tongs, mustard spoons, hullers, palette knives, nutmeg-graters, basting brushes, whisks, mashers, mallets, spatulas and his must-have Christmas accessory, the grapefruit knife. If only such care had gone into his gifting. Previous Christmas offerings had included a copy of

He might recognize it in Latin?

Records of Social and Economic History in Lincolnshire 1377–1381 for me, a sturdy set of fondue forks for Hilary, and for Jack and the children, as I think he often forgot how many we had and what ages they were, a CD of Noel Coward songs that he had bought from a garden centre just outside Bath. Jack, who was five at the time, was less than impressed.*

*Still, it's better than those stupid monks.

As for Uncle Peter and Auntie Vera, they were by now pretty immobile. Peter had recently had a stroke and was sleeping on a camp bed downstairs. A World War Two veteran, Peter was not a frugal man when it came to alcohol and there were many occasions in my youth when he would turn particularly testy post-Christmas lunch after I had woken him up by pulling a cracker next to his head, while my brother Barry burst a few balloons in his vicinity. And here we were many years later with Peter dozing in front of the fire when Jack appeared in his brand-new pink Power Rangers outfit [shudders], courtesy of Hilary, which he'd accessorized with a toy gun that when fired let out a piercing buzz and a flash of light. The gun was fired centimetres from Peter's good ear, causing him to wake up in a panic.

**Ironically, Power Rangers were originally from Japan.

'Fuck, I thought I was back in the jungle!' shouted Peter.**

'Uncle Peter has just said fuck,' said Jack, having rushed into the kitchen.

Three years of fighting the Japanese in the Burmese jungle, and it was a pink Power Ranger that got Uncle Peter.

'I can't believe he used that word,' said Vera. 'I do apologize.'

'I can,' I said to Jack. 'And you have only yourself to blame.'

'There was a very funny chap hanging around here while we were waiting for you to get back from the abbey,' said Auntie Vera. 'I think he was trying to deliver something.'

Every Christmas, Hilary's cousin Uncle Billy gave her a crate of beer, although fully aware that she was not, and never had been, a beer drinker. Hilary was also required to ferry this unwanted gift back from Kent in her car. But this Christmas he had decided not only to deliver it by hand, but also on Christmas Eve.

'Billy's coming to see you, he's driving up in the camper van now,' Woose had said on the answerphone. 'You forgot to take your beers when you were down here last, so he figured he'd run them up to you himself.'

In fact, they had been left behind on my instructions, by the dustbins, in the vain hope that the dustman would take them as a Christmas box.

So Billy arrived while we were at church and Vera and Peter were sitting in their car waiting for our arrival home. They had never met Billy before and given his unique style, unkempt being the kindest way to describe it, they were not about to leap out of the car and challenge him as to what he was doing prowling around our front garden.

Billy rang the doorbell several times and, having padded around the drive for ten minutes, eventually got bored and drove off, unfortunately leaving the beer in a flowerbed. Beer that had been bumped along in that horrible van of his and was probably so fizzed up it was ready to explode.

We were subsequently told by Hilary's brother, Andrew, that Billy had driven from our house to theirs in Kent. Andrew opened the front door the following morning and discovered Billy had parked his camper van on their drive. He went upstairs to break the news to his wife, Amanda.

'I've got good news and bad news.'

'What's the good news?' she asked.

'It's Christmas morning.'

'Hooray,' she said, smiling. 'And what's the bad news?'

'Billy's parked his mobile home on our front drive.'

Billy, never the easiest of house guests due mainly to his eccentric and forcefully put opinions on pretty much everything remained with them until the day after Boxing Day.

Another interesting delivery he once made was to Hilary's parents at their diamond wedding anniversary family dinner at the Hotel du Vin. Billy left the restaurant and returned moments later pursued by the doorman, wheeling a brand-new aluminium wheelbarrow past shocked diners before parking it up next to the table.

'Here's your present. I thought you'd like a new wheelbarrow.'

Family functions that Billy attended were always edgy affairs. On one occasion he walked out of a wedding when he discovered the priest was a woman. This was, however, a unique moment in our relationship, when Billy and I actually agreed on something. It was never to happen again.

At Woose's birthday party a flustered Jack came back from the Harvester salad buffet and informed me that Billy had sidled up to him and, while helping himself to potato salad with his hands, told him that he shouldn't masturbate or God would punish him. I suggested Jack ignored this advice and told him that having the odd one off the wrist never did me any harm.*

*And this remains one of the most harrowing things my dad has ever said to me. Billy got his way, though, as I couldn't bring myself to masturbate for about a year, as every time I tried to all I could hear were my father's words ringing in my ears. A likely story!

Molly too was constantly being criticized by Billy for crimes such as wearing too much make-up and for the length of her skirts, and warned about the evils of sex before marriage. This advice seemed premature at the time as she was only ten. I steered a very wide berth around Billy as I had been married before and in his eyes was a bigamist. There seemed little point in attempting any social contact with him and for the most part I was able to avoid him whenever our paths crossed. In fact, the last time I spoke to Billy was at another family function when he had restyled his beard into thick bushy sideburns across his cheeks.

I couldn't resist complimenting him on his new look. 'Ah, Billy, that's a very impressive pair of bugger's grips you've got there,' I said.

For once in his life Billy was lost for words. We have not spoken since.

**Is there any event in my life that Nigel Havers wasn't at? Your eighteenth birthday at the Garrick Club. He had a prior engagement.

So back to Christmas Day and we were joined for lunch by Nigel and Polly Havers, who lived nearby.**

Before they arrived I was setting the table for lunch and lighting the Christmas candles in the dining-room with Molly and Jack.

'Did they have candles when you were a boy?' asked Jack.

'Yes, of course there were candles,' I replied. 'Your grandparents always enjoyed a nice candlelit supper.'

'No, I mean did you live by candlelight when you were a child?' he said.

'Well, not really, Jack,' I said. 'People tended to have electric light in their homes from around a hundred years ago and gaslight for a hundred years before that. It was a long time since they wandered around by candlelight. Why?'

'It was just that I was talking to a friend of mine at school and he said that you were much older than the other fathers, or did you just look older? And then we were talking in class about going to bed with a candle in the olden days and he wondered if you did.'

'Nice friends you have, Jack,' I said. 'Perhaps he'd like to have a look at my birth certificate?'*

'What's a birth certificate?' said Molly.

'When Daddy was a boy he didn't have a bed,' said Jack. 'He slept on a straw mattress with the dogs.'

'Very amusing, Jack,' I said. 'Shall we talk about something else?'

Christmas day went smoothly. Neil tried to make the best of it when the timer malfunctioned and he burned the roast potatoes. 'Not a great loss,' he said. 'I would normally roast them in goose fat but you didn't have any.'

Neil had brought us five-dozen mince pies from his local baker in Pucklechurch, who claimed to supply mince pies exclusively to Buckingham Palace. This seemed a little unlikely as the Pucklechurch pies, although delicious, were enormous, more like pasties than pies, and we were still trying to work through them well into January. As we were tucking into them, Neil went off to the cellar to get the Vacherin he had brought from a newly opened speciality cheese shop he had discovered in Bath.

'What is that disgusting smell?' chorused the children as he came back into the dining room.

'Wow, that is a corker,' said Nigel.

I had been to the kitchen to get some cheese biscuits, and when I came into the dining room the smell of cheese made from the unpasteurized milk of cows from the Jura region hit me like a brick wall.

*Which was written with quill on parchment. Piss off.

'Oh, Neil, that is disgusting! It smells like it has been made in one of Billy's old socks!' I said.

'Don't be ridiculous, Michael. It will be delicious,' said Neil.

'It's making me feel rather sick,' said Vera.

'I'm afraid you can't eat that in here,' I said.

'But I know it will taste sublime, Michael.'

'I don't care how it tastes, it's not staying in here,' I said firmly. So with that Neil picked up his cheese and made for the kitchen.

'I'll join you,' said Nigel as he followed Neil.

As he made to sit down in the kitchen, Hilary added, 'And I don't want you stinking out my kitchen either, Neil. You'll have to eat it in the garden.'

'But it's getting dark,' said Neil.

'There's a light out there. You'll be able to see what you are doing,' I called out to him as he went out through the back door brandishing the previously gifted fondue forks, which were presumably given knowing that the Vacherin was on its way.

The Vacherin affair, as it became known, has not been forgotten by Neil to this day, and by way of trying to avoid any further cheese unpleasantness he brought a truckle of English Cheddar for the post-mince pie cheeseboard the following year.*

*Even I found that last paragraph a bit too posh.

A good old English ham with some French cheese.

Nigel Havers on the pull again.

Uncle Peter was very apologetic that he couldn't stand for the Queen's Speech, a tradition in our house, and I assured him that he had earned the right to remain seated. Peter had had a good war – Dunkirk, Burma – and had risen to the dizzy heights of major. He wouldn't have anything to do with his former enemies, no Japanese or German products were allowed in his house, so he was very concerned to find himself about to watch his monarch addressing him from a TV with Sony emblazoned across the top of the set. 'I can't watch it on that thing,' he said. 'Do you have another set?'

'a good war'? What's 'a bad war'? When you die?

By the time we got him up to our bedroom, with the help of Neil and Nigel, he was very breathless and the Queen was about to begin. Fortunately he didn't notice that he was now watching it on a Grundig.

Boxing Day usually meant our friends the Mullinses' party in Barnes, where they now lived. A cold collation served on paper plates with plastic knives and forks, this was always a challenge for me, as Jack would invariably manage to send lumps of forked ham flying around the room and, on one disastrous occasion, he temporarily blinded an aged relative by launching a cocktail sausage into his eye.

It was you! Why are you referring to yourself in such a cryptic way?

But this particular year it was Hilary who let the side down in a big way. The Mullinses' youngest daughter had just got engaged and the Boxing Day party had been designated as an easy way to introduce all members of the wedding party to one another. Molly and Barnaby were to be bridesmaid and pageboy at the upcoming summer wedding and Hilary had excitedly been discussing every detail with Anne and the bride-to-be, Selina.* She was therefore keen to meet Chris's (the groom to be) parents in order to put faces to the names she had been talking about. On arrival in the sitting room, Hilary plonked herself down next to a large guest with a slightly bristly chin.

*Didn't want to be a pageboy anyway.

'You must be Chris's father,' she said by way of introduction.

'No, I'm not. I'm Edwin's aunt!' she replied tersely.

It is not often I have seen Jack's mother dumbstruck, but this was up there as one of the best.

'That was mortifying,' said Hilary as we went through for lunch.

'Well, she could have had a shave before she came out,' I said by way of reassurance, not realizing she was standing directly behind us in the ham queue. The rest of the party was spent with guests sniggering behind their hands as they heard about Hilary's faux pas.

Eventually Jack brought Chris's father over to meet Hilary.

'This is Chris's real father,' said Jack.

'So now you can put the correct face to the name, Hilary,' I said.

Thus ended another Whitehall family Christmas.

1. I am totally with my mum on this. It was not her fault she made that mistake, as Edwin's aunt had bigger bugger's grips than Uncle Billy.

2. You claim that the issue of female vicars is the only thing that you agree with Uncle Billy on. Do we assume, therefore, that you were happy for Molly to have premarital sex at the age of ten?

3. Surely there isn't such a thing as a mustard spoon?

CHAPTER 16

My Christmas

– JACK WHITEHALL –

Christmas at the Whitehall residence has always been traditional with a capital T. We'd spend it at our home in Putney, and Christmas 2004 was no different.

In the past we'd have a lot of people to stay for Christmas – a mixed bag of friends and relatives, as my dad has just described. But over the years nearly everyone had been struck off the invite list for one reason or another. My mother's family weren't invited for fear of mad Uncle Billy turning up in the camper van. My dad's Uncle Peter and Auntie Vera had sadly died; his brother Barry had been frozen out due to his seemingly insatiable desire to talk about the various motorways and A roads he'd taken to get to our house, or what his company car was doing to the gallon.

Even if you managed to steer Barry off the road, his other great passion was discussing any medical ailment he was suffering from and, more specifically, the various forms of medication he was on. One Christmas Uncle Barry* had a nasty backlog of ear wax and proceeded to tell us all with much enthusiasm about how he was battling the condition.

*For once, a genuine uncle.

'I was using carbamide peroxide, but that didn't work, so they moved me on to Exterol, which is a far more heavy-duty form of aural irrigation,' he told us. We were all on the edge of our seats, desperate to be the first up if Mum needed any help in the kitchen.**

**That was a rarity!

The final straw came when Uncle Barry started to remove his shoes and socks before lunch to show us all the extent of the damage that had been caused by a particularly aggressive bout of athlete's foot. We looked on in horror as Barry unsheathed his swollen foot and started waving it around the room like a butcher selling meat from a van.

It looked like a hock of ham.

'Look at the fungal inflammation of the toenail bed,' he announced. In response, my sister just cried, and my father added another name to the list of forbidden Christmas guests.

By 2004 the only person who remained eligible to stay was my father's best friend Neil, an honorary member of our family. He also has the distinction of being the only person I know with a temper as short as my father's.* He's in many ways a more extreme version of my dad, maybe what my father would have been like if my mum hadn't been around to drill in some basic social skills – and, yes, as the 'Uncle' might suggest, there was no Mrs Stacy. Neil lives in an apartment in a seventeenth-century house in Gloucestershire owned by the National Trust. It is set in a deer park with extensive lawns; Neil's only regret about living there is the fact that the house and park are open to the general public for much of the year and one thing that Neil doesn't like is the general public.** His only interaction with them is waving his walking stick at them and shouting expletives at dog owners when their charges attempt to foul the park. Surprisingly he never has any such qualms when the deer do so. The same stick and expletive routine is reserved for any errant children who might be foolish enough to stray on to a prohibited area of grass; Neil appears from nowhere, like the Woman in Black, and, with Twinkle-like efficiency, makes sure the culprit is so traumatized they would not dream of reoffending.***

*Don't be ridiculous, Neil Stacy is a very patient man with a wonderful temperament. How dare you insult my friends like this?

**My kind of man.

***If it wasn't for the care and selflessness of men like Neil Stacy, many of our great stately homes would simply fall into disrepair. Is that what you want? Because that's what would happen.

My father's favourite tradition of going to Westminster Abbey on Christmas Eve came to an abrupt end that year, thanks to my mother's insistence on preparing every element of her Christmas lunch the night before because Jamie had said so.

'Jamie says you should make the gravy well in advance, so the flavours have a chance to develop,' she'd tell my father. As if he cared. He is a man who still likes to have everything he eats cooked to within an inch of its life, obliterating any subtlety of taste.

HIM & ME

Vegetables should be boiled for days, to the point where they could practically be consumed through a straw. Meat should be incinerated, as though the chef is trying to destroy evidence linking it to a murder they've committed; short of taking a hammer to it, or dumping it in a lime pit, the chef should go as far as humanly possible to make this meat unidentifiable. Oh, and then cover everything in industrial amounts of salt, just in case any flavour had snuck through.*

Meals that have been seasoned with anything other than salt he refers to as 'food that's been mucked around with'. My mum once gave him a chicken breast with some paprika on it and he acted like she'd dusted it with anthrax, spitting it out on to his plate and then heading upstairs to have a lie-down because, quote, 'Your mother's tried to poison me.' Good food, in short, is wasted on him.**

So for Christmas 2004, instead of a trip to the abbey, we set off for Midnight Mass at our local church. Neil decided that it was a bit downmarket, so offered to stay at home and keep our terrier Charlie, with whom he was obsessed, company, although I thought that this was probably a ruse and that he wanted to get his hands on my mother's new paring knife. When we got to the church, though, my dad was given the shock of his life. The church had a new vicar. And this new vicar was a woman.

My father is a lapsed Catholic. His faith may have waned, but his views on how the church should be run have remained steadfast.

Reverend Lindy – or 'that woman dressed up as a vicar' – had short hair and bright lipstick. She was a very warm person and conducted a really nice service, but her gender meant she didn't stand a chance with at least one member of her congregation.

'She's got a shaved head! What's that all about?' he asked my mother during Lindy's sermon.

'Be quiet, Michael,' hissed my mother.

'She's probably like those women you play hockey with,' he whispered. 'Those women you play hockey with' is my dad's way of inferring that a woman is a lesbian. It sounds bizarre, but compared to his euphemisms for gay men it begins to seem actually quite normal. Favourites include a man who *winters in Florida*, *mints his peas* or *takes the bus to Penge* (the etymology of this last euphemism is unknown but my mother informs me it may have been linked

*I have a very refined palate. Take everything Jack has just said with a pinch of salt.

**So speaks the boy who spends his life in Kentucky Fried Chicken and Nando's!

to an incident that occurred at some point during the 1960s when my father was propositioned by a man on a bus to Penge).*

'Look at her boots!' he said to me. Under Lindy's vestments you could just about make out the capped toe of a rather chunky black-leather Dr Martens.

'You wouldn't see the monks at Ampleforth wearing those!'

'Well, we won't be going there again,' announced my father as we walked home. 'Wait till I tell Neil about this.' Neil, like my father, was also a lapsed Catholic . . . sorry, I mean was also a bit sexist.**

Christmas morning came. My parents gave me the PlayStation I'd asked for; they were given a couple of book tokens I'd won at school in return. Then we were on to Neil's gifts, a dreaded moment of any Christmas. He handed me a badly wrapped, worryingly book-shaped object. Damn it, Neil, I felt like saying, I've just got rid of some book tokens and now you're laying this shit on me?

'Well, this is far too big to be *FIFA 04*,' I said instead.

'What's Fee Far?' Neil replied. I hadn't been holding out much hope.

It turns out that Neil had given me a Gordon Ramsay cook-book. On paper, it's a much better result than some of his previous offerings, the worst of which was a VHS box set of *Duty Free*. I'm interested in cooking, plus I liked some of the recipes in it. I knew I liked some of the recipes in it, however, because Neil had given me exactly the same book the year before. He'd clearly bought it on a two-for-one offer in a petrol station in Bath.

'Thanks, Neil,' I said unconvincingly. 'I'll put it with my other one.'

'He means his other book. The boy can hardly read, you know?' said my dad, making it clear I was not to offend his friend.

'His presents are rubbish,' I told my mum later as I chopped up the Brussels sprouts aggressively. 'Why would I want a stupid book?'

'Don't be so ungrateful,' she said. 'Anyway, it could have been worse. He could have given you one of his books.'

A lot of Christmas was spent making sure we didn't upset Uncle Neil. It was wise not to cross him. The year before he'd nearly assaulted me when he found out I'd put an expensive cheese he'd given us into the fridge.

'This is an Époisses, you imbecile!' he shouted. 'It's ruined! I told you to put it in the cellar. What are we going to eat with the port now?'

A parson wearing Doc Martens. What kind of world do we live in? Well, for a start one where no one uses the term 'parson'.

**Nonsense!

'I think there are some Cheestrings in the fridge,' I replied, trying to be helpful.

It was then time for me and Molly to watch *Top of the Pops*. That year's number one was the Band Aid 20 version of 'Do They Know It's Christmas?' and as we sang along merrily, Neil and my father wondered whether or not that chap on the telly (Robbie Williams) *danced at the other end of the ballroom*.* It was then time for another tradition. Neil and my father are ardent royalists. Where most normal people's Christmas highlight might be the presents or the turkey, for those two relics it was all about the Queen's Speech. Neil was such a diehard monarchist that he'd caused at least one spectacular meltdown in the Whitehall house before.

I think we concluded that he probably 'brunched' with Martha but took afternoon tea with Arthur.'

A couple of years previously my mum had invited round some of her friends from the hockey team and their husbands, or 'beards' as my father called them. In Dad's eyes marriage is no proof of heterosexuality.

Oscar Wilde was married with children!

My father had asked Neil to provide moral support. What Neil actually provided is – to give it its scientific name – a shit-storm.

The conversation that evening ended up on the subject of Princess Diana, a favourite topic of my mother's. My mother and her friends were unanimous in their praise of the People's Princess. They spoke movingly of the Queen of Hearts hugging the little AIDS boy and rearing two fine sons despite their awful, adulterous father. My dad was able to let their attacks on Prince Charles slide** thanks to years of practice, but Neil couldn't let such a slander go unchallenged. He'd been tight-lipped until they started wittering on about Al Fayed having a decent case and how dreadfully the royal family had treated that lovely Paul Burrell. Burrell was to be 'the rock' that broke the camel's back, and Neil blurted out the immortal line: 'Queen of Hearts? She was a shameless, brazen hussy who threatened the stability of the monarchy!'

Only just.

Stunned silence. He wasn't invited to any dinner parties for several months where normal guests (closeted or otherwise) were present.***

***He said no such thing, Jack!**

Come the Queen's Speech the whole house went into lockdown. We were forced to bolt our Christmas pudding – it was disrespectful to eat during Her Majesty's address. We were also made to stand by Neil and my father, not just for the national anthem, but for the duration of the speech.

'Why do we have to stand?' Barnaby moaned.

'Because she is your queen, Barnaby,' snapped my dad.

This happened every year. During the Queen's Jubilee, when all the commentators were saying it was tough on the Queen being forced to stand throughout the royal pageant on the Thames, I was probably the only person in the country thinking, 'That's payback, Ma'am'!

The Queen's Speech is always followed by a Christmas stroll. This event is entirely pointless, bearing in mind it gets dark at three forty-five.

'It's all very well for you children to moan about going out,' my mother said. 'I've been busy cooking, and your father and Neil have put the Church of England to rights. And poor Charlie has had to cross his legs all day!'

Really my mother's so keen on this walk not because the dog needs a wee but because she lives in hope of meeting neighbours she could have a Christmas gossip with.

'Who the fuck was that?' said my father, after one of my mother's lengthy stops.

'Joan Felsham, Michael. She was on the Putney Common Association Committee with you.'

'Never clapped eyes on her in my life! Wait, is she the barren one at number five?'

The only thing that eclipses gossiping is a celebrity spot. My mother once thought she saw Michael Ball on the towpath by the Thames, and she was so excited that she nearly fainted into the river.

Christmas Day 2004 ran to the normal schedule, then. But there was one major difference to our routine: the plan for Boxing Day.

Normally we would go to Edwin and Anne Mullins' Boxing Day lunch party to catch up with friends, or allow my mother an opportunity to question an elderly stranger's gender, but this year my mother had bought us a joint family Christmas present: tickets to watch Leicester City versus West Ham at Upton Park.

Neil wouldn't come as he was a big Millwall fan and didn't want to set foot in Upton Park . . . OK, not really, he wasn't remotely interested in football, so instead opted to stay at home and make the dinner.

'He could make something from my Gordon Ramsay cookbooks. Maybe cross-reference the editions,' I said as we set off.

My mum is a lifetime supporter of Leicester City. She doesn't get to go to many of their games, though, so this was a major treat. There was, however, a slight problem. The only tickets she could get hold of were in the home end – in the infamous 'Chicken Run', where all of the toughest fans *and* Danny Dyer, sit.

Now, my father likes football, but he is more of an armchair fan. The few live games he has attended were mostly at Fulham's ground, Craven Cottage, which was within walking distance of our house in Putney. The Cottage (their ground) is a civilized affair, even during the fieriest of fixtures. It was at a Fulham match that I heard the most middle-class bit of terrace abuse ever. One of the mid-fielders gave the ball away and was promptly accused of being a 'charlatan' by the man sitting behind me eating some breadsticks.

That's the kind of hooliganism you get at Fulham. They don't throw coins at the players, but you might see the referee getting handed a Coutts gold card at the corner flag. Nothing could prepare my dad for the Chicken Run on a cold Boxing Day Championship fixture.

Once into Upton Park, we sat down next to a man who turned to my father and said, 'We're gonna rape the Foxes today, mate.'

As a Leicester City fan my father might have challenged this assertion, were it not for the fact that his new-found 'mate' was a twenty-five stone, gaudily tattooed, shaven-headed man mountain, whose breath was boozy enough to render anyone he was talking to over the limit.

We sat through a pretty boring fixture, with me and (more wor-ryingly) my little brother Barnaby, being subjected to some of the most colourful language you've ever heard coming almost exclu-sively from my dad's neighbour. What made the tattooed man's swearing all the more unnerving was that Barnaby wasn't the only child in his immediate vicinity. Next to him was a boy of about seven or eight who much to our surprise started referring to the man as 'Dad'. We realized the little boy was his son! Amazingly this did

'We're forever blowing bubbles!'

nothing to censor his language. And the tirade of abuse continued. It was all of a theme: 'The referee's a WANKER!', 'Oi, ref, you're a WANKER,' and, to ring the changes, the odd 'This ref's a fucking WANKER!' It was all pretty uncomfortable to witness.

At about the eighty-minute mark, after hearing this stuff on a constant loop throughout the game and having been egged on by my mum at half-time to 'have a word with that oaf', my dad finally plucked up the courage to confront the man mountain about his choice of language. 'I'm sorry, sir,' said my dad firmly but very politely, adopting the tone of voice I've only ever heard him use when talking to scary builders he suspects might be ripping him off, 'but I cannot understand how you can use those words in front of your son; he's a child.' The man was stunned, as clearly no one had ever had the balls to call him up on it before. He was lost for words, though not for long, as he collected himself, looked down at his son, then back at my dad and said brazenly, 'It's all right, mate. Cos he –' pointing at his son – 'thinks the ref's a WANKER as woll!'

As we left the ground ten minutes before the end of the match ('avoiding the crush at the tube station' was the official excuse, though I suspect it was to also get home so that my father could change his underpants), my little brother enquired about some of the new vocabulary he'd learnt that afternoon.

'Daddy, what's a WANKER?' he asked.

'Peter Mandelson,' said my dad.

When we got home Neil told us that the Gordon Ramsay book was shit.

The following year we didn't return to West Ham for the Boxing Day football. It was back to the Mullinses' party, where the only person that might cause offence was my mother.

1. These allegations about me and food are all vicious lies. The chefs of many of London's top restaurants are always hugely appreciative of any input I can give them on their signature dishes. You will often see me chatting with Jeremy King or Chris Corbin

at the Wolseley or the Delaunay about the construction of their Croustade of Quail's Eggs and Hollandaise or the mix of ingredients in the Wolseley Fish Stew. I have also had many exchanges of correspondence with Jeremy or Chris on topics such as the excellent texture of the meat in their Boeuf Bourguignon at the Brasserie Zedal or the ratio of garlic to butter in their exceptional Escargots, a regular favourite of mine. As you well know, good food is one of my passions.

He's only mentioning restaurants he likes now in the hope that he might get a free meal. Pathetic. So pathetic actually that it's making me feel quite hungry. God, I could do with a lovely, tasty Nando's.

2. Prince Charles is one of the finest men this country has ever produced and my only regret is that he is not yet a member of the Garrick Club. My life's ambition is to put this to rights.

3. I wouldn't want anyone to think I am a genuine Leicester City supporter, more of a Fox by marriage.

Part VII

Hapless House Guests

CHAPTER 17

Nannies

– MICHAEL WHITEHALL –

HILARY INTRODUCED HERSELF to our new neighbours, Tom and Gilly Gutteridge.

'How lovely to have a young family moving in next door,' Gilly cooed.

'Wait till you see my husband,' said Hilary.

After Hilary had Molly she was very ill with double pneumonia and pleurisy. Woose still worked full-time as a social worker so was unable to come and help. Therefore a live-in nanny was required, as Jack was sixteen months old and only just walking, although the whole thing filled me with horror. I'd heard so many gruesome stories from people about their nannies.

'You'll loathe having a nanny in the house, Michael,' said Edwin. 'They spend all their time on the phone to Australia or wherever they come from. And, whatever you do, don't leave any cash around.' Advice from other helpful friends included: 'Keep your drink locked up – our nanny drank a whole bottle of Cointreau one evening and was sick all over the nursery carpet,' and 'Never leave your nanny in the house alone – we got home early once and found her in bed with some bloke, and she was in *our* bed!' And then there was the South African nanny who smoked in bed, set fire to the sheets and narrowly avoided burning down the house.

Despite her illness, Hilary was in charge of interviewing the likely candidates and I was invited to attend but to observe in a non-speaking capacity, much like the role undertaken by my good friend Nick Hewer on *The Apprentice*.

Due to over-demand and lack of supply, there was never much of a choice.

'Don't go on looks,' said Hilary. 'The good-looking ones are always out on the town. The plain ones are best.' She would say that, wouldn't she?

Jenny Wilson, our first nanny, was certainly plain. She was six feet two and wore size ten shoes. A big unit in all departments.

Finding good nannies is quite a skill and one that I never acquired. Agencies back then charged a hefty commission and often hadn't met the girls that they recommended, nor indeed knew much about them, so we tended to get ours through a magazine called *TNT*. How could we have entrusted our children to the care of people who read a free magazine left in piles on the pavements of the Earls Court Road? The 'Nannies Wanted' ads were next to 'Bar Staff Required' and attracted a similar clientele – girls looking for temporary accommodation and some money while they explored London.

'I gather you drive,' I said to Jenny at her brief interview. Naturally the non-speaking part I had been allocated was not one I could play for long. 'How long since you passed your test?' She was only eighteen and I wasn't too keen on her roaring off in the new Volvo estate with our precious baby Jack strapped into the back and her size tens slammed on to the accelerator.

'Well, I've only recently passed my test but I've been driving for twelve years,' she replied.

'So you've been driving since you were six, eh?' I said.

'My family are farmers in New South Wales and we had a Mini Moke that I was allowed to drive to the end of our sheep station; we had 50,000 acres. I left the car by the road, caught the bus to school and back, and then drove home. My father taught me to drive when I was six, yes, although, of course, I wasn't allowed to drive on roads until last year.'

A tall, strong, practical girl – perfect, I thought, and indeed she was in every respect, bar one.

Jenny was cursed with the most virulent, overpowering and heinous BO. That distinctive strain of BO that hits you at the back of your throat and causes your heart to miss a beat as you attempt to exhale it. The one that lingers on the air for hours after the original blast. It had that trademark aroma of overcooked mince and never properly left the house from the day she took her size tens off in the hall when she first arrived to when she put them back on for the last time six months later and returned to New South Wales.

'I've tried everything,' explained Hilary. 'Slipping canisters of deodorant into her handbag, leaving roll-ons lying around her bedroom, giving her presents of body wash and perfume; I even bought her a gift pack of Wright's Coal Tar Soap, but all to no avail.'

It was obviously all outdoor showers and tin baths under the stars back in the old country, with the sheep and cattle masking more rancid aromas, and as all her best friends probably came from similar locales, there had been no one to tell her.

I came down to the kitchen one evening to find Hilary talking to Jenny about her social life, which seemed to be non-existent. She'd been out once in the past month and was back that evening by nine thirty.

'Is it shepherd's pie for dinner?' I asked as I was hit by the aroma of cooked meat.

'No, fish actually,' said Hilary, 'and I haven't started cooking it yet.' Jenny smiled sweetly.

As a leaving present we gave her an expensive set of toiletries – body washes, deodorants, bath oils, scents, creams and lotions, but after she'd left we discovered that they were still in her room. Maybe they'd come in handy for the next occupant, I thought.

We then had two false starts. A New Zealander whom we got through an agency – we were so desperate we'd now gone down the more official route – and who arrived with a large woolly-haired black mongrel and told us that she never went anywhere without it.

'Nobody's ever complained about Mr Mandy before,' she told us. The dog had in fact been christened Mandy as the girl had originally thought the dog was a bitch, but on discovering her mistake she re-named him Mr Mandy. Was this a person we wanted looking after our children?

We told her that we would sadly have to do without her and her dog, and sent her back to the agency in Gloucester Road, which had no idea of her canine attachment.

And then another Aussie, who was working in Bristol but wanted to move to London. She was due to join us on a Saturday morning but didn't actually appear until the Sunday evening and was unable to be reached by phone.

She walked into the hall carrying a large suitcase.

'Sorry I'm a bit late. I overslept!' she said.

'What, for two days?' Hilary asked.

'I thought you wanted me today,' she replied, 'Sunday.'

'No, yesterday. Saturday,' said Hilary, annunciating the word 'Saturday'. 'But that was yesterday, today we don't want you at all!' I handed her her suitcase and she headed back to Bristol.

'Poor girl,' said Hilary, 'perhaps we should have given her a week's trial.'

'And waited until she'd forgotten which shop she'd left Jack and Molly in?'

As we were going on holiday shortly after that, Hilary decided that it would make more sense to 'hire' the Mullinses' daughter Selina as a temporary nanny to accompany us on holiday, rather than rush into yet another false start. She was at that point seventeen and studying for her A levels, but had the huge advantage of already knowing the children and being very willing. Unfortunately, two days before we flew to Spain, she was attacked on Putney Common by a vicious dog, which inflicted three puncture wounds in the back of her leg. So, although she was willing, this meant that there was absolutely no swimming allowed at all. Not perfect on a holiday with a swimming pool just outside the sitting-room French windows and the beach half a mile down the road with two very small children to be entertained, but we were too near to departure to make alternative arrangements.

We were joined on this holiday by Martin Jarvis, Ros, and Neil Stacy. On the first afternoon Hilary, Ros and Selina headed off to the supermarket for supplies, leaving Martin, Neil and me in charge of Jack and Molly. We were all happily splashing around in the shallow end of the swimming pool as the shopping party drove off. Within a few minutes the car came crunching back up the drive.

'I can't believe you're still all in the pool!' called Hilary as she leapt out of the car.

'Why, what's wrong?' I asked. 'Jack and Molly are having a great time.'

'And what if they got out of their depth?' she asked. 'How would you cope with that?'

'Well, we'd . . .' said Neil.

'Swim and get them . . .' spluttered Martin.

'But none of you can swim!!' said Hilary crossly.

And, of course, none of us could. Well, I could just manage a width of a small pool as long as I didn't breathe, Martin and Neil were much the same, and Jack and Molly couldn't at all.

Hilary ordered us out of the pool. 'How could I have left three men who can't swim in charge of my two beautiful children in a swimming pool. I must be raving mad,' she said.

Martin, Neil and I sat grumpily by the side of the pool as Hilary dried Jack and Molly off, dressed them and put them in the car.

'See you guys later,' said Ros. 'Is there anything we can get you in town?'

'How about three sets of water wings?' I asked

'Don't joke, Michael,' said Hilary, 'they're already on the list.'

I had been 'taught' to swim by a monk at Ampleforth who stood at the side of the pool with a long pole, in full Benedictine habit, shouting instructions. Totally unable to float, let alone swim, but not wanting to look stupid, I engineered an impressive crawl stroke with my arms, while I bounced along the bottom of the pool with my legs. I then spent the next ten years of my life pretending I could swim.

Donald Sinden told me that his parents had never taught him to swim and that although he was involved in lots of seafaring films he never actually did his own swimming. In *The Cruel Sea*, Nicholas Monsarrat's story of life and death on an Atlantic corvette during World War Two, Donald had a double for the long shots of him struggling in the oily seawater after the ship had been torpedoed and, for the close-ups, two deep-sea divers holding him upright as he swam to the safety of the lifeboats.

On our return home, we engaged our first English nanny, not that we would have guessed it from her accent. Uncharacteristically, Hilary had hired Sharon, a pretty twenty-two-year-old from Essex. Pretty on the eye but not on the ear.

'Say ta!' she told Jack, having put a spoonful of mashed swede into his dribbling mouth. 'Don't you want no juice?'

I told Hilary that I really didn't want our children being taught English by Sharon.

One evening Jack walked into my study as I was talking to Patrick Macnee, aka secret agent John Steed, in Los Angeles. 'Have we received any residuals for *The Avengers* recently?' he asked. He had a cash-flow problem.

'I want toilet!' shouted Jack.

Hilary and I discussed how best to approach this potentially lethal problem before we were awash with cruets, greens, toilets, lounges, settees and, worst of all, serviettes.

OK, this might be the single most arbitrary, needless name-drop in all my dad's chapters. Quite a feat.

'Well, I can't tell Sharon not to speak to the children, and I don't think leaving a copy of Nancy Mitford's *Noblesse Oblige* on her bedside table would have any more success than that can of Sure in Jenny's bathroom did.'

'It just needs constant monitoring,' I said helpfully. 'Every time Sharon says "lounge", interrupt her and say "sitting room", and at the merest mention of the word "couch", get straight in with "sofa". And definitely, definitely stamp all over the word "toilet".'

I then heard her admonishing Molly rather loudly after she'd burped up some juice with the words: 'Say "pardon"!' Followed by an almost unforgivable: 'Posh children say "pardon"!' Things were getting out of control. Metaphorically her bags were packed and in the 'porch'.

Fortunately as Jack was only three, Molly two and Barnaby newly born, their vocabulary was still pretty limited, comprising mainly of different degrees of gurgling, so when Sharon left us a year later, no lasting damage had been done.

A couple more mistakes followed Sharon's departure. Nikki Jenkins from New Zealand played fast and loose with our ex-directory telephone number.

''Allo, is Nikki there?' said a rasping voice at the other end of my home phone.

'Yes, I think so, may I ask who's calling?' I replied.

'Just put her on!' said the voice aggressively.

I put the phone down and went upstairs to talk to Nikki.

'I'd really rather you didn't dish out my phone number to anyone you happen to meet. Who was that person? He sounded like a bailiff.'

'He's called Bob and he's really nice. I met him on the twenty-two bus last night. I had a chat with him outside the Spencer Arms and gave him your phone number.' The Spencer Arms was our local pub and the end of the twenty-two bus route.

'And what does Bob do?' I asked.

'He was the conductor,' she replied.

Nikki left a few weeks later and got a job behind the bar at the Spencer Arms, very handy for Bob.

Rosie Jones was a newly qualified opera singer from Perth, Australia, who had made her way to the bright lights of London seeking fame and fortune with one of the big opera companies here. We were mutually attracted by the common ground of a love of the arts. A cultured, educated and willing girl, I thought she might be able to reverse some of the more Essex-based interests that the children had picked up from Sharon.

'What is that deafening din, Hilary?' I asked on the first morning of Rosie's employment. 'It's six thirty a.m. for God's sake!'

Hilary knocked on Rosie's door.

'Come in,' she trilled.

'Could I have a word, Rosie?' she said.

'Sure.'

'I wonder if you might do your vocal scales and arpeggios at another time during the day? Perhaps when the children are at school?' she asked politely.

'Oh, this is just the first set of the day. I'll need to repeat this another three times.'

'She won't have time to fit in looking after our children, with all that singing to get through,' I remarked.

That clearly was never going to work, so we parted amicably with Rosie.

'Adolf Hitler did some good things for the German people, one shouldn't forget that. He was not a bad man.' Not a quote from David Irving or Nick Griffin of the BNP, but from our next nanny, Hilde Buchmann.

A squat nineteen-year-old South African, Hilde was not unhappy to have left her native Pretoria following the recent breakdown of Apartheid. She was ultra-efficient and undoubtedly master of her brief when it came to looking after small children. She'd been with us for a few weeks and we were watching England v Germany on television. She was clearly supporting the wrong team and explained that her grandfather had been an Obergruppenführer in the Waffen-SS and had exchanged* Berlin for Cape Town at the end of the war, and married his South African wife in 1947.

*As my dad and I concluded, for 'exchanged' read 'fled'.

'He often talked to my father about the efficiency of the Third Reich,' she told me over a TV supper in the kitchen one evening. I think we might have been watching *The World at War*.**

**He has genuinely made us watch that as a family during dinner.

'Well, they were certainly very efficient at carting tens of thousands of Jews off to the death camps,' I said, feeling it was important that Hilde knew exactly where the Whitehall family stood vis-à-vis Nazi Germany.

'Winston Churchill killed people too,' said Hilde.

'She'll have the children goose-stepping up and down the play-room next,' I said to Hilary later in the evening. 'She's got to go!'

'But she's the most organized nanny we've ever had – she even tidies your sock drawer –' this is of course the great advantage of having a pro-Apartheid nanny, one's sock drawer is strictly separated between whites and coloureds – 'and you'll never find anyone answering the phone like that,' Hilary added.

Before Hilde's arrival nannies either ignored the ringing phone, answered it with a disinterested 'yeah?' or left people holding on while they changed nappies or washed up trainer-cups. Not Hilde. Before the first ring had ended she grabbed the phone and announced in her clipped South African accent: 'The Whitehall residence – can I help you?'

The Whitehall residence – I liked that – it had a certain something to it and we hadn't even asked her to do it.

'Michael is showing major signs of *folie de grandeur*,' said Neil to a mutual friend of ours. 'He insists on his nannies answering the phone with "The Whitehall residence" and now they're all at it. His cleaning lady does it and so do his children. It's all deeply embarrassing.'

After Hilde had returned to South Africa and married a boy whose father had been a leading light in the Hitler Youth, we were now on the final lap, and for the first time looked to Eastern Europe for help in the form of an au pair from Macedonia called Svetlana. We went to meet her at Victoria coach station fresh off the bus from Skopje – well, maybe not that fresh. As the doors powered open the smell of a rancid dustbin in a heatwave engulfed us. As we steadied ourselves a mass of sleepy-eyed, dishevelled-looking teenagers poured on to the pavement. But which one was Svetlana? The pretty auburn-haired one with the pink scarf, the fat one bursting out of her leather jacket?

Hilary held up her card with 'Whitehall' written on it in heavy felt-tip pen. And then, just as a stunning-looking blonde girl started to get off the bus and gave me an 'I'm Svetlana' look, a voice from behind us said: 'You Whyhole?'

I was being approached by a hooker – dyed red hair, heavy make-up, topplingly high heels, a very short and very crumpled skirt and far too much cleavage for a chilly November evening.

In the car on the way home Svetlana explained in her basic English that she had arrived in London on an earlier bus and had been filling in time wandering around Victoria.

'Victor nice town,' she said 'nice boys.'

Five-year-old Molly really liked Svetlana, especially her wide range of beauty products and high heels. Svetlana considered herself to be a bit of a dab hand at make-up application and one evening she appeared in the kitchen for supper, followed by Molly.

'I have big, nice surprise for both,' she announced. 'Molly beautiful,' she said and ushered her into the room.

'Svetlana's made me up, Daddy, do you like it? It's my new look!'

Molly looked like a child prostitute, probably much like those found on the backstreets of Skopje.

'Pretty, no?' said Svetlana.

My thoughts entirely. If I thought that wasn't bad enough, I hadn't seen Jack. He leapt into the room behind Molly with a 'tah-dah!', looking like a miniature transvestite.* Not only had she made him up, but she had dressed him in some of her best 'going out on the town' finery. I was furious.

'Hilary, you must know that the last thing on earth this child needs is the slightest encouragement to dress itself up as a woman!' I thundered.**

'She's very good, Michael, and is a sweet girl. Don't you go upsetting her. It was only a bit of fun; she means well,' said Hilary.

*I looked fantastic.

**I'm literally a child called 'it'.

'Well, as far as I am concerned, she's on borrowed time.'

Svetlana was a very willing girl, always ready to help, but shortly before she returned to Macedonia she caused havoc with my horticultural plans. Our garden roses were looking worn out, so on the recommendation of Edward Fox, who had just replaced his roses, I went to an upmarket grower called David Austin.

The catalogue was full of ravishing roses in full bloom. The plants that arrived were obviously less attractive as we were still in the middle of winter, though not inexpensive, but I checked them all and was particularly impressed that each plant had a brass tag attached to it with the name of the rose.

I left the twenty plants by the back door on Friday night so that I could start planting them the following morning. A well-invested £150, I thought.

When I came down for breakfast on Saturday morning the kitchen looked very spick and span. Good old Svetlana.

We had an incinerator at the end of the garden where Hilary used to burn unwanted boxes and assorted detritus; she liked a good burn-up.

'Eins, zwei, drei, vier...'

'I get rid of old papers in cinemator,' said Svetlana as I was boiling myself an egg. 'And old boxes,' she added.

'Well done, Svetlana, Hilary will be pleased. I'm going to be doing some gardening this morning, so I'll take the children outside with me,' I said, looking across to the back door where I had left the roses.

'And I burned those old twigs that you left by the back door,' she said, beaming.

'Svetlana . . . no, please . . . not my roses . . . please . . . no!'

I ran down to the end of the garden and at the bottom of the incinerator was a smouldering heap of grey ashes, and dotted around them little clusters of brass labels.

I pulled them out of the embers: Old Blush China, Glamis Castle, Constance Spry, Rosa Mundi.*

Her borrowed time was up and, indeed, it was time to say goodbye to nannies and au pairs for good. What I didn't know at the time was that looming round the corner was the prospect of having lodgers on the premises, but at least they would be paying me rather than vice versa.

*Aren't those the names of Bob Geldof's children?

1. I find it worrying that my parents appear to be far more relaxed with their childen being raised by a neo-Nazi than by a woman from Essex.

2. What's wrong with the word 'toilet'? 'Bog' may be a bit informal, 'shitter' I might be concerned, but everyone says 'toilet'! Big deal.

3. You describe several nannies in this chapter as being very 'willing'. Please don't refer to young women as being 'willing'. It sounds really dodgy.

4. Rosie the Opera singer. Isn't that the one Mummy caught you flirting with?*

*No

CHAPTER 18

Sacha's Laundry

– JACK WHITEHALL –

'We're hard up for money,' announced my father.

It was true. The burden of three sets of school fees and a pen-chant for expensive menswear had hit him hard.*

The accounts didn't make for pretty reading. (Don't worry, this isn't the sob-story chapter where I talk about how tough life was for me growing up in Putney. Things were tough but it was hardly *Angela's Ashes* . . . we still had an AGA.)

'Why doesn't Jack get a job?' he suggested.

'Because he's twelve, Michael, and we aren't living in the Industrial Revolution or in China,' said my mother 'Why don't we ask my mother to lend us some money?'

My father would rather have lived in China or during the Industrial Revolution than borrow Woose's money.

'Over my dead body. I'm not being indebted to that woman,' my dad replied. His hostility to the idea was partly due to his sense of pride, and partly (mostly) because he'd always been quite scared of Woose. She was a formidable woman and very much the head of the family.** If you owed her money, she would definitely exploit the situation to her advantage. And, as with all criminal master-minds, if it wasn't paid back swiftly Woose would make you an offer you couldn't refuse . . . like spending Christmas down with them in Hampshire in their freezing-cold sitting room with its three-bar electric fire. My father certainly didn't want that.

*Not to mention the cost of feeding your mother's obsession with having your teeth fixed.

**Debatable.

My mum's friend Felicity, whose family were also having a few money troubles,* had helped boost their coffers by taking in a lodger. They had a student from the Royal Ballet School called Sabrina, who'd lived with them for six months now. Sabrina paid rent, did her part of the housekeeping and helped Felicity with the school run from time to time. It sounded perfect.

My dad got the number of the Royal Ballet School and my mum prepared a room for our new guest.

'It'll be like having the fourth child you never let me have,' my mother said to my dad as she placed bottles of sparkling and still water next to the pristinely made spare bed. This is her go-to piece of passive aggression, and it usually guilts my dad into doing whatever she wants. I'm certain the thought of a fourth set of school fees, though, made my father privately congratulate his prudent seed-sowing.

Not that he wasn't excited about the lodger. His friends had been very jealous when he told them an attractive young ballerina was coming to stay. He clearly pictured a woman much in the mould of Sabrina: petite, lithe and perennially dressed in little skirts.

The smile was wiped off my father's face when Sacha arrived on his doorstep. Sacha was a very slender, incredibly camp first-year ballet student. He was half-Peruvian, had thick blow-dried hair and a pout to make Eddie Redmayne jealous. He was certainly not what my father had been expecting.

'We could send him back,' he said to my mum as Sacha unpacked his vast arsenal of bags upstairs.

'Don't be silly, Michael. He's not from John Lewis,' she said as Michael looked knowingly undersold. 'Anyway, you haven't even got to know him yet. Give the boy a chance.'

A week went by with Sacha in residence. He was a really nice guy, and Molly and I especially liked him. When he came home from school he'd entertain us by demonstrating what he'd been learning that day.

One evening I went into my father's study as he was looking over a script he'd been developing with the theatre in Guildford, no doubt to crowbar one of his out-of-work clients into. I decided that he needed a little respite from all that hard work in the form of a little theatrical performance of my own.

'Hey, Daddy, look what Sacha showed me,' I said while performing a faultless pirouette. There was no invitation for an encore. In fact he reacted like I'd shown him '2 Girls 1 Cup'.

'Have you seen what he's got my son doing, Hilary?' railed my dad. 'As if that boy needed any more encouragement.'

My house was very quickly turning into a sort of middle-class *Billy Elliot*.* This wasn't my first brush with the silk slipper. As a child, my mother had actually sent me to ballet lessons along with Molly. I'd originally been signed up to learn karate but, because these combat classes were held in Hammersmith and my sister's ballet school was in Richmond, my mother found the car journey a bridge too far. One of us was going to have to make a sacrifice.

Molly wasn't keen on having to hang up her tutu, no matter how much I tried to persuade her that every young girl should know how to throw a karate chop, especially living somewhere as dangerous as Putney. So, alas, I ended up being the only boy in Richmond taking ballet classes. And worse still, I loved it. I even took my Royal Academy of Dance pre-primary exam and got a top mark.

Unfortunately when my father got wind of this he suddenly became more than happy to help out with the picking-up and dropping-off duties. His little white swan was plucked from the arms of Richmond's ballet instructors and thrust straight into the Sensei's flying eagle embrace, where I kicked planks of wood with little visible effect and learnt how to count to twenty in Japanese, a skill I'd later use to annoy my father's war-veteran uncle, Peter.**

But back to Sacha. It was as if God had designed this young man to annoy Michael Whitehall in every conceivable way. For a start, Sacha was very, very messy. Dishes were left lying around the bedroom, and his vast array of cosmetics and face wipes were wantonly scattered about, not only his bathroom but the communal bathroom as well. This did not go down well with my father, a stickler for tidiness and obsessed with bathroom hygiene in particular. So much so that one of our cousins, who shall remain nameless,*** has never been invited back to our house, as on a previous stay he left a very large and very hard souvenir of his visit floating in the immaculate guest loo.

The problem was that whereas Sabrina had acted as a sort of

What is that? Don't ask!

*The only difference being that in this version the father was very pro-Thatcher.

**How dare you? If it wasn't for Uncle Peter, you'd be writing this book in German.

***Henry Whitehall.

live-in nanny, Sacha treated our house like a hotel. This was partly down to my mother making it seem like one. The bottles of water by the bed, offering to make him breakfast every morning, newspapers outside his door – she even suggested putting a chocolate on his pillow. That was vetoed by my dad, but he couldn't stop her from doing all Sacha's laundry.

This wasn't the arrangement my father had had in mind. Maybe he would have done the lissom Sabrina's delicates, but this was going too far.*

As a ballet dancer, Sacha had vast amounts of washing. Every time my dad went to put a shirt in the laundry basket, it would be overflowing with sweaty leggings, tracksuit bottoms and other soiled regalia.

'Why can't Sacha be a normal boy like Jack and wear the same pants for a week?' my dad moaned one evening, suspending for a moment his view of me as being more or less a freak.

'Jack is not a normal child,' replied my mother.

'Why's Sacha got a truss?' my dad asked her. He'd picked up a garment from the basket she was loading into the washing machine. 'Isn't he a bit young to have had a hernia?'

'That's not a truss, that's a jockstrap.'

'Oh, my God!' my dad screamed. He dropped it and tried to kick it into the washing machine, but the jockstrap's pouch became entangled with the toe of his Church's brogue, leaving him dancing about on one foot trying to free himself from the gusset. After this, Sacha was on borrowed time.

One afternoon, Sacha came back from a hard day's ballet and made the fatal error of slinging his bag down and shouting into the kitchen, 'I think I'm going to hit the hay. There's whites and colours in there, so make sure you separate them, darling.'

'I beg your pardon?' a male voice came back at him. It had been my father in the kitchen, not my mother. 'Maybe you'd like me to make you some tea, Sacha, or run you a bath. Bubbles, candles, the porcelain garnished with rose petals. How does that sound? I wouldn't want you putting yourself out at all in *my house*!'

When my mum was around, Dad was made to behave. She'd said it in jest, but Sacha really had become a bit like her surrogate son. What he made of it all is anyone's guess. I'm sure most lodgers aren't encouraged by the mother of the house to dine with the family every night, to come on family outings and even to meet the relatives. When Sacha was introduced to Woose I could see my father in the background, wondering if a Kent Christmas was really all *that* bad an idea.

I certainly think that my mum would have loved a son as exotic as Sacha.

'Our lodger, Sacha, is from Peru and so handsome,' she'd say to her friends in Timothy Williams Hair Design, Barnes, hairdresser's-cum-gossip epicentre for the whole of south-west London.

'Oooh,' cooed the excited mothers, probably not quite sure where Peru actually was. My mum's pride in Sacha living with us, meanwhile, was matched only by my dad's deepening embarrassment.

Having a 'flamboyant' male dancer living with him was a cause of constant discomfort, the pinnacle of which came on a trip to the doctor's on Glebe Road to have his ear syringed.

While in the waiting room, leafing no doubt through that week's *Heat* to see if Sir Donald Sinden had made the 'Spotted' section,* my dad was sat next to a man in his late seventies called Spencer. Spencer, a former civil servant, had been married for most of his adult life, until his wife had passed away a couple of years before. Her death had promptly liberated Spencer to discover 'the real him'. And if he didn't quite chuck his wedding ring into the crowd at the Royal Vauxhall Tavern during the chorus of 'I Am What I Am', it turned out that the real Spencer was a man who *makes his own hats*. He was seen with a different young man on his arm every week and was even spotted once by my mother coming out of a notorious cottaging area in a graveyard near Putney Common.

'I just saw Spencer down by the cemetery walking his dog,' my mother told my dad.

'But he doesn't have a dog, he never has,' said my father.

Suffice to say, everyone knew that Spencer was now out. Good on the old codger, I used to think, living his life to the full. My father, perhaps inevitably, was less enthusiastic. Is this what happens to men of a certain age when their wife dies? No wonder he started insisting my mother wore her seat belt.

*I have no idea what Jack is talking about here, but any publication having Sir Donald writing for them would be very fortunate.

Anyway, Spencer turned to my dad in the doctor's packed waiting room and started up a conversation. He was talking into my dad's blocked ear so was promptly encouraged to 'speak up', so in a stage whisper loud enough for the rest of the waiting room to hear he said, 'I heard about the South American boy you've got. Where can I get myself one of them?'

My dad was so shocked at hearing this that, by the time the doctor saw him, I doubt he needed to have his ear syringed any more. Spencer's comment had cleared it out.

'People think I've taken some sort of male concubine! That I'm the kind of man *that has a lead without a dog*,' my dad raged. 'He's got to go.'

'But we need the money, Michael,' said my mum. She knew that – while she had this excuse – Sacha had a stay of execution. But if

'Be a darling and put this load on for me.'

HIM & ME

Sacha had one positive effect on my dad, it was making him double (maybe even triple) his work-rate. Clients who'd been out of work for years[*] suddenly got jobs. Dead and buried scripts were dusted off and given a second push to channel executives or production companies. Respected, classically trained actors were ushered into lucrative panto productions by their desperate agent. My dad knew that if the money came flowing in, then Sacha could be flown out.

Of which there were very few.

Two months later, at the end of Sacha's agreed first term of tenancy, my parents' finances were firmly back in the black, that script he'd been developing with Guildford had been green-lit with Peter Bowels in the main role and Nigel Havers was having his costume fittings for Captain Hook. We bid our farewells to Sacha, but he left an indelible mark on our family, and quite a few items of clothing, which were discovered wedged under the bed and down the sofa.

It is spelt 'Bowles' not 'Bowels'.

Years later we were watching the news during a TV supper and a story came on about a mudslide in Lima.

'The community has rallied together,' said the reporter, 'and the clean-up mission is well under way.'

'There you are,' said my dad. 'Some Peruvians know how to clear up.'

1. *I don't recall ever referring to Woose as 'that woman'. I have the utmost respect for my mother-in-law and am very fond of her. I am definitely not scared of her. In the very unlikely event of my having to borrow money from her I can't believe that she would force me down to Hampshire for Christmas as punishment for not paying it back. A midwinter weekend break in a B & B in Eastbourne would be more her style.*

2. *I do not dispute that my dear friend Spencer rides his bicycle side-saddle, but he is a very kind and interesting man, excellent company and a very popular member of the Garrick Club.*

3. *I don't know what 'cottaging' is, but my son clearly does. Maybe it was something he was introduced to by Sacha.*

4. *Nigel Havers was a fabulous Captain Hook.*

CHAPTER 19

Dirty Den

– JACK WHITEHALL –

One of the things you learn growing up as the son of an agent is how fleeting so many of the relationships are in this industry. My father would have clients he was incredibly close to, young actors he'd plucked from drama school, nurtured, spoken to on a daily basis and even, with some, gone on holiday with. Then with one phone call they were gone, never to be spoken to or of ever again. I remember my dad telling me that one of his clients who he had represented for over twenty years had sacked him by letter, saying that he 'felt like a rudderless ship'. 'More like a rudderless shit,' observed my father. I won't name the client to save his blushes, but let's just say he was to the manor born. (Oops!)*

My dad never seemed to take it personally and always accepted that it was just part of the game, and although he was often upset to see clients leave, he didn't beat himself up over it, at least not in front of me. I guess once you've seen so many come and go it gets easier. My dad was like the Katie Price of the agenting world, filing for divorce without a flicker of emotion.**

Of course, there were some clients he never forgave. Richard E. Grant, or as he's known in our house Richard E. Can't, and on other occasions the Grant replaced with a word that's similar to Cant, was a client whose perceived 'betrayal' left deeper scars.

*I can see what Jack is trying to imply here, but I will have you know that Peter Bowles and I parted company on extremely amicable terms and we remain close friends to this day.

**I don't fully understand or approve of this analogy.

Whenever he comes on TV,[*] I can see my dad dry-heave slightly. My father took on Richard E. Grant when he was completely unknown and desperate for an agent. He signed him up and fought especially hard to get him the part in *Withnail and I*. Producers had originally wanted Daniel Day-Lewis, another of my father's clients at the time, but when Daniel's diary didn't work out, my dad pushed them really hard to consider a young actor from Swaziland. 'Daniel's busy – but you must see a new client of mine called Richard E. Grant. He's very funny.' After much agenting, endless meetings and several screen tests, Richard finally got the part and the rest is history. He became a star, went to America and then out of the blue, following a phone call from LA, Richard was gone. He wanted to move on to do more challenging projects, work with bigger directors; he'd had coffee with Terrence Malick, and the American agents he signed with a week before said they could set up meetings with Spielberg and Scorsese. Within a few years Richard was starring in *Spice World*; I forget who directed it but I don't think it was Terrence Malick. I remember seeing the pictures of the premiere in London and

Me and my good friend Peter Bowles.   Me and Richard E. Grant.

[*] *Which I note doesn't happen that often any more.*

thinking if that guy hadn't sacked my dad I could have been hanging out with Baby Spice. Bastard. It wasn't till my teens that I got round to watching *Withnail and I* and I'm ashamed to say he's so amazing in that film that I've kind of forgiven him.*

*I haven't.

But for every Richard E. Grant, there is a Richard Griffiths or an Edward Fox, your one-club men, the Ryan Giggs of the thespians. By that I mean loyal, not sleeping around. I don't know if Richard or Edward were into that but I think it's highly unlikely. Edward Fox was one of the more 'old-school' clients on my father's books; he had an incredible vocabulary and he spoke like he was in a Wodehouse novel.** But when it came to modern technology Edward made my dad look like Mark Zuckerberg.

**How would you know, you've never read a Wodehouse novel?

He's the chap that invented that Twatbook. He invented Facebook, which is a separate entity to Twitter, which is spelt with an 'i'.

The device that seemed to cause him the most confusion was our answering machine. For years our answerphone message was me, my sister and brother when we were toddlers speaking in harmony: three little angelic voices saying, 'Hello, this is the Whitehall family, please leave a message after the tone.' It was sweet, but for Edward it always came as a surprise every time he heard it. He thought we were really there for real, not thinking it odd that the three of us were answering the phone together and also failing to notice that my voice, when I was seventeen, had still not broken.

'Hello, this is the Whitehall family, please leave a message after the tone . . . Beeeep.'

Daniel Day-Lewis just after I'd advised him not to do My Beautiful Launderette.

'Hello, children, greetings and salutations to you all. Now be a set of darlings and fetch your father, will you?' Then a long pause. 'Children, where have you gone? Children!?'

These messages would last for several minutes, with Edward bellowing out our names in the hope we'd come back to the phone. I suggested to my dad that he would avoid this happening if he could get Edward to email him instead. He would have been better off buying Edward some parchment and a pigeon.

Another of my father's loyal clients was the slightly less distinguished Leslie Grantham, better known as Dirty Den. My dad had stuck by Leslie as an agent and friend through many career highs and lows, from being the most famous villain on TV in *EastEnders* to fronting the ill-fated game show *Fort Boyard*, a truly bizarre concept.

'What's the pitch?' You could imagine some slick TV commissioner asking a producer.

'Imagine *The Crystal Maze*, but in the middle of the ocean . . . with dwarfs.'

'Let's do it!'*

For poor Leslie, though, the lows came rather thick and fast, and the final nail in the coffin of his television career was in 2004 when he was exposed in a tabloid newspaper assuming all manner of lewd poses, including the infamous finger In mouth, on an Internet webcam while slagging off fellow cast members. The nation was shocked. Leslie was fired from *EastEnders*. The revelation that struck me as the oddest was the detail 'while slagging off fellow cast members'. Suggesting that the woman on the other end of this webcam, who, we can only assume, Leslie was trying to turn on, was really into such 'dirty talk'. I mean, I've heard of people wanting some weird things in the bedroom, but the idea that such defamatory details might get someone's juices flowing struck me as particularly odd. Just as you're about to push her over the brink into climax, leaning in and whispering sexily in her ear, 'You know Pat Butcher's always late on set.'

Or maybe: 'Shane Ritchie shouts at runners.'

But, hey, each to their own.

'Adam Woodyatt once left a floater in the honey wagon after lunch.'

*All I can say is that it sounded very strong on the page. Bearing in mind such legendary programmes as Celebrity Juice, Chris Moyles' Quiz Night and The Million Pound Drop, there is a danger here of stones being thrown from glass houses.
You were on
The Million Pound
Drop with me!

Who ate all the pies?

OK, I'll stop.

Leslie's public humiliation did not completely spell the end. Its one advantage was that Leslie was in demand for press interviews, grovelling apologies on breakfast-television sofas and even a lucrative book offer, an offer that my dad negotiated and signed off for Leslie. The only snag with this book deal was that finger-cam meant Leslie's wife, for obvious reasons, refused to let him use their home computer. Leslie's wife was a strong character; she definitely wore the trousers in that relationship. Well, I mean she obviously did. If the videos taught us anything it's that Leslie wasn't keen on wearing trousers at all. Poor Les was left with no option but to call upon his old friend and agent for help.

'Mike, I need a computer to write the book on and I can't write it at home cos the missus won't let me near it,' he said over the phone, 'and I can't go to a bloody Internet café, can I? So I was thinking, you've got a computer over at your office, could I use it?'

'Of course you can, Leslie,' said my father without a moment's hesitation.

'Sure Hils won't mind?' added Leslie.

'Of course she won't,' said Dad.

She did. She minded because my dad's office at the time was situated in our house and my father, without asking her permission, had invited the most famous 'sleaze' in Britain over to have unlimited access to our family computer.

'I can't believe you've allowed this, Michael!' I heard her say behind the closed kitchen door. 'What next? Maybe you could call up Broadmoor and see if they have anyone to babysit the children or perhaps we could get hold of Harold Shipman to do a check-up on my mother!'*

The argument went on for some time but my mum hit a brick wall and eventually it was agreed that Leslie would be allowed to come round and write the book on the proviso that she could monitor him. Which she did like a hawk.

'Would you like a coffee, Leslie?' she'd say as she burst in through the door, expecting to find him hunched over the Apple Mac, kecks** around ankles.

'No thanks, Hils ... As I said to you five minutes ago, I'm not really thirsty,' replied a bewildered Leslie.

'Crumpets?' she asked, coming in five minutes after that.

Cucumber sandwiches, biscuits, cake, hot-cross buns, a glass of wine, cold meats, tonic water, breadsticks, Pot Noodle, crostini, miso soup, Berocca and so on. Leslie was offered anything she could find in our larder just to check he wasn't on that webcam. She observed him like a guard at Guantanamo. Poor Leslie, it must have been like being back on *Fort Boyard*. This went on for weeks until Leslie finished the book and it was released in all good book shops that Christmas – *Life and Other Times*. Although I still think my mother's idea for a title was far better.

'We're trying to think about what Leslie should call his book. Any ideas?' Daddy threw open one dinnertime to the family. 'We're thinking either "Life and Other Times" or "Hello, Princess".'

'I know what you could call it,' said my mother, '"Leslie Grantham: Den of Iniquity".' The rest of the meal was spent in silence.

My mum never quite forgave my dad for letting Leslie write his book at our house, but for me it was a godsend. I was seventeen at the time: a pubescent horny little son of a gun who, in the Internet

*Woose would have sussed out Shipman in five minutes.

**Where's all this Northern vernacular come from? I knew you shouldn't have gone to university in Manchester.

age, had at times allowed his dirty wandering mind to get the better of him. Where most kids might have been busted by eagle-eyed parents and lectured at length on the dangers of onanism, I had the perfect excuse.

'Jack, I need to have a word,' my mother said ominously. 'I have just checked the Internet history on our computer and it says someone visited a website called www.dirtychicksandcougars.com.* Would you know anything about that?'

'Well, Mum, it was probably Leslie.'

Leslie also holds the dubious honour of being the man that finally caused my dad to retire for good as an agent. He'd been thinking of winding his agency up for a while; he was enjoying his new calling as a theatre producer and had also employed an assistant some years previously who was taking his agency in a different direction, the wrong direction to his mind. My dad had always prized himself on the quality of his client list, never signing anyone he didn't deem 'classy' enough. He'd repped Dame Judi Dench and Dame Dorothy Tutin, so he didn't want any 'riff-raff' on his books. You can imagine his dismay when his slightly less selective assistant had signed a dame of her own, Christopher Biggins. My father was very fond of Christopher, but more as a dining companion than a client, and to make matters worse, as his clients were listed alphabetically, Biggins would have appeared immediately above Sir Tom Courtenay, which neither my father nor, one imagines, Sir Tom, was too thrilled about. My father had spent the majority of his career working out multi-picture deals for his top talent or golden handcuff contracts with television networks; he was not going to start calling up theatres to argue whether Christopher Biggins or *Hollyoaks* star Paul Danan would be getting the number-one dressing room when they appeared together in *Aladdin*. But if the Biggins saga was a minor irritation, it was an evening in the company of Leslie Grantham that was to be the final nail in the coffin. Leslie's career was stumbling along like a seasick dwarf and he was starring in a touring production of *Misery* that had reached its final week at the Ashcroft Theatre in Croydon. Dad had put off going to see it and by the time he got round to it decided it was a good idea to take me and my mother along for moral support. We arrived with spirits low

*www.dirtychicksandcougars.com is, I think, a wildlife website specializing in poultry and mountain lions. I seem to remember reading about David Attenborough having something to do with it.

in monsoon-like conditions after a long traffic-hit journey. Though, hey, if there's anything that's bound to perk you up when you're feeling down, it's the notoriously upbeat and fun-filled play *Misery*.

'You can't park the car here, sir,' said a man in a high-vis jacket drenched in rain outside the theatre.

'I'm Leslie Grantham's fucking agent. I will park where I want,' came the reply.

It was a disabled bay. We moved.

We went into the theatre and there was a sea of people in the foyer.

'Well, at least it's doing good business,' my mother observed, and she was right. It wasn't the youngest, hippest crowd; there were a fair few hearing aids on display and the smell of talc, but at least it looked like it was going to be a full house. I have noticed over the years how this is always the demographic of regional theatre. When I walk in I tend to bring the average age down from about a hundred. Recently I got in trouble with my dad on a theatre trip to Guildford when I took a picture of the back of everyone's heads in the auditorium and tweeted 'fifty shades of grey'. He said it was disrespectful, but, as I pointed out, I doubt any of them are on Twitter. They looked like they'd struggle to work out how to use an electric kettle.

'Final call for *Misery*,' said the usher, but none of the crowd moved.

'They're leaving it late,' said my dad.

'Maybe he needs to shout louder because they're all deaf,' I added.

'Aren't you going in?' my mother asked an old woman.

'Oh no, dear, we're not here for the play. We're seeing the Wurzels.'

It turned out that the crowd in the foyer weren't even there to see Leslie, they were all there for the Fairfield Halls, which is attached to the Ashcroft Theatre but shares a foyer. The West Country rockers the Wurzels were performing their hits that night.

We took our seats in the auditorium and the play began. The lights went down pretty quickly but I think I counted ten heads in the stalls, which could seat about five hundred.*

'This is so depressing,' said my dad in a grump.

The play began and out came Leslie; there was a sharp intake of breath from the elderly couple sitting behind me. Impressive, I thought. Even though he's had his day, Leslie still has the charisma and gravitas to make the diehard fans gasp in their seats through his

*He's exaggerating, there were at least fifty people.

*Forty-eight!

sheer presence on stage. The couple got up and began to shuffle out.

'Sorry, we're in the wrong venue.' A couple of stray Wurzels fans had got the wrong auditorium. We were down to eight.* This wasn't the only damage the scrumpy and western band caused to that evening's performance. Although the Ashcroft Theatre is a wonderful space, acoustically it leaves a little to be desired and as Leslie arrived at the emotional climax of the first act it was hard to be drawn into the drama, as all you could hear through the walls were hundreds of drunken pensioners singing 'I've got a brand-new combine harvester'. The play creaked on.

'We're going at the interval,' whispered my father. 'We'll go to the pub across the road, get a drink and then we'll go backstage to tell Leslie he was wonderful and get back to London as soon as we can.'

This was a tactic that my father had deployed before. If he really, really didn't like a play he'd been known to make a sneaky exit at the interval. When this occurred he always managed to blag and bullshit his way through a post-theatre drink or dinner with the star.

Leslie embarks on some vital research for his book.

'What about you, then?'[*] he'd ask, not knowing whether the second half had been a disaster or a triumph. 'I loved that final act; you really nailed it.'

*A phrase that covered all eventualities.

The only time he truly fucked up is when he'd been to see a client in a play, left at the interval and slipped off home for an early night. The following day he rang the client to congratulate him on a second-half performance that had in actual fact been suspended due to one of the cast members collapsing. The quality of Leslie Grantham's *Misery* meant that such a risk was worth taking. Thank God we were getting out soon, I thought. Only twenty minutes, I reckoned, till the interval. But twenty minutes was not enough for one couple who were (sat) down the front.

Once again, your English seems to have deserted you! It is sitting, not 'sat'.

The play had reached a moment that involved some sound effects of a thunderstorm and during a clap of thunder we heard a woman turn to her husband and say, 'I can't take it any more.' As the storm intensified, they got up out of their seats and stomped towards the exit. The woman, who seemed distressed by how bad this play was, looked at us in our seats and said almost apologetically, 'I just couldn't stand it any more.'[**]

**Who could?
***Oh, how I envied them!

'Well, that's why we're fucking leaving!'[***] said her husband loud enough for the actors on stage to hear. Leslie seemed momentarily stunned, but gathered himself to complete the finale of the first half just in time for the Wurzels' 'I Am a Cider Drinker' to completely body-slam his final speech.

We went to the pub at the interval, but much to my dismay my father had a rare moment of conscience and started feeling sorry for Leslie, and told us that, even though he didn't want to, we should go back in and see it through to the bitter end. We downed our drinks and with stiff upper lips returned to our seats for the second half.

'Don't worry, Jack,' said my mother, 'the second half is always shorter. It'll whizz by.' I felt like I was in there for days. The second half was not much better, and the constant sound effects of thunder and lightning meant that it was impossible to even go to sleep.

Afterwards we met Leslie at a nearby restaurant and had to endure an hour and a half discussing every nuance of the production. My dad told him it was a triumph and that London producers were out of their minds not to be bringing it to the West End. Good old Dad.

In the car on the way back he announced that he was going to pack in the agency business for good. Thirty-three years was long enough.

'Come on, Dad, it wasn't that bad, was it?' I said, trying to rally him.

'Wasn't that bad? Jack, it was the worst play I've ever seen. The only way you could get me to sit through that again would be if you hobbled me!'

1. After the incident to which you refer I have never again risked walking out of a client's play. However, I have frequently walked out of plays that I do not have clients in. One such instance is the performance of Peter Weiss's Marat/Sade at Marlborough College. Though you're well aware of this, as you were in it.

2. Regional theatre has a loyal and discerning middle-aged audience, a far cry from the rank lowlifes and yobbos that frequent your seedy comedy nightclubs.

3. I should make clear that Leslie was merely the catalyst for bringing my career as an agent to a close. I was actually very fond of the old bugger (if he'll forgive the expression). And he was wonderful as Dirty Den. Besides, ten years later I still haven't quite given up the agency business. Maybe I never will!

4. We have never had Pot Noodle in our larder. Maybe you're confusing my house with your ghastly student lodgings.

Part VIII

Holidays & Other Disasters

CHAPTER 20

The Tom Cruise Ship

— MICHAEL WHITEHALL —

I HAVE NEVER HAD MUCH LUCK HOLIDAYING in the West Indies. I took Hilary there on our honeymoon, and it is a honeymoon I will never forget for all the wrong reasons.

On our first day we settled into a pretty standard routine. Hilary sunbathed while I sat in a beachside café reading. It was there I met Serge.

'You like to snorkel? I take you snorkelling by the bay,' he said.

'No thank you,' I replied.

I didn't want to get into a lot of detail with this man, like telling him I couldn't actually swim. Fortunately Hilary came up from the beach and took over. They had a long conversation about rocks, fish and snorkelling and Hilary said that she'd catch up with him later.

We saw rather a lot of Serge after that. While we were eating breakfast in the hotel Serge again invited us to go snorkelling with him. Hilary explained that I was not a strong swimmer but she would be delighted to join him for a swim around the bay that afternoon.

'Do you think I'll be all right with Serge? I'm going to put a T-shirt under my swimming costume, it might well be cold out there.'

I assured Hilary that all would be fine and that Serge seemed a really nice chap.

'OK, if you think so. I'll be back in an hour. See you later.'

Hilary left the room and I dozed off. When I woke up it was six o'clock - two hours since she'd left; she was probably having a nice drink with Serge.

The door burst open. There she was in the doorway: cold, wet, dishevelled and bleeding.

'Thank God I put that T-shirt on under my bathing costume,' she said.

She then told me all. Having snorkelled around for half an hour the water had become choppy so they swam to the shore of a small cove. Unable to find any sand she hitched herself up on to a jagged rock, cutting herself. Serge got out of the water and joined her, and pulled down the straps of her bathing costume in one experienced double-handed movement.

'Hilaria, my love, I sex your body now!'

Hilaria was definitely not looking for sex – a towel or a plaster for her cut leg, perhaps, but not sex, and certainly not sex with Serge.

'Serge, please,' she said. 'I'm on my honeymoon.'

'I have many honeymoon girls,' said Serge, hoping to reassure her.

'Michael would kill you,' she told him.

'Michael, he is your father?'

'No! He's my husband, Serge, we've just got married.'

Serge, sensing that this particular body-sexing was going to require more groundwork than usual, changed tack. 'He is too old for you, he is like your grandfather, you should have younger man like me.'

At this point Hilary wasn't looking for marriage guidance but decided, with her bathing costume being the only protection between her and Serge's manhood, to change the conversation. 'Were you born on the island?'

They then had a chat about Serge's childhood, his parents, his siblings and his hopes for the future.

'One day I plan to go to America, I like American girls, they are always very friendly.'

Sensing Serge might be heading back in the direction of body-sexing, Hilary jumped off the rock on to the narrow beach.

'I must get back to the hotel. Michael will be worrying about me.'

She headed up the grassy bank in the direction of the hotel, pleased to discover, on looking back, that Serge was still sitting on the rock pensively, presumably having lost his primal urges after his long chat.

'I'm going to kill him!' I said, leaping to my feet. 'Bloody little shit, where is he?'

Now, Serge was clearly a fucker, and indeed a shit, but he certainly wasn't little; he had the look of a young Arnold Schwarzenegger and I undoubtedly would have been the loser in any beach-based altercation.

'Let's just forget it, Michael,' said Hilary.

That evening Serge appeared at the bar with some friends.

'Right, I'm going to chin the little shit!' I said, pulling up my Bermuda shorts. But Hilary was insistent. 'Please, Michael, just leave it alone, please.' So in a cowardly way I did. I would have decked him.

* * *

Some years later we were back in the West Indies, this time *en famille*. We had arranged to meet up with Trevor McDonald and his family, who were holidaying there at the same time. Our Jack, now aged ten, was still close friends with Trevor's son Jack – they were in the same class at school – and they wanted to play together. The original plan had been for them to come over to our hotel, but as this had turned out to be a bit of a dump, and seemed to involve more self-catering than we had anticipated, we arranged to have dinner with the McDonalds at their more upmarket hotel the Colony Club, which happened to be within walking distance.

Pre-lunch drinks in the midday sun quickly turned into a dash for cover to the restaurant when black clouds, thunder and lightning took over. Trevor, born and bred in the West Indies, sagely assured us that the thing about these tropical storms was that their bark was worse than their bite and that it would blow over in five or ten minutes.

An hour later, having sat in silence unable to hear ourselves speak, such was the force of the rain crashing down on the roof of the restaurant, we were faced with two options. Either making the short but potentially perilous journey back to our hotel along the now flash-flooded roads, or bunking up with the McDonalds.*

We opted for the former. Contrary to Trevor's predictions, the bite of the storm had been pretty bad and the rising water was already up to the children's waists as we waded down the street. By now, Molly was on my shoulders and Barnaby was on Hilary's, which meant that Jack could only hold my hand.

'Don't let go, Jack,' I said.

'I won't, Daddy,' he replied.

What Jack had forgotten was that he could swim and I couldn't.

*I don't really remember this story but please tell me it ends up with my dad spooning Trevor McDonald!

It's suddenly turned into Titanic! 'I'll never let go, Jack!'

As we approached our hotel I was aware of a large broken pipe coming out of the side of a building. It had clearly been damaged by the storm, and was gushing out muddy water that was sweeping past us at the side of the road. As soon as I got a whiff of it, I realized it wasn't muddy water but something altogether more sinister.

'Jack, don't look to your left!'

'Is it a shark, Daddy?' said Barnaby from the safety of Hilary's shoulders.

Jack looked scared but for once did as he was told, and consequently didn't see what I can only describe as a school of turds sweeping past his midriff.*

We eventually got back to the hotel safely but on reflection maybe topping and tailing with Trevor would have been a better option.

*I think the correct collective noun for this is actually 'a colony of turds' or, if they're on dry land, 'a nursery'.

* * *

One piece of hospitality we had been offered on a previous trip to Barbados was less attractive. Filling in time on a long, hot Monday afternoon, the receptionist at our hotel suggested that we might like to take a trip down to the harbour in Bridgetown, the capital of Barbados, as the largest cruise ship in the world, the *Monarch of the Seas,* was moored there on a short stopover during one of its Caribbean cruises. Jack was keen to see this great liner and also look at some of the luxury yachts moored there and I was keen to meet some friends of mine for a late-afternoon drink, as looking at other people's boats was something that didn't hold much appeal for me.

On arrival at the harbour we were greeted by a very jolly chap in a jaunty uniform who informed us that he was the harbour master and if we wanted to do anything it was going to need his approval. We explained that we had heard that the *Monarch* was in town and wondered if there was any possibility of having a look around her. Not a problem, said the harbour master, who proceeded to give us directions to the correct berth. 'You'd better get a move-on, though, she's due to leave this evening,' he added as we strolled off in search of our quarry.

As we rounded the corner of the passenger buildings we were greeted by the sight of the most enormous seagoing monolith we had ever seen. It was amazing and rose like a small city out of the water. We raced towards our target like a group of excited schoolgirls!

To our great disappointment, when we arrived, our path on to the ship was barred by several cruise-company employees, who very calmly but firmly explained that there was no way we could come on board as they were busy getting ready for the next leg of their cruise.

'Everyone is far too busy and, besides, it would breach our security procedures,' said one of them.

Jack, aged four, was having none of this. He had been told by the harbour master that it would be all right and no one else was going to tell him any different! After much arguing, cajoling, persuading and bribing, we managed to calm Jack down sufficiently from his mega strop, with the promise of finding another ship that we might be able to look around. We walked off down the quay, more in hope than expectation, in search of pastures new.

Docked in a prominent position on the next quay was another not quite so huge white cruise ship, but one, nonetheless, that would have given Roman Abramovich pangs of envy. As Hilary and the children were looking admiringly at the boat and I impatiently at my watch,

'Hey, can I offer you folks a refreshing beverage?'

Jack suddenly hared up the ramp on to the deck and into the waiting arms of a clean-cut man in full-white naval uniform, with a look of Richard Gere in *An Officer and a Gentleman* about him. He came down the ramp with Jack in his arms. Not a tall man but tanned, flashing white teeth that looked like they belonged in someone else's mouth and with one of those extremely annoyingly high-pitched American voices, he said, 'Hi, folks. How are you guys? I'm Dan. Welcome to the *Freewinds*.'

I managed to parry his attempt at a warm welcoming hug.

'Are you the captain?' asked Jack

'No, son,' he replied in a slightly patronizing manner.

I resisted telling him that it was an easy mistake to make, bearing in mind his uniform was adorned with more gold braid than your average admiral of the fleet.

'Please can we look around your ship?' asked Jack with his most winning of winning smiles.

'I'm afraid we don't have time,' I lied. 'We're meeting some friends for a drink.'

'Oh, surely you guys can spare half an hour? It would be my pleasure to show you around. Come on, kids, say "pleassseee, Grandpop".' And with that he raced up the gangplank, Jack still in his arms, with Molly in hot pursuit behind him. I now hated this man.

On arrival at the top of the ramp I looked to Hilary for support, but being six months pregnant she had clearly decided that the potential for a half-hour sit-down was quite appealing. As we entered the ship beneath a golden sign that read *The Bridge to Ultimate Freedom*, we were confronted by a huge white marble staircase of Las Vegas proportions, at the top of which was an enormous garish portrait of a deeply unattractive trout-faced redheaded man. Up and down the stairs rushed assorted blonde women and clean-cut young men in clinging white uniforms, all carrying clipboards. It was like we were on the set of *Moonraker*.*

'Look, Daddy, it's your friend Winston Churchill!' Jack said, pointing at the portrait.

'No, son,' said Dan, 'it's our founder, L. Ron Hubbard.'

I shot a look at Hilary. 'He's the freak who runs that Tom Cruise cult,' I whispered.

'Be quiet, Michael. They're Scientologists. I'd already worked that

*Incredible that you managed to mention Moonraker without name-dropping that one of your clients was in it. *Didn't have a client in it but did have a couple of friends — Sir Roger Moore, of course, and good old Walter Gotell.*

one out for myself,' said Hilary.

'Would Jack and Molly care for a refreshing beverage?' asked Dan, who by now had extracted the names of my children from Hilary, but before I'd had a chance to tell him that we had no interest in joining his cult he was off to get Jack and Molly's 'sodas' and Hilary's tea.

'Do you realize what's going on here?' I said to Hilary. 'We're being softened up for brainwashing. First it's a Coke, next thing they'll be injecting us with something.'

One of the white-uniformed blondes sashayed up. 'Are you kids hungry?'

'No thank you, they've just eaten their lunch,' I said.

'I'm starving,' said Molly.

'Me too,' said Jack helpfully.

We were shown into a cabin where chairs had been arranged round a table piled high with cream cakes and sandwiches, which the children needed no invitation to tuck into.

'This is how their so-called "religion" works,' I whispered to Hilary. 'Lure you on to their floating prison, then shower you in fizzy drinks and fast food until you are too fat to leave. No surprise this cult has mushroomed in America.'

'Sshh, Michael.'

As I reluctantly followed them into the room the whole ship lurched. I panicked and dashed to the porthole, fearing that they'd

The brainwashed child tries to pull his mother away from the non-believer.

raised anchor and *Freewinds* was heading off to some Pacific island where we would spend the rest of our lives being indoctrinated. My fears were allayed by the returning Dan, who assured us it was merely a freak wave associated with the departure of the *Monarch of the Seas*. He handed the children their 'refreshing beverages'.

By now I was desperate to get back on to dry land, so with a promise to return the following day, a promise I had no intention of keeping, we started to head for the exit. But with his impeccable sense of timing Jack announced that he needed to go to the loo.*

'All right, but be quick,' I barked, not wanting to spend a second longer in the company of the creepy Dan.

Jack was taken up the white marble staircase by yet another blonde, or was it the same one as earlier? It was very hard to tell as they all looked identical. I sat down listening to Hilary trying to make polite conversation with Dan about what had been happening on our very uneventful holiday to date. As Hilary was wrapping up an anecdote about a blocked sink in our villa I began to worry about Jack. Where was he? After ten minutes alarm bells were ringing. Jack was not one to linger in the loo, as he seldom lifted the seat and never washed his hands afterwards.**

'I think we're going to have to crack on now, Dan. Our friends will be wondering where we are. Could you get one of your . . . um –' I paused for thought – 'blondes, to retrieve my son.'

He smiled. 'Sure thing, Mike.'

I winced. I am not a Mike.

'If you want, you folks could stay for dinner. How about it? We have a DJ on the boat tonight. It's gonna be a lot of fun.'

Frustrated that I wasn't getting through to him, I decided to take a different tack. 'Look, Dan, we don't want dinner or DJs! I want my son, and then I want to leave.'

Dan looked upset.

'I'm sorry, I do apologize,' said Hilary. 'That was very rude of Michael, but I think he's feeling a bit seasick from that lurch. Please forgive him.'

'Apology accepted, Mike.'

I felt like throwing him overboard but resisted for fear we might never see Jack again.

Dan led us to the top of the marble stairs but still no sign of Jack.

'This is typical, Hilary,' I whispered. 'I know what they're up to. He's probably locked up somewhere having wires hooked into him.'

Yet another blonde appeared. 'Jack is such a sweet little kid.'

'What the fuck have you done with my son?' I snapped.

'We've given him some cookies and he's watching a movie in the cinema,' said the blonde, ignoring my bad language.

I whispered to Hilary, 'I told you they were brainwashing him. It will be one of those weird propaganda films, like the ones they show Russian dissidents in the Gulag.'

'You're being ridiculous, Michael!' said Hilary.

At which point the blonde opened the doors to the cinema to reveal Jack stuffing his face with biscuits and roaring with laughter at *The Lion King*.

'Right, Jack, we're off!'

'Hakuna matata,' Jack started singing.

'Look, Hilary, they've got him chanting one of their mantras!'

I grabbed him by the arm.

'But, Daddy, I still haven't met the captain.'

We headed off down the marble staircase and as we stepped on to

Serge prepares for his 'chinning'.

dry land Dan returned to overfamiliar mode and had to be rebuffed from giving me a farewell double hug, which looked suspiciously like it could have turned into a kiss. He then brandished a goody bag of chocolates and sweets for Molly and Jack, who by now looked like he was on the verge of another major strop.

As soon as we were out of sight of *Freewinds* I commandeered the bag with a view to disposing of it as soon as possible. 'The chocolates are probably drugged,' I said to Hilary as I flung them into the water. 'Don't you remember *Village of the Damned*? I could have sworn that Jack's eyes were beginning to take on a very weird stary look while he was eating those cream cakes.'

Jack slowed into one of his sluggish sulking walks. 'You promise we can go back and see the captain tomorrow?'

'Yes, of course, Jack. When I make a promise, I stick to it. You must know that by now.'

We never met the captain.

1. My father is painting Dan as some sort of disturbing David Koresh figure. What little I can remember of this event is that a charming man invited a group of holidaymakers on to his boat and was generous enough to show them round and offer them refreshments. There was nothing sinister about it at all.*

   *See, I told you they'd got to him.

2. I am upset to learn that during a flood Molly and Barnaby were immediately hoisted to safety above the water on my mum's and dad's shoulders but I was seemingly left to drown in a torrent of rainwater and human excrement. I feel like the daughter in *Sophie's Choice*, except at least she only lost out to one sibling.

3. What I don't understand re the honeymoon story is that if nothing happened between Mummy and 'Serge' then why would she have decided to come home and tell you about it? Particularly as she would have known exactly what your reaction was going to be. Surely she'd only say something if in fact she was trying to cover up something that did happen, but didn't want you getting suspicious.

4. Why was Mummy so quick to go on this 'snorkelling trip' anyway?

5. Is Serge my real dad?

CHAPTER 21

Disney World, Florida

– JACK WHITEHALL –

Going to Disney World, Florida, may be every child's dream but, for my father, it turned out to be more of a nightmare.

'Florida is for fat American pensioners and Paul Burrell, neither of whom I have any interest in seeing,' he'd told my mother when she first pitched the idea of a family visit to the Disney resort in Lake Buena Vista.

Unfortunately for him my father was still worming his way back into his wife's good books after a spectacular fail at the book launch of one of my mother's close friends, Clare Byam-Cook, a breast-feeding guru. My father had struck up a conversation with a stranger at the bar by saying, 'So, how do you know Titty?' What he'd failed to recognize was that the man in question was 'Titty's' husband, and he wasn't very amused at my father's little nickname for his wife, and even less amused as he had, in fact, not only already met my father but indeed had been to dinner with him on a couple of occasions. Once the story got back via Titty to Hilary, Michael was deducted several house points for this social faux pas. The flights to Florida were duly booked, if only to paper over Tittygate.

The hotel we stayed in was jam-packed with kids. Not only that, but everything was geared towards children having the best holiday of their lives. Adult comforts were definitely of secondary concern ('adult comforts' sounds dodgy – I should clarify that I doubt there were happy endings to any massages received in the spa area, given that the masseurs were dressed like Pluto and Donald Duck*).

*Ironic, as all those Disney films have happy endings.

All the lifts played loud pop music; the swimming pool had a web of slides, luges, fountains and wave machines; every restaurant was manned by teams of tanned, beaming servers, all frustrated children's entertainers, desperate to hone their skills on the excited diners with balloon shows, jokes, songs and dances.* Imagine they'd released nitrous oxide into the air supply of a T.G.I. Friday.

*A far cry from Timmy Twinkle!

My dad felt like he had entered Dante's descent into Hell. For a man who had a tiny appetite, detested jollity and couldn't swim, the week was going to feel like penal servitude. I believe he even took up reading Dostoevsky – having never clicked with tales of back-breaking misery in Siberian salt mines before now, suddenly my father became the Russian's biggest fan.

There's nothing wrong with jollity in its place, but the American version of jollity verges on the manic. Ditto most non-British countries.

Every day brought him a fresh trial. At an early point during our stay, I managed to lose the key to our room.

'You've lost it, Jack, so you will have to go down to reception and obtain a replacement,' my father told me over the top of *Crime and Punishment*. 'You have to learn the consequences of your carelessness.'

I trudged down to reception for a lengthy and fruitless exchange with the intransigent helper behind the desk, who explained that – as I was not the credit-card holder (being ten years old) – they were unable to furnish me with a replacement. They would need my father to come down. I went back upstairs to explain the situation to him.

'This is the Colosseum all over again!' barked my father.

'Oh, don't start, Michael,' pleaded my mum.

The Colosseum incident was an example of my dad at his most stubborn. We were on a visit to see one of my mum's old school-friends, Fuzz, who'd married an Italian and ended up living in Rome.

A very tricky short Italian judge, called Roberto . . . it didn't last.

We'd visited Fuzz one Easter for improvement and education. In fact, the highlight of the trip for Barnaby and me was getting to see Roma play Milan at the Stadio Olimpico, their home ground. Even Dad had enjoyed this, as it was built during the Second World War and had a certain Fascist flavour; he particularly liked the monument to Mussolini that still stands at the front gate.**

**I've always had a slightly soft spot for good old Benito — he did at least keep the trains running on time.

That particular morning, we went to the Colosseum with Fuzz's son, Hugo. Hugo was the same age as Barnaby but bilingual, and he acted as our tour guide.

'Two adults and four children please,' my father said to the man in the Colosseum's ticket office. Hugo translated. There was a brief discussion.

'He says he needs to see proof of age that we are all under sixteen,' said Hugo.

'Do they look over sixteen?' my father exploded.*

The rather weaselly man behind the glass looked at Hugo, who obliged with a translation. Further discussions ensued.

'He still needs to see proof of age,' said Hugo.

'This is ridiculous,' retorted Dad.

'I don't think he's going to let us in without it,' said Hugo.

At this point, Dad grabbed the ten-year-old Barnaby, lifted him up to the window, pushed him against the glass and thrust his face in the direction of the man. 'Does this child look like it has taken its GCSEs?'

The queue behind us was beginning to look a bit uneasy at the show unfolding in front of their eyes.

'Michael, just pay the full price. This is embarrassing,' whispered my mum.

'Leave this to me, please, Hilary. Negotiating is one of my major strengths.'

The ticket man looked unmoved and directed his reply back to Hugo.

'He needs to see proof of age, Michael.'

'Unbelievable. We find the only Italian who won't run away from a conflict with his tail between his legs,' he bellowed. 'Hilary, you'll have to go back to the apartment and get the children's passports.'

'Michael, is it really worth it to save five euros a ticket?'

'It's the principle, Hilary. I'm not having some Italian jobsworth getting one over on me!'

So my mum trudged off on the forty-five-minute round-trip** to get the passports from Fuzz's apartment, as we watched some out-of-work actors dressed as gladiators fight while our father lectured us about how 'at least the Germans stuck to their convictions to the bitter end'.

Back in Florida my father returned to our rooms fuming, having turned a relatively simple procedure into a long and angry discussion, during which he called Disney World a nanny state and made ludicrous remarks about Walt Disney being 'a Nazi sympathizer who had rolled out the red carpet for Leni Riefenstahl'.

The holiday apartments were crammed together round communal porch areas. Our immediate neighbours were a jolly American couple and their teenage son, Eric. Mr and Mrs Renner were not the slightest of individuals. Indeed, every time Mrs Renner stepped on to our shared porch to ask if we were heading to the pool, she more or less eclipsed the sun. As the temperature was scorching, however, this came as a welcome relief.

Eric was a very strange child, but his strong suit was that he was also very silent, unlike his parents.

'Hey, Mike,' she'd say, and every time my father would affect to look around for the 'Mike' she was addressing. 'Me and Harvey are going to the pool. Want us to save you folks a lounger?'

'No thank you,' said Dad from behind his new book, *The American Way of Death* by Jessica Mitford, having given Dostoevsky a break.

Mrs Renner's efforts were gallant but doomed. My father spent the majority of the holiday in our hotel room, refusing to come out and talk to people. Up until this point, the only prolonged interaction he'd had with anyone other than his own family (and the woman he'd accused of being but a cog in the nanny state) was with a man dressed as Goofy, who'd tried to help him with his bags, and whom he'd told to 'get out of his fucking way'.*

*I didn't say anything of the sort; I told him to go cock his leg somewhere else.

'Come on, Michael, be sociable,' said my mum, taking the book out of his hand and throwing some more suntan lotion into her bag.

'I don't want to go and sit by the pool with that gross woman on my own.'

Mrs Renner was not especially mobile and, when my father made this remark, she had only wobbled all of ten metres from the porch. She may well have heard him, had it not been for the cacophony of screams and splashes that geysered from the busy pool area pretty much 24/7.

'Let's hope she doesn't fall asleep down there,' added my father. 'People might think she's been beached.'

Sensing defeat, my mum left him to his back-up book, Kitty Kelley's *The Royals*, which he'd stashed under the bed like a naughty schoolboy hiding his smut.**

**This book was a major disappointment. A load of rubbish, full of mindless tittle-tattle from largely unattributed sources, and even the attributed sources were ridiculous, being from such august publications as Women's Wear Daily, the Buenos Aires Herald and the San Antonio Express News.

The main attraction of this holiday was obviously the Magic Kingdom. I was obsessed with roller coasters and insisted that we rode everything, usually more than once. Before we set off my mother took a series of precautionary measures. She'd been told by her friend Fiona that – according to the *Daily Mail* – Disney World had suffered recently from a spate of child abductions.

'They snatch the child,' she'd said earnestly, 'and whisk it off to the toilets, where they change its clothes and dye its hair.'

'That sounds a little far-fetched,' my dad had replied.

'The only thing they can't change are the shoes, because they don't know the size of the child's feet,' added my mother. 'So we have to make sure Jack, Molly and Barnaby are wearing very distinctive shoes.'

'Hilary, you're being ridiculous,' my dad said, no doubt struggling with the logic that any would-be child-catcher might be deterred from kidnapping a child by garish footwear.

But he knew he wasn't going to win this argument. Once Fiona got an idea into my mother's head, nothing on earth was going to get it out. It's like the time she told her that eating tomato ketchup can heighten your chances of getting cancer (another myth dreamt

The weird-looking man at the back with the Bruce Forsyth chin had the definite look of a kidnapper about him.

Look at those ridiculous goofy teeth.

up by her favourite newspaper). We were confined to eating mayonnaise with our chips for years. If I came back with a takeaway and she found a sachet of ketchup in the bag, she acted like I'd brought meow meow into the house.

I presume this 'meow meow' is like 'piri-piri'.

So off we set for the Magic Kingdom, wearing a selection of the most colourful and outlandish shoes Disney World had to offer. If my father felt embarrassment it was soon eclipsed by a Mrs Renner-sized problem. The queues for the attractions were massive, some snaking back for what seemed like miles, with waiting times of over two hours.

'Why don't we just pretend Molly's ill?' asked my dad. 'Sick children always get put to the front of the line.'

He knew this from hearsay only. The last time we tried to take him to an amusement park, we'd been staying at some friends of ours in Stoke-on-Trent, near Alton Towers. My father had inevitably thrown a tantrum, so whilst my mum and I enjoyed Oblivion and Nemesis, he went round the Etruria Industrial Museum on his own.*

Rather than wasting your time on some overpriced funfair ride you could have joined me at the museum and marvelled at the world's oldest working beam engine. An afternoon I shall certainly never forget.

This time, though, he'd run out of luck. My mum put her foot down and insisted he spend quality time with the family. Her definition of 'quality time with the family' consisted of him standing with us in the queue and then, while we went on the rides, standing by the exit holding our bags, cameras and snacks. Needless to say, he was in a pretty foul mood. He had also made it clear to us that he didn't wish to appear in any photographs, not wanting anyone to know that he had set foot in the place. Why he thought anyone would want to photograph an irate man under a heap of lunchboxes and a sweaty Panama hat is anyone's guess. My suggestion was that we wrap a beach towel round his head to make a turban and just pretend that we were being followed around by Jafar from *Aladdin*, but this idea was vetoed by my mother.

'Well, Mrs Renner certainly wouldn't like this one,' he said as we boarded Big Thunder Mountain Railroad. 'It's got a weight restriction.' The only way for him to retain his sanity, it seemed, was to be continuously unpleasant about the poor woman.

The Magic Kingdom's centrepiece was Space Mountain, an outer-space-themed steel roller coaster with tunnels, high-speed 180-degree turns and loop-the-loops, all in darkness. This much-in-demand attraction had an appropriately mammoth queue. As we joined the end of it there was a sign indicating that the wait from that point was approximately one hour and forty-five minutes. My father's mood deteriorated even further.*

*Wouldn't get queues like that at the Etruria Industrial Museum.

'Daddy, there's a wasp buzzing around me,' said Barnaby as we hit the hour point in the queue.

'Well, leave it alone, Barnaby. It's not interested in you,' replied my dad coldly. 'Wasps never attack people unless they are provoked.'

The large wasp, which actually looked more like a hornet, continued to whizz around my brother, who was beginning to look distressed.

'Please, Daddy, kill it. I don't like it!' said Barnaby.

'Now listen to me, Barnaby,' came the response. 'You have my word that if you just ignore it, it will go away. I will not tell you again.'

Barnaby's lip quivered. And the wasp did not go away; it continued to pester my little brother for the next ten minutes. My father, who is a stubborn man at the best of times, ignored it, not considering for a moment that his advice might be wrong.

As we approached the front of the queue, having been in it for nearly two hours, the buzzing stopped. My dad looked smug.

'See, Barnaby? Daddy was right. If you just ignore them, they fly away.'

There was a scream.

'Daddy, it's flown up my shorts!'

'Barnaby, there is no way that wasp has flown up your shorts!'

At which point the wasp stung him. Barnaby yelped with pain as my mum tried to rip his shorts off him. Before she could achieve this, the wasp had helped itself to a couple more stings, leaving Barnaby in floods of tears and jigging around in his new Mickey Mouse underpants as if he was dancing on hot coals.

'Would you folks mind coming out of the line and stepping to one side? You're holding up the queue,' said the bubbly server, with a hugely insincere smile on his face.

Dad blew a gasket!

'I have no intention of stepping aside,' he said, fumbling for his mobile phone, 'until I have consulted my lawyer, Brook Land.' Brook was a high-powered corporate lawyer who specialized in film and television, he's wasn't exactly Claims Direct. 'My family have been subjected to a vicious attack by vermin on your site and I shall be looking for substantial compensation!' At this point he grabbed Barnaby and thrust his groin into the server's face. 'This child could be disfigured for life!'

Suddenly a burly security man appeared on the scene and suggested that we discuss this further in his office.

We didn't get any compensation, but my father did manage to negotiate a compromise whereby we were given priority passes to skip the queues for any rides we wanted to go on. So, for once, we had to concede that my father was right: a poorly child does help when it comes to queue-jumping. Though Barnaby has never believed anything Dad's told him from that day to this.

1. What do you mean 'for once'. On numerous occasions you have had to concede that your father is right.

2. Jack says that I 'made ludicrous remarks' about Walt Disney's Nazi sympathies. Let's look at the facts. This is Leni Riefenstahl talking about her time in Hollywood promoting her film Olympia, a four-hour homage to Hitler's 1936 Olympic Games: 'American film directors didn't dare to receive me because of their financial dependence on the Jewish money men. An honourable exception was Walt Disney, creator of Snow White, who warmly welcomed me and showed me his extensive studios and even his latest work.' The quote is taken from Steven Bach's definitive biography Leni. The Life and Work of Leni Riefenstahl. Who sounds ludicrous now?

3. At that time I'm sure there would have been a number of more relevant features to deter a potential kidnapper from abducting Jack than colourful footwear. His tantrums, inability to eat anything without getting it all over his hands, face and clothes, habit of nose-picking and the constant need for trips to the loo, which would certainly hold up any speedy kidnapping opportunity.

CHAPTER 22

Four Weeks in Provence

– MICHAEL WHITEHALL –

WE WERE ON HOLIDAY SHARING A RENTED VILLA with some American friends in Provence. We were staying in the main farm-house with Jack (just five), Molly (three and a half) and Barnaby (eighteen months), and Avery Chope, a Californian banker, and his wife Jane were billeted in a garden annexe with their seven-year-old twin girls. We were also accompanied by our new nanny, Brandy Bush.* Brandy was a blue-eyed busty blonde from Bondi Beach in Australia. She was a beach babe in the *Baywatch* tradition and busty was probably too mild a word to describe the phenomenon that was her chest. Happily she was also very bubbly in a way that busty blondes often are but, unhappily for us, very light in the brains department.** However she was a welcome addition to the family after the Jennies and Hildes of previous years.*** Her bust was a constant source of worry to her; skimpy dresses and plunging necklines were not an option for Brandy. Containment was her priority. Throughout our holiday, she had to wear a T-shirt under her bikini to prevent unwanted side seepage, and when in the pool a loose-fitting shift was added. Jack, by now a red-blooded five-year-old, found Brandy's bosom a source of both comfort and constant amusement. He would refer to it as Brandy's 'boo-boo', although we attempted to prevent him from doing this within her earshot.

On day one of our holiday, as I was dozing by the pool, she leant over me, her bosom eclipsing what remained of the late-afternoon sun, and asked if I'd seen her bra. Why did this girl think that I would be able to locate misplaced items of her underwear? Perhaps she'd

*That sounds like a porn name but she was actually called that.

**You've managed to sound pompous and pervy at the same time.

***She used deodorant and had renounced apartheid.

This has not changed, I still have a similar relationship with bosoms.

noticed the look of stunned amazement on my face when she'd first stepped into the swimming pool earlier that week, the loose-fitting shirt not hiding her assets in the least.

'I'm afraid I can't help you there, Brandy,' I said as she padded off in search of it.

A few minutes later she returned. 'Sorry to disturb you again, Michael, but have you by any chance seen Barnaby anywhere?'

I couldn't help. She was, after all, the one looking after him.

'You seem to be misplacing quite a lot of things this afternoon, Brandy,' I said. 'First your bra and now your Barnaby.'

'Yes, I still can't find my bra,' she said. 'Hilary and Molly didn't take Barnaby to the supermarket, did they?'

'No, I don't think so. He's not really into shopping,' I replied, 'and the Chopes certainly haven't taken him with them on their day out.'

The sun had hazed over, so I headed off into the house calling for him.

'I put him down to sleep in my room, but I've just looked through a crack in the door and he's not in his travel cot. I've looked everywhere,' said Brandy.

I began to worry. Well, at least he wasn't at the bottom of the swimming pool. I checked and rechecked all the other rooms in the house and annexe, and just as I was about to start panicking I heard Jack shouting at the top of his voice, 'I've found him! He was asleep on Brandy's bed.'

And with that Jack came into view. It was a vision worthy of Omar Sharif's entrance in *Lawrence of Arabia*: Jack in his French Foreign Legion hat dragging a now giggling Barnaby 'hammocked' in the missing bra, head in one cup, bottom in the other and Jack at the top of his voice making loud train noises, accompanied by chants of 'all aboard the boo-boo choo-choo!'*

*Again, little has changed as this is still a chant I say when confronted with large breasts.

* * *

The Chopes liked their days out. They wanted to make the most of being in continental Europe and made sure that no sight was left unseen, no historical monument missed and no artisan market unvisited or local delicacy unsampled. Avery was a great enthusiast, he loved travelling and wanted to pack as much as he could into every hour of their holiday. He wanted his girls to experience all that France had to offer. I'm not convinced that they were totally behind this need for outings, but generally they went along with his plans. Every breakfast was dominated by Avery running through the day's itinerary. Maps were produced, Michelin guides pawed over, newspaper cuttings and written recommendations from various friends read out. We Whitehalls had very different expectations for our holiday. I wanted to read several books and Hilary wanted to sunbathe or play around with the children in the pool. I certainly had no desire to drive for hours, battling our way into car parks and then jostling with crowds while we went around ancient cities like Les Baux-de-Provence, spending fortunes on lunch, which the children wouldn't eat because they were all far too hot.

During the time the Chopes spent with us, Jack's behaviour was a source of bemused consternation to them, particularly as he seldom wore any clothes.

'Barnaby's just eaten three crickets, Daddy,' Jack announced proudly to us after breakfast one morning. Barnaby was standing behind him with the remains of a cricket hanging out of his mouth and a handful of bugs that he had collected from the patio.*

'I can't believe that you let him do that,' I said. 'I told you to look after him.'

'But they were only crickets,' Jack replied, 'and Barnaby said he was hungry.'

Later that morning Betsy announced that Barnaby had thrown up

*(Sung in a reggae style) Barnaby don't like crickets, oh no. He loves them.

Did you only have the one holiday shirt?

A serial flasher is escorted from the beach by his father.

So that's where Brandy Bush's bra had got to.

HIM & ME

all over the kitchen table and his vomit had some 'bits of bug in it'.

Jack's supervisory skills took a further backward step when he was asked to hold Barnaby's hand while Hilary backed out the rented Peugeot 406 estate for a trip to Aqualand. I had selflessly volunteered to remain at the villa to get on with some urgent paperwork and the Chopes, deeming Aqualand not to be up to scratch culturally, had gone off for the day to Saint Rémy. As Hilary was shifting into reverse, Jack decided it was the right time to go in search of a fizzy drink and within seconds Barnaby was under the wheels of the car.*

As we sped to the hospital I tried to convince Hilary that tyre marks on a child were not necessarily a cause for alarm as they were very bouncy at his age but she seemed unconvinced.

'*Mon bébé est mort!*' she cried as we rushed through the swing doors of the hospital, sweeping concerned nurses out of our way. It was like Jean-Luc Godard had directed an episode of *Casualty*. The doctor assured us that the '*bébé*' was not, in fact, '*mort*' and that although he'd incurred no serious damage it was probably best to supervise him when he was around reversing vehicles.

On our return to the villa Jack looked very concerned and upset, but sadly not for Barnaby's condition. He wanted to know whether or not we were still going to Aqualand. When told that we weren't he strutted off in a sulk and didn't speak to anyone for the rest of the afternoon.

However, this didn't prove to be the end of our medical escapades. A couple of days later Jack was tasked with keeping Molly out of the midday sun.** He had not only allowed his sister to wander into its glare but also to take her hat off. By mid-afternoon she had a raging temperature and was showing signs of being photophobic. And by the time she started vomiting I knew some action was needed.

'I think it's heatstroke,' I said. 'We'd better call a doctor.'

I headed off to the kitchen and worked my way through a list of local doctors attached to a pin board, with some reluctance ending up with a German doctor, who promised to come out later that day. Meanwhile Hilary was tending to an increasingly wan Molly with icepacks, but being constantly interrupted by Jack, who wanted his supper.

'Please can I have some crisps, Mummy?'

'No, Jack, not at the moment.'

'Can I have a drink?'

*Nonsense! I went in search of suncream because I was worried my brother might be burning.

**Where'd this nanny gone? Why am I always having to look after my siblings?
She was probably looking for her underwear.

'No, Jack.'

'Can I watch a cartoon on television?'

Hilary lost it. 'Jack, for God's sake, for once in your life can't you think of anyone other than yourself? Can't you see how ill Molly is? She could be dying!'

At which point Molly, who had been lying in complete silence with her eyes shut, sat bolt upright and screamed, 'Am I *really* dying?' before bursting into tears.

'Now look what you've done, Jack,' said Hilary. 'What do you have to say for yourself?'

He pondered for a while. 'Can we go to Aqualand after the doctor's been?'

'No, don't be silly, Jack,' I said.

'Can I have a Calippo?'

Later, by now early evening, the German doctor arrived, a humourless fifty-year-old woman with the look of a *Gruppenführer* about her and a very sketchy command of the English language. Having inspected Molly she kept referring to her inflamed 'meninges', which Hilary mistakenly took to mean she had meningitis, but in fact my diagnosis was correct and it was only heatstroke. The doctor prescribed suppositories.

'Madam,' I told her, 'just because we're in France I have no intention of stuffing medication up my daughter's backside. Kindly prescribe the oral version.'* Which she did reluctantly and Molly made a swift recovery, with no thanks to Jack, whose only medical advice to his little sister was that an immediate trip to Aqualand might cool her down.

*This is my favourite line in the whole book.

The doctor's parting shot as she left was, 'This child has a major infestation of the head lice. You will all be treated immediately due to cross-contamination. These lice must be destroyed.' As she wrote down the name of a special shampoo, she said, 'This is the final solution!' (Those may not have been her precise words.)

Having picked up the chemical-laden shampoo and a nit comb at the supermarket, we delivered the news to the Chopes.

'Oh no, what a nightmare,' said Jane.

'Well, at least we are all in this together,' I said helpfully.

'Easy for you to say, Michael,' replied Jane. 'Have you seen the length of the girls' hair? This is going to take ages!'

The day before we were due to fly home Jack had one final contribution

The naked photo bomber strikes again.

Barnaby and Molly sit next to their caring and responsible older brother.

to make to our already eventful holiday. As the Chopes had been on the move for most of the time Jack decided that he would try a bit of bonding with the twins and, in an attempt to make up for lost time and fresh from the pool, kicked open the double doors of their annexe, naked and dripping wet, and invited them to go skinny-dipping with him. Unsurprisingly, they declined this invitation, which made Jack all the more determined. He leapt soaking wet on to their bed and started jumping up and down, shouting for them to come and join him.

They were seriously unamused and immediately reported the incident to their parents. Avery suggested to me that Jack was clearly a flasher* and even though I pointed out that my son had probably only done it as a joke Avery insisted that Jack be made to apologize to his daughters, who, he said, were 'deeply traumatized'. I don't think Jack ever did issue an apology.**

*I was five!

**Damn right I didn't!

So the holiday ended on a low note.

* * *

Time is supposed to be a great healer and ten years later we found ourselves returning to Provence; different house but same cast. The twins were by now nearly eighteen and Jack was sixteen and at the peak of his toxic teenage years.

***1. It's drum and bass music.
2. Exit is a rock festival.

The holiday did not get off to a great start, as Jack had wanted to go to a music festival called Exit which specialized in 'bass and drum' music*** and, even more worryingly, it was held in Serbia, a nation known for very little apart from sex-trafficking and a modicum of success in the Eurovision song contest!**** I put my foot down and

****I don't think he got that description straight out of the Lonely Planet guide.

said that he was too young to go, and if he disobeyed me the only thing he'd be exiting was my house.

'I don't want you being arrested on foreign soil for shooting up marijuana or snorting drugged cigarettes or whatever it is you do at these music festivals,' I said. 'Haven't you ever seen *Midnight Express*? Over my dead body. You can come with us to France.'

Relations were further fractured when Jack, without my consent, got his hair dyed peroxide blonde a few days before we were due to leave. He came back from the barber's looking like the kind of chap you might find lurking around a podium in a Soho nightclub. I was furious about this 'statement' that had clearly only been made to get back at me for vetoing his festival trip. Tensions were certainly running high.

So by the time we got to Provence, neither Jack nor I were in the mood to play happy families. His usual daily regime at that time was to appear grumpily for lunch, eat but not clear up, and then settle down with all the curtains closed in the sitting room in front of the television for the afternoon, to watch such gems as *Cash in the Attic*, reruns of *Bargain Hunt* and *Trisha*.

One morning after the Chopes had departed for the day Jack came downstairs and spoke to us for possibly the first time during the holiday.

'I couldn't get to sleep last night my head was so itchy. I think I've got nits.'

'Oh, God,' said Hilary. 'Jane will go nuts! It's Sunday, the pharmacy will be closed. I'll have to call Jo, she's bound to have some nit shampoo in tow.' Thankfully our friends the Williamses were staying in a villa nearby, so we arranged to meet that evening for supper.

We encouraged the Chopes to visit a local Michelin-starred restaurant they'd been banging on about, but for once they decided that it would be 'fun' for us all to dine together. Typical. We met the Williamses in a local bistro, with Jack placed strategically at the opposite end of the table to the Chope twins. He was wearing my finest Panama hat,* which Hilary had insisted he wear as an extra precaution to disguise the infestation. I was not happy about this but decided that it was a sacrifice I was willing to make for the greater good.

'When I put my hat on in the morning I do not want my hair contaminated with livestock,' I told Hilary when she initially floated the idea.

'Not even the most determined head louse could conceivably stand

*Yes, he has a collection.

a chance of clinging on to a strand of your thinning hair,' she had replied rather scathingly.

Hilary's attempts to complete the shampoo handover with Jo were dealt an added complication when Jane decided to plonk herself between them. Therefore the two women had to head off to the loos midway through the main course and complete an exchange that Hilary remarked felt a little bit like a drug deal.*

*How would she know?

The evening didn't get any easier. Jack and Barnaby had by now abandoned the table in favour of kicking a ball around the square in front of the bistro, and when we called them to come back for pudding they made a quick visit to the loo. Jack exited first and slammed the heavy metal door so hard that it jammed shut. As hard as we tried it wouldn't shift. Barnaby, trapped inside, became hysterical.

'Oh, this is typical of you, Jack,' Jane said.

'I only did it as a joke,' said Jack.

'Where had I heard that before?' added Avery, clearly still sore from the flashing incident over a decade on.

Barnaby was by now lying on his tummy, speaking to us through a very narrow gap underneath the door.

'It's so dark and smelly in here, Daddy,' he said. 'Please, Daddy, tell me I'm not going to die!'

'I promise you're not.'**

**We all know about your promises.

Jack was sent off for help and returned with two burly French locals

Blondes have more fun — or less fun if their dads ban them from going to a music festival in favour of a stupid holiday in Provence.

from a bar in the square, who managed to prise the door open.

'I'm glad you managed to make use of that schoolboy French I spent so much money on you acquiring,' I said. 'I told you it would come in handy one day.'

* * *

We returned home in separate cars, still managing by some miracle to have kept Jack's scalp from making contact with the girls' hair. We eradicated the dreaded lice and covertly disposed of the shampoo container in the bin.

The next few days were thankfully incident-free and Jack even began to help out a little and managed to engage in conversation with the twins, albeit to a fairly limited extent. So the holiday drew to an amicable close and we said goodbye to the Chopes.

'We'll see you back in Provence in ten years,' said Avery jokingly as he put his bags into the back of the cab.

'Mum, I think I might have had an allergic reaction to the chlorine in the pool,' said one of the girls. 'I've got a really itchy head.'

'So have I,' her sister piped up.

'Bye!' I said, hastily slamming the door on the cab. 'See you in 2014!' and off they went.

1. I am very fond of those twins, they are really nice, but aged seven they used to freak the shit out of me. The flashing incident: I'd been skinny-dipping and was jumping up and down on their bed to dry off when they suddenly appeared at the window like those girls in *The Shining*. If anything *they* were peeping on *me*.

2. I find it hard to believe that I needed to tell my mother that I had head lice. She had a sixth sense when it came to lice; she'd know I had them before I did. I'd come home from school and sit in front of the television and she'd be watching me like *The Predator* — the merest scratch of the temple and it would be up to the bathroom for a once-over with the dreaded nit comb, the teeth of which were so sharp it felt like you were getting a head massage from Freddy Kruger. Put simply, if there were nits in my hair she'd know.

3. The following year I made it to *Exit*!

Part IX

A State of Undress

CHAPTER 23

The Naked Truth

– JACK WHITEHALL –

I grew up in Putney. It's a nice area. 'The right side of the tracks,' my dad says, though this didn't stop him telling people that we actually lived in Barnes, which he thought sounded classier.

Even though Putney is in London, where we lived, by the common, had a sort of village feel. In the houses around the common, everyone knew everyone. Although you could count on the fingers of one hand the neighbours we were still on speaking terms with.

The Whitehalls no longer spoke to the Tittle family at number fifteen because their son, William, had exposed Molly to the practice of 'tongue-kissing' while they were at nursery school together. One night, when Molly was three, my father went to give her a kiss goodnight and got a bit of a fright when she whipped out her tongue.

'What the hell was that?' said my dad.

'It's a tongue kiss, Daddy. William Tittle showed me.'

My dad made sure this story got round the neighbourhood pretty quickly. Before you knew it the Tittles were social pariahs, and their three-year-old son branded a sexual predator.

The whole incident was made even more surprising by the fact that Mrs Tittle was a rather sour-faced Christian. She had the look of a woman who'd neither given nor received a tongue kiss in her entire life.

At the end of our road lived Lord and Lady Rix. Brian Rix (of trousers-down fame) and his wife, Elspet, had a swimming pool in their back garden, which they were kind enough to let us use from time to time. However, this offer was retracted after an incident involving Barnaby having an accident in the shallow end. Though a legend in the world of farce, Brian Rix showed very little sense of humour on that occasion.*

The posse that ran Putney Common, SW15, comprised an all-female group of dog walkers. 'The Dog Squad' – Watson, Laithwaite, Brass – were the area's chief gossips. They'd meet up on the common every day. This was ostensibly to walk their dogs, but, in reality, the animals provided cover for a good old nosey natter.

It was like a scene from a slightly tawdry Putney-based *Desperate Housewives* knock-off. The Dog Squad knew literally everything about anything going on in the neighbourhood. When the Wardles at number three had their son expelled from Oundle, the Dog Squad knew about it prior to the poor boy returning home. They were telling people about the sale of number twelve before its recently bankrupted owner had even exchanged contracts. And when the Tittles ended up getting divorced the Dog Squad knew about it in advance of anyone else, including Mr Tittle (who was probably axed for taking his son's cue on the tongue-kissing).

The Dog Squad also exemplified that incredible phenomenon whereby each woman looked exactly like the dog she owned. Whether all these similarities were coincidental or deliberately engineered, I don't know.

Julie Watson was a local artist: all flowing dresses, Laura Ashley scarves and organic sandals. She owned an equally free-spirited Afghan hound called Salvador. Mrs Laithwaite had a dog called Herman, an old grey schnauzer with a put-upon look. Herman was so similar to his owner that if you'd put Mrs Laithwaite's glasses on the dog and taken him off to a photo booth you could definitely have got away with using the picture as her passport photo.

And, finally, the leader of the Dog Squad: Penny Brass. Penny had a big beige duffle coat with off-white fur trimming, a deep brown all-year fake tan, and an enormous bouffant of highlighted blonde hair. She, of course, owned a golden retriever called Leonard.

*I can't believe that you are framing your brother for this incident. You know and I know who urinated in that swimming pool.

Of the group Penny Brass was definitely the nosiest. Under the pretence of having taken up bird-watching, she even took to walking the common with a large pair of binoculars slung round her neck. They helped her get a better view when peering into other people's houses.

'She's so pokey-nosey, that one,' said our decorator Tommy, who'd been doing up our bathroom. 'All morning she's been looking up at me. What's she think I'm going to do? Wave my dick out of the window?' He was very distressed.

'Tommy's just overreacting,' said my mum later. 'I'm sure Penny Brass has better things to do than spend her afternoons spying on us.'

She didn't. Although she'd never set foot in our house, she was always the first to know about any changes to the décor, however insignificant.

'I like the new lamps you've put in your bedroom,' she said one day when we met her on the common. 'They work so well with the curtains. And I see you've got yourself a new grandfather clock for the hall. That can't have been cheap,'* she added as her and Leonard's brows rose in unison.

*It wasn't cheap, it was an antique London Long case by Bateman of Great Tower Street.

* * *

As you can imagine, there wasn't much crime in Putney. The closest we ever came to a turf war was an ongoing dispute between the Putney Cricket Club and the Putney Common Association (of which Brass was a prominent member) about the length to which the common's grass should be cut. Yeah, that's right, homies, welcome to thug life. That particular dispute worked itself out, not with a bloody gangland-style shoot-out, but with some fencing round the wicket, which the cricket club paid for. The outfield was left longer for the Dog Squad. High-octane shit, all this compromise, right?

Then, one summer, completely out of the blue, a spate of muggings broke out in SW15. My mother was terrified. She went door to door** warning people to be careful, insisted her children all carry panic alarms and started picking us up from the bus stop in the car, even though it was only a two-minute walk home.

'I spoke to Fiona Azis,'*** my mum said, flustered.

Here we go, I thought.

**Egged on by her friend Fiona.

***Again!

'Fiona had tea with Julie Watson, who'd talked to Mrs Laithwaite, who'd been told by Penny Brass that the gang use knives and nun-chucks.' Well, if Fiona Azis had heard it from those reliable sources, then it must be true! I doubted whether Watson, Laithwaite or Brass would recognize a nunchuck if you took one to their faces, but I let it go.

One weekend my mother and sister were away. Late on the Friday night after a few drinks in the pub Barnaby and I decided to head home to play some *FIFA*. As we neared our house we realized that a group of youngish guys in hoodies were following us on the other side of the street. We knew they were gangsters because one of them was riding a tiny little BMX bike, making him appear both comical and scary at the same time, like a sort of stabby clown or angry circus midget.

'Do you have your panic alarm, Barnaby?' I whispered to my brother.

'They're not going to rape us, Jack,' he replied, clearly not as worried as I was.

'Well, if they do, you're first. That way they'll be too tired to bother with me!' I replied, ever the protective older brother.

We upped our pace, doing that kind of fast walk that looks a bit like you've shat yourself (which the closer the hoodies got became more and more of a possibility). Thankfully we got to the front door without being raped. We went in, but the group of guys remained outside, lighting up cigarettes and peering in through the sitting-room window like a gang of slightly more menacing Penny Brasses.

'Pull down the blind!' I told Barnaby. I didn't want them to see stuff that they potentially might want to steal, conveniently forgetting that my father's sitting room is predominantly decorated with large twentieth-century British paintings – swag that I doubt has a particularly high street value.*

'What are we gonna do? Shall we call the police?' I said.

'They haven't actually done anything,' replied my brother.

'Maybe we should wake up Daddy?'

My father goes to bed around ten thirty p.m. and was fast asleep. He wears earplugs because my mother snores, and sleeps

*How dare you! Maybe not on Wandsworth High Street, but certainly on Cork Street or Bond Street they would change hands very quickly.

~ We're nearly through this book and you're still not speaking properly.

with them in even on nights she's away. He therefore took quite a bit of waking up.

'What do you want?' he groaned on finding his two sons shaking him in what was for him the middle of the night. 'Has one of you wet the bed?'

A bizarre suggestion bearing in mind my brother and I were in our late teens at the time.

'Daddy, there are some guys outside,' I told him. 'We're not sure what they want, but we're worried they're sizing the place up. One of them definitely got a glimpse of *Polo Ponies Returning from Hurlingham* by Algernon Newton.'

My dad got out of bed, wearing only socks* and earplugs. He looked out of the window. One of the boys was gently kicking our wall. The one on the mini bike was smoking a ciggy.

'They're just yobbos, Jack. For God's sake, have a sense of pro-portion,' my father said.

Then the boy took a final drag and flicked his cigarette into our front garden. It landed on my father's camellia.

'Little shit!' growled my dad. He was off.

He grabbed his dressing gown and headed downstairs, swinging open the front door. 'Right, get the fuck off my drive!' Dad shouted very loudly, the earplugs giving him a false sense of the volume of his voice.

The boys looked slightly shocked but stood their ground.

'Fuck off, old man,' one of them said.

Barnaby and I were cowering behind my dad; it looked like things were about to get ugly. Five athletic boys versus a sixty-year-old man who loses his breath ironing a shirt, half-heartedly backed by his two equally physically inept sons.** I didn't fancy our chances.

Then nature intervened. In the rush to get downstairs my father had been unable to fully fasten his silk dressing gown. As one of the boys squared up to him, presumably to punch him or (if my mother was to be believed) apply some nunchuckery, a gust of cold wind shot up the dressing gown. The garment billowed open, dramati-cally revealing my father's body in all its glory, his manhood caught in the glistening moonlight.

'Eurgh, what the fuck?' one of them said, before staggering back aghast.

*I NEVER wear socks in bed. Even if your mother and I have had some impromptu intimacy, requiring me to derobe hurriedly, I will always ensure that I am sockless before entering the bed.

Hydrangea!

**You said it, not me.

They all looked at each other, not knowing what to do. They'd clearly not been in this situation before. My father made an unsuccessful attempt to rerobe himself, but in his hurry made it look like he was fanning both flanks of the dressing gown in order to draw attention to his nakedness.

'Go on, fuck off,' he repeated as he finally grasped both panels of the dressing gown, momentarily forming a sort of silk-eared elephant complete with fleshy trunk.

This time the boys turned and fled, clearly terrified.

My father walked back inside triumphant, the dressing gown now fully fastened at the front, but not before another little gust briefly flapped it up at the back to give any stragglers a flash of buttock. Then he got back into bed and went to sleep as though nothing unusual had happened.

We never saw the boys again. The muggings also stopped. So it appears that the lesser spotted Whitehall pecker is the best and most comprehensive anti-crime device around. The police should harness its power by inviting my father to late-night patrols. If there's any trouble at closing time outside a Wetherspoon's my father could stand on the bonnet of the police van and do his elephant trick. Trust me, the crowd would disperse pretty quickly.

A few days later my mother was at Waitrose unloading her things on to the conveyor belt by the till. She saw that the basket in front of her contained several bottles of St. Tropez instant tan and a few tins of dog food. It was Penny Brass.

What's she going to have noticed this time? thought my mum. The new rug in the sitting room, maybe, or the Bart Simpson poster that had gone up on Barnaby's bedroom wall.

'I was walking Leonard across the common the other night,' Brass began, 'and I had my binoculars just in case I chanced upon an owl.'

My mother raised an eyebrow but said nothing.

'There was rather a commotion outside your front door, Hilary. I do hope,' Brass continued, her voice quavering slightly, 'that Michael is, um, *all right*?'

When she came back from Waitrose we filled my mum in on what had happened, and took much pleasure imagining Penny

Brass stood on the common in the dead of night, peering through her binoculars and getting an eyeful of the lesser spotted Whitehall pecker. The ultimate deterrent – Penny Brass hung up her binoculars and never spied on us again.

1. This story is hugely exaggerated but I assume you have included it to take the focus off all your own naked activities at school. As you well know, this was a rare occasion when I wasn't wearing pyjamas and frankly it wasn't my fault that Mrs Brass got a macro-visual eyeful.

2. It's extremely ungallant of you to mention your mother's snoring. She is by no means a loud snorer and I'm sure I have far more unpleasant bedroom habits than she does. *

*Ergh!

3. I think it is grossly unfair that you have focused on the nudity element and deliberately tried to distract from the thrust of this story. Namely the tale of a father gallantly protecting his hapless, cowardly sons from a gang of hooded ne'er-do-wells. **

**Hooded ne'er-do-wells!!?

CHAPTER 24

Don't Let's Be Beastly to the Germans

– MICHAEL WHITEHALL –

JACK ALWAYS HAD A THEORY that if you had a non-skiing father you would never learn to ski, because he would never take you on a skiing holiday. It has to be said that a skiing holiday was not top of my wish list as I had tried it once and hated it. I also hate the cold and, as has been made clear several times now, don't generally embrace anything much of a sporting nature. But he had a point: why should my dislike of it hold back the rest of the family? He also reckoned that if he could get his mother hooked he would have a better chance of adding skiing to the annual holidays. So when Hilary suggested that we go on the Dragon School ski trip, as a try-out, on the basis that it would all be organized for us, Jack was very keen. Jack had left the Dragon by now, but the trip included staff, pupils, parents and old pupils. This would be nice for the children as loads of their friends were going with their families, and Hilary would have the added bonus of a week of chatting to all the parents. However, it held considerably less appeal for me as I could never remember who anyone was, let alone remember their names or who their children were.

'But, Daddy, Freddie spent half-term at our house,' Jack said to me when I described a boy and his mother who had come up to me and said hello in the wine department at Sainsbury's.

'Well, I can't be expected to remember everyone, especially out of context,' I said.

'He was the one you liked because he kept unloading the dishwasher,' said Jack.

'Oh yes, lovely manners. What was his name again?'

So it was off to Davos in Switzerland for a week with the Dragon School. I spent most of the trip sitting in restaurants with Paul Baker, known affectionately as Pabs, a non-skiing schoolteacher, talking about prep-school politics.*

*You guys know how to party!

The holiday got off to a bad start when a toboggan trip went disastrously wrong. We went to St Moritz, where we could embark on a long toboggan run for a couple of miles down a hiking road, at the bottom of which was a restaurant for lunch, where Pabs would join us.

When we arrived we got off the train and queued up to get our toboggans with almost everyone else who had been on the train, which amounted to something like two hundred people all jostling to get started on the hair-raising sledge down the mountain. It was decided that I would go down with Barnaby, and Jack would go with Hilary, Molly being off up the mountains with her friends. But just as Barnaby and I pushed off ahead of Hilary and Jack, I remembered what Pabs had said to me earlier. 'Be careful, Michael – I haven't done a full risk assessment on this activity.'

Twenty minutes later, Barnaby and I ended our run and headed for the restaurant. Slowly the tobogganers from our party joined us and we waited until everyone arrived before we ordered. Forty minutes passed and no Jack and Hilary. I was very concerned, but Pabs kept trying to reassure me that all was fine, that perhaps they had just taken a wrong turning and got lost. At last, Jack threw open the doors and announced that Hilary had had an accident.

'What happened, Jack? Where is she? Is she all right?'

'She's just cleaning up in the loo,' he replied.

'But what happened?' I asked again.

'We took a bend way too fast and came off the toboggan at speed. I was thrown to the side, but Mummy was thrown into the middle of the track. Her face was directly in the path of all the oncoming toboggans. The next people round the bend were two of the biggest German men I've ever seen and they were stopped in their tracks by Mummy's face. It was horrible, there was blood in the snow and everything. When she got up, her first question to me was "Are my teeth still there?" Fortunately they were. She was very shaken up and we had to walk down the rest of the run.' Jack went on, 'Her face is in a pretty bad way, but try not to react too much when you see her.'

At which point Hilary walked through the door.

'Fuck me!' I said as I saw her. Jack shot me a look. 'Um, fuck me . . . it's not as bad as I thought it was going to be. You look fine,' I lied.

She didn't. She looked like she had done three rounds with Henry Cooper* I turned to Pabs and said, 'Right, we've done a risk assessment on this tobogganing lark, Pabs. It's risky!'

'I'm so sorry, Michael,' spluttered Pabs.

'Typical Germans,' I said. 'I hope you got their insurance details.'

*Is this really the most modern boxer you could think of?

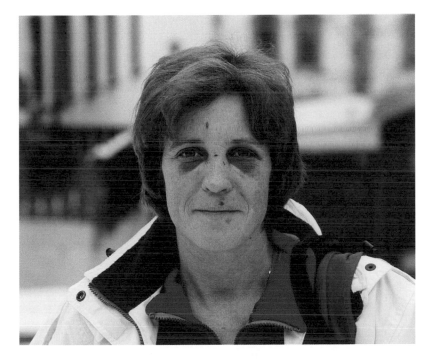

When the neighbours saw Hilary, I had a lot of explaining to do.

* * *

Staying in.

Anglo-German relations came to the fore again when I had an altercation with a German couple occupying the room opposite us in our hotel. Our two rooms were off the main corridor in a little enclave of their own, separated from the main hotel by a door which fulfilled no purpose and which we always left open and they insisted on closing. The Germans were certainly not in Davos for the skiing and they seldom left their room, apart from coming out to shut the intercommunicating door. They clearly didn't come out to eat, as there was always a pungent aroma of fried food emanating from under their door. It was difficult to guess why they were there, apart from to annoy me.

In fact, nearly everything about that trip irritated me. Our room was a dark and dingy affair, set just below street level, so we could see people's feet walking along the street and the occasional car tyre whooshing past and throwing up slushy snow on to our window, but nothing of the 'breathtaking views of sunlit peaks' mentioned in the brochure. It was also incredibly small, which meant that the bed had to be upended into a cupboard on the wall during the day in order to give enough room to be able to move around and do basic things like get dressed.

It made me more irritable than usual. A day or so later when we returned from an afternoon's extremely expensive shopping there was a note pinned to the door: KEEP THIS DOOR SHUTTED.

Turned into?

I turned into Basil Fawlty.

'Who the hell do these people think they are? Bloody Krauts!' I said to Jack, who was struggling down our bit of the corridor with two heavy bags in the pitch dark.

'And put those lights on! Why do they turn the bloody lights out all the time?' I raged. I grabbed the note, screwed it up and threw it on the floor. We went out for supper that evening and on our return discovered another note on the door: TURN LIGHT OFF.

'I can't believe those Germans are at it again!' I bawled. 'Having to turn my lights off because of the Krauts, it'll be blackout curtains next. It's the Blitz all over again. Have they forgotten who won the bloody war?'

*He then explained to me at length exactly why it wasn't 'just a lightbulb'.

'Two wars actually, Daddy,' said Jack, 'but don't get so annoyed, it's only a light bulb.'*

226   HIM & ME

The following day was Saturday and there was a party in the hotel that evening for all the parents, staff and children on the trip. This included a sit-down dinner, a quiz, some competitions and lots of dancing – all very un-me, but it's amazing what a couple of large V&Ts can do. So as not to disturb the other guests, the evening started early at six thirty p.m. and finished at ten thirty p.m., and was a very jolly affair. When we got back to our corridor, the door was closed and the light switched off, resulting in my tripping over a pair of ski boots, which were drying off outside our room, and hitting my knee on the doorstop.

My ski boots. Oops!

'For Christ's sake!' I shouted, my language going to pot having rather overindulged in a bottle of dessert Mosel after dinner.

'These Germans are fucking mad.'

Back in our room Jack, Molly, Barnaby and Hilary chatted as I prepared for a relaxing bath. I'd brought with me some light après-ski reading but just as I was about to step into the bath there was a bang on the door.

'You please be silent, my wife cannot sleep with your noise!' said the German to a startled Barnaby.

'It is only ten forty-five,' said Hilary. The man looked like a comedy sleeper – a striped nightshirt and even a matching nightcap. What was he doing in our room? How dare he?

Had I actually been in the bath, I might have let it go, but the temptation was too great.

I charged out of the bathroom, now in full Cleese mode, following the retreating German across the corridor.*

*No doubt hearing Winston Churchill's 'We'll fight them on the beaches' ringing in his ears.

'Daddy, you've got no clothes on!' screamed Molly as I wedged my bare foot in the door that he was attempting to shut. At the last moment I used the book I was holding to cover myself.

'What the hell do you think you're playing at, you ridiculous people?' I bawled. Behind Mr Kraut was his wife in bed, the room strewn with an array of cooking utensils and a camping gas stove, which had no doubt been the source of the smells that had permeated the corridor earlier in the week.

'How dare you leave ludicrous messages everywhere about shutting doors and putting out lights, and how dare you bang on my door and intimidate my wife and children! I shall be taking this up with the hotel manager immediately!'

'Not without any clothes on, you won't,' said Hilary as the German slammed the door in my face.

As I turned back round, I noticed a look of surprise on Hilary's face, which was probably due to the fact that covering my manhood was a copy of the second volume of Ian Kershaw's biography, *Hitler*.

I spotted Pabs coming up the corridor on his way back from the party.

'Those people in the room opposite are completely mad and I want them, or us, moved to another room. They're making our lives complete hell!' I said as I stormed down the corridor to accost him.

'Why haven't you got any clothes on, Michael?' he asked.

'Because I'm trying to have a bath. I'm serious; you've got to sort this out tonight, Pabs!'

At which point Hilary appeared behind me, put on my dressing gown, apologized to Pabs, who was trudging off back in the direction of the reception, and frogmarched me back to my room. 'Now calm down, have your bath and read your book,' she said. I got into the bath and turned to chapter three, 'Marks of a Genocidal Mentality'.

Over breakfast the following morning Pabs told us that the Krauts had left.

'Well, we can chalk that up as three wars won,' I said to him.

As we returned upstairs, there was a team of industrial cleaners arriving to attack the now vacant room opposite ours. 'You're going to need a hell of a lot of elbow grease and chemical help to get rid of the smell of bratwurst and sauerkraut from those curtains,' I said as we disappeared into our room.*

Jack could say *auf Wiedersehen* to any more skiing holidays. It was back to the Caribbean for us from now on.

*As Davos is 86% German-speaking I'm sure they really appreciated this particular bit of Germanophobia.

1. This one is entirely true.
   Are you suggesting that some of them aren't?

2. I must point out that I have tried and failed, on numerous occasions, to make my father aware that not all Germans are Nazis. So any German readers we might have, entschuldigung.

'Did someone order bratwurst?'

Part X

The Family Disappointment

CHAPTER 25

Acting Up

– MICHAEL WHITEHALL –

JACK'S EARLY ACTING CAREER was a rather hit and miss affair, veering more towards the miss.*

*What a lovely way to open a chapter. Seriously, don't pull any punches.

Apart from Fiona Azis, who says it was her favourite television programme of all time, few people in the entertainment business, apart from Mrs Whitehall and myself, are still talking about LWT's comedy drama series *The Good Guys*, starring Nigel Havers and Keith Barron. The concept, which was dreamt up by me on the back of a very, very small envelope, was an imagination-stretching story of two men, both called Guy, who crash into each other on Richmond Hill and end up sharing a flat together and accidentally get involved with solving crimes.** A pair of modern-day Miss Marples. Awash with my clients in the acting roles, not to mention the directors and writers, I also managed to shoehorn a young and attractive actress called Hilary Whitehall into the series. This was a major achievement, having failed miserably to cast her in my first production for ITV, *A Perfect Hero*, the previous year. On that occasion the director, an old hand, had treated me, a first-time producer, with contempt, and although I had developed the project and cast the two leads, James Fox was to partner Nigel Havers in the series, he made it very clear that *he* was in charge. I attempted to get Hilary an extremely small part of an RAF driver, a piece of minor casting, which would normally have been nodded through by the casting director. But, no, Mr Cellan Jones would have to interview Hilary along with several other actresses and predictably

**Can anyone else smell BAFTA?

decided Hilary wasn't 'right' for the part. In fact, the girl he cast was the same age as Hilary and looked identical; in fact, she was different from her in only one respect – she couldn't drive! This meant that we had to find and then employ a driving double for her. To save money the crew often pushed the car while she mimed driving it.

This time, in *The Good Guys*, I had managed to cast her as a semi-regular character and she appeared with her two children, Jack and Molly.*

In series one Jack made his TV debut, aged three, with a lot of mournful looks and a few moments of toddler talk, but in the second series, by now a more mature four, he had a full-on speaking part playing a child kidnapped by a jealous husband, played by Michael Kitchen. Michael Kitchen, known affectionately as Michel Cuisine, not the easiest of actors then or now,** was happy up to a point to play his lines as written and to react to Jack's responses. However, Jack was not a generous actor, then or now, and took to making farting noises with his mouth over Michael's dialogue. On the third time this happened Michael looked ready to explode and I decided to step in before he stormed off the set. So now I had to sit in for Michael on all Jack's lines and reaction shots, with Jack playing scenes to me, his father, rather than to Kitchen's character. Occasionally Jack would start delivering a line to me and then suddenly stop and say, 'Daddy, why do I have to keep saying this?'

All of the crew found this most amusing, but from the sidelines Michael Kitchen definitely didn't get the joke. I suspect he is an actor of the 'don't act with animals or children' persuasion. Have you ever seen any animals in *Foyle's War*?

Having been warned by Nick Elliott, the controller of drama at ITV, not to use drama commissions as a way of employing my entire family, and that having most of my client list in them should be more than enough, Jack was dropped from my next production, *Element of Doubt*, a thriller starring Gina McKee and Nigel Havers, but Molly, Barnaby and Hilary managed to slip through the net. The director Christopher Morahan*** had his patience severely tested, and he was not a man with patience as his strong suit when Barnaby needed sixteen takes to deliver the unmemorable line: 'Mummy, I've cut my knee.' Part of the problem was that Hilary wasn't playing Barnaby's mother, which was a leading role and which I think Nick Elliott would have spotted,

*My mother got these parts on her own merit as well. Before she even met my father she was an actress of some distinction and has been in numerous shows that he has not produced: Inspector Linley, The Bill, London's Burning, The Knock and, most impressive of all, Woof, the hit children's show about a boy that turned into a dog and solved crimes.

**Probably because you kept calling him 'Michel Cuisine'.

***Yes, another client.

but confusingly for Barnaby she was playing a small part of an estate agent in the same scene. Needless to say, three-year-old Barnaby kept delivering the line to her.

Jack's only contribution to this production was to seriously piss off his godfather Nigel by escaping from his nanny Hilde and roaring around the hotel landing that we shared with Nigel on his scooter, singing at the top of his voice at six o'clock in the morning.

Jack's next professional engagement was the part of a young shaver in Martin Clunes's *Goodbye, Mr Chips*.* For this one I was demoted from producer to chaperone and it was not a happy time for me. A very precocious child called Casey, who was playing one of the leads, showed us around the set as though he was producing the show. After the conducted tour he told me to sit in the trailer and not watch the filming from the sidelines as it would 'ruin the magic'. Little prick!

* The first job I'd got on my own merit.

Jack followed this playing the part of Ben Whiston in an episode of Noah's Ark for ITV, a series about a veterinary practice created by Johnny Byrne of *All Creatures Great and Small* fame. There had already been a few mutterings from Nick Elliott and Carlton's head of drama, Jonathan Powell, especially as Johnny Byrne was a client of mine, as were the two stars of the show, Anton Rodgers and Angela Thorne. The director was happy to take my word that Jack would be able to cope with the part, which consisted of a couple of short scenes in the vet's surgery, co-starring with a supposedly aggressive rabbit. What no one had allowed for, however, me included, was that Jack seemed to have developed a severe lisp and that the word 'rabbit' was to prove a bridge too far for him. In the scene Ben Whiston's rabbit bites Anton Rodgers's finger.

Back to my dad's shows.

'This animal is a menace,' says Anton.

'It's not a menace, it's a rabbit,' replies Jack.

Very high-class dialogue in this show, I recall. But poor Jack suddenly turned into Jonathan Ross and kept saying 'wabbit', which, although quite enchanting from a parental point of view, was not a huge plus on the production side.

It was a bold character choice. I think this may have been the start of your mother's obsession with getting your teeth fixed.

'We'll have to dub him,' said Nick, who was making a visit to the set that day. 'And isn't that boy Michael Whitehall's son?' he said to the director. 'I can't believe he's sneaked him in again! And I'm sure I recognize the extra who's sitting next to Jack in the waiting room?'

This man is showing me his post-modern magic trick where he pulls a top hat out of a rabbit.

'Yes,' said the director, 'that's Stephen Scutt, Michael's accountant, with his dog, Clarence. They've been here all day and Michael is keen for us to try to find something for Clarence.'

It had always been a policy of mine to cast friends and relatives as extras in my productions, as it was a great treat for them and they were always so grateful.

Bullshit, you cast them so you could scrimp money on the budget.

Hilary's parents had made their small-screen debut as a couple of well-to-do farmers with a lame pig, a backstory that they created for themselves and had difficulty in expanding as they had no dialogue and twenty seconds of screen time. Any saving made on not having to pay them was lost many times over after Woose had finished pilfering the catering wagon. Another ruse was offering work as an extra as auction prizes at school fund-raising events. On one occasion the Pattinson family bid the highest amount and Robert made his on-screen debut. Sadly for him, the director featured him just fleetingly and only in long-shot; sadly for us it does not appear on his IMDB page.*

After six or seven takes, Jack found his Rs for a brief moment, but the writing was on the wall vis-à-vis his acting career, certainly with ITV anyway.

*I'd be more proud to have that on my CV than Twilight.

My father grooming me for future BNP membership. It starts with a flag.

A few years later I produced *Bertie & Elizabeth* for ITV but by then Jack's reputation had preceded him and he and Barnaby appeared in strictly non-speaking roles as two urchins on a bombsite during a royal visit to the East End. Being unencumbered with dialogue, Jack was required to wave a flag at the actors playing the royal couple, which he did with great aplomb and Nick Elliott and Jonathan Powell didn't even notice he was there.

And then in 2000 an opportunity arose for Jack to put all his disappointments behind him and become an international movie star. He was to audition for the name part in one of the greatest film franchises of all time – *Harry Potter*!

The casting director had contacted the Dragon School in Oxford and asked the head of drama, Ian Murchie, if he could put together a shortlist of children who could audition for the principal roles. The assistant casting director would then visit the school and whittle down the candidates in an open audition. Jack was eleven at the time, the right age for Potter, and had more than a passing resemblance to the character, and even if he wasn't getting glowing references from the bigwigs at ITV he did at least have a very solid CV by this stage. Could this be it? I rang Mr Murchie.

'To be honest, Ian, an open audition with an assistant casting director is probably fine for most of your chaps, but I think I can do better than that for Jack. And, anyway, open auditions like this never find the stars. You might cast the odd supporting part, a Weasley twin or a Longbottom, but believe me the leads are dealt with in a very different way. As with so many things in our business, Ian, it's who you know.'

I was slightly flattering Ian, as I didn't honestly think they'd even cast the supporting parts at an open audition, but I didn't want to appear too grand.* I got to work the following day. Jack's godfather Richard Griffiths was already signed up to play Vernon Dursley and I asked him to call the director of the film, Chris Columbus in Los Angeles, and tell him to call off the search, we'd got his Potter.

My old friend Norma Heyman, a distinguished film and television producer, was my next port of call, as her son David was producing the film. I had also planned to talk to the casting director personally, but thought that as we had the producer and director in our pockets I needn't go that far down the food chain. A few days later I had a call

*Then you failed.

from her assistant Rebecca, with a date for Jack to come in and read for the part.* I told her that I would be accompanying Jack in my capacity as his personal manager.

We arrived at the casting director's office. There were no other actors there. Impressive, I thought. Jack's the only one they're seeing.

'Jack, whatever you do, don't cock this up,' I told him. 'We're in really good shape. We've got the producer and the director in the bag and although I don't want to be too confident, this looks to me like a shoo-in.'

'Have you had a chance to look at the short speech we sent you?' asked Rebecca.

Jack nodded.

Had he had a chance to look at it? His mother had been rehearsing it with him for the last week, with me reading Dumbledore. He was word perfect.

'I must say you do look very like Harry Potter,' she said.

Jack preened.**

One of the reasons for that was because his mother had constructed a whole outfit for him based on the detailed descriptions of Harry Potter in the books. She had got her hairdresser Timothy Williams*** of Timothy Williams Hair Design, Barnes, to recreate the Harry Potter haircut and had even borrowed a pair of round-framed spectacles from Leighton's Opticians in Putney to replace his rather bashed Adidas frames. Unfortunately she hadn't had time to get Jack's prescription lenses into the Potter frames.

To be honest, I think, had I not intervened, she would have gone as far as scarring his forehead, but even without the trademark bolt Jack *was* Harry Potter. It was now looking like this whole experience was going to be a mere formality. The role was his and I was even beginning to wonder what kind of deal they'd be offering. Obviously seven pictures, but would we be starting at a million dollars or even higher? I could almost taste that first dry Martini at the Chateau Marmont and momentarily spared a thought for poor Ian scrabbling around back at the Dragon, trying to convince some assistant's assistant that one of his kids might be right for a Weasley twin.

'Before you start reading, Jack,' said Rebecca, 'let's just chat about the book.'

*This is because Ian Murchie, my drama teacher, called the casting director, as my dad had still not heard back from his 'friend' Norma Heyman.

This was never cleared with me.

We hadn't.

It wasn't.

**I have never preened!

***The only man allowed to touch what's left of my father's hair.

Awaiting the 'formality' of an audition.

Hilary had bought Jack hard- and paperback versions of the book, including a signed copy of the *Chamber of Secrets* inscribed with the words 'Good Luck, Jack, Love J. K. Rowling', which she had stood in a queue for three hours outside Waterstones in Putney to secure. Rebecca was clearly impressed by the fact that we had the personal backing of J. K Rowling with her 'good luck' inscription in the book, another distinguished name to add to the ever-lengthening list. Hilary had added her own annotations and I had impressed upon Jack how vital it was that he read the book carefully and indeed had an in-depth knowledge of the text.

'Casting directors hate it when actors come in for roles and they are unprepared,' I told him. Jack assured me that he had read the book several times and knew his stuff.

'Who's your favourite character?' she asked.

'Harry,' Jack replied without a moment's hesitation. Shrewd, I thought. So far so good and his Rs were as sharp as a knife.

'Well, everyone loves Harry. Is there anyone else?' she added.

'No, just Harry,' came the reply.

'And what about the baddies? Who do you think is the scariest?'

Jack was clearly stumped and, in a flash, I suddenly realized that he'd never read the books. He-who-must-not-be-named became just that as Jack scrabbled around for an answer.

There was a long pause. 'Ummm . . .'.

I attempted a whisper that came out rather louder than I intended

'Voldemort,' I said, nudging him in the ribs.

Jack didn't hear me, his mind was too busy struggling for a response. He found one. 'The orcs,' he said nervously.

Orcs, I thought to myself, there aren't any fucking orcs in *Harry Potter*. I hadn't even read the book and I knew that. It was clearly time for me to intervene.

'I'm sorry, Rebecca, he's obviously mixing this up with *Lord of the Rings*. He's just finished reading the trilogy.* Incidentally, I hear on the grapevine that they might be making them into a film. Jack would, of course, be wonderful as Frodo.'

But I felt that things were slipping away and I was getting the impression that the game was up. Jack got through his speech but it was clear by now that Rebecca had lost interest.

*I hadn't.

I drove Jack back to Oxford the following morning where Ian was waiting, desperate for news. He'd even got the headmaster with him.

'How did it go, Jack?' he gushed.

'It went really well,' I replied. 'They loved him, but I'm not sure they know what they want. The thing is Ian, even if they did offer him the part, we'd all have to think about it very carefully. These long-option deals can be so hit and miss, and Jack wants to have a serious career in this industry, not just be a flash in the pan.'

When the letter of rejection arrived the following week I told Ian over the phone that Jack had ticked all the boxes for them but unfortunately he was too tall for the part. I thought it would be polite to ask Ian how the open audition went, although I had already anticipated a negative reply.

'It seemed to go OK.' he said, 'There's a girl in year five who they were quite keen on for Hermione.'

That will never happen, I thought to myself.

'Her name is Emma Watson.'

* * *

A year later Jack and I were guests of Richard Griffiths at the premiere of the film. I had taken Jack rather than Hilary, on the basis that if this Radcliffe boy had not been any good I would have Jack in the producers' eyeline as a potential replacement. At the party at the Savoy afterwards I found myself sitting next to Alan Rickman.*

'Wonderful performance, Alan, you stole the film for me. I think they have undercast Potter, but what do I know?' I said to him. 'You probably don't know this, but Jack was their first choice for Harry, but they felt he was just too tall for it and also we had diary problems. A great shame, as I think he would have been a lot more convincing than Radcliffe.'

The film was, of course, a massive success and inexplicably everyone seem to love Radcliffe. I hadn't given up hope of getting Jack into the franchise. I realized that even a supporting part could do wonders for his career and, having now read all the books up to date, had identified the part of Cedric Diggory as a perfect fit for him. I called David Heyman's PA to set up a meeting with him but was told, rather tersely I thought, that he was tied up for the next couple of months, so I floated

*An actor with whom you might have had more to talk about had Nigel got that John McClane part all those years ago.

the idea past his PA but it seemed that someone else was already in place to play the part. When we finally got round to seeing *The Goblet of Fire* on a family outing to the Odeon Putney (and I didn't think Daniel Radcliffe had got any better), I was keen to see who had been cast as Cedric. You can imagine my surprise when I saw who had got it.

'Isn't that the boy from Tower House whom I told not to bother being an actor?'

His name was Robert Pattinson.

*I greatly resent the word dodgy. My productions included work by some of our finest actors – Dame Eileen Atkins, Sir Alan Bates, David Suchet, Edward Fox, Simon Ward, Elizabeth Hurley and, of course, Nigel Havers.
Is Liz Hurley one of this country's finest actors?

**Why must you be so crass?

1. I never asked to be in any of my father's dodgy productions.*

2. My father's delusions of grandeur have got a little out of control here. It wasn't a one-on-one casting for *Potter*, there were dozens of other children present. Norma Heyman never called him back because she had no idea who my dad was (neither did her son) and Richard Griffiths was probably asleep when he was asked to talk to the director.

3. I think I would have made a great Harry Potter, though I wouldn't have been totally faithful to the books. If I got given an invisibility cloak I wouldn't be off searching for the philosopher's stone, I'd be trying to get a butchers of Hermione's Gryffindor!**

CHAPTER 26

Ungainful Employment

– MICHAEL WHITEHALL –

JACK DEVELOPED A LOVE OF COMEDY very early on in life. He watched countless stand-up comedians and comedy shows as a young boy and comedy was something that we were able to bond over . . . sometimes. He would make me watch whatever his latest obsession was, be it Alan Partridge (yes), *The Fast Show* (yes) or *The League of Gentlemen* (hmm), and I introduced him to the far superior comedians and comedy shows of yesteryear: Tommy Cooper,* *Dad's Army*** and a particular favourite of mine, *To the Manor Born*.*** I dug up old vinyl records I had of Stanley Unwin and Bob Newhart, with the driving instructor sketch becoming a favourite of both of ours.

    It was inevitable that Jack was never going to be content with just being a viewer of comedy. In school plays, he managed to find the comedy in the most unpromising of supporting parts. He would always add a gurn, a costume embellishment or a prat-fall somewhere, never being one to shy away from the cheap laugh. One early perfor-mance that I particularly enjoyed was an incredibly over the top take on Oberon in *A Midsummer Night's Dream*. Jack took his role as the king of the fairies as a licence to camp it up; it was a turn that Frankie

*Yes.

**Yes.

***Hmm.

Howerd would have been proud of. One person who was not so enamoured of it was the play's director, Mr Brien, who you will remember as Jack's football coach. Hearing from Jack about Mr Brien tearing his hair out during rehearsals, as time and again Jack refused to 'tone it down', gave me much pleasure. Though it's probably the reason he kept substituting him in those football matches.

On another occasion Mr Brien had done his usual trick of casting his son in the leading role, this time as Scrooge in *A Christmas Carol*, something that I personally felt was deeply inappropriate.* He had cast Jack in the role of the undertaker.

*The only thing Mr Brien and my father had in common was that neither of them shied away from blind nepotism.

'I'm not familiar with the role of the undertaker,' I said when Jack told me. 'I didn't know there *was* an undertaker in *A Christmas Carol*.' This was a play I had seen many times and indeed had sat through both halves to the very end, as various clients of mine had played Scrooge: Stratford '*Z Cars*' Johns and Anton Rodgers, to name but two. I definitely didn't remember an undertaker. However, by the end of Mr Brien's production everyone knew the undertaker. At the curtain call, his son was greeted with a polite round of applause for his two and a half hours on stage. Jack, on the other hand, was greeted by whoops and cheers for ten minutes of high-camp comedy, a homage to the great Leonard Rossiter of *Rising Damp* fame.**

**Although sweet, this is a massive exaggeration.

* * *

By sixteen, bored of losing out to Mr Brien's son in the casting stakes, he was writing sketches and performing stand-up in front of the school, as well as in local pubs, having persuaded the landlords to let him put on shows in their back rooms. And after a trip to the Edinburgh Fringe Festival that summer he was introduced to a whole new world. Although always supportive in whatever path he chose, I had major reservations about Jack choosing stand-up as a viable career. This was a completely different end of the business to the one that I operated in and I knew virtually nothing about it. I told Jack that I thought he should at least try other things before he made any firm decisions. He could by all means carry on doing his gigs in the evenings, and entering comedy competitions, but he would still have to go to university and he would definitely have to get some properly paid employment to help towards his board and lodgings.

HIM & ME

Up until this time Jack hadn't shown any signs of anything that could be remotely described as a sensible entrepreneurial spirit. Not the faintest hint of a high-flying career with Goldman Sachs, making millions of pounds for his clients and even more for himself. By no stretch of the imagination the makings of a FTSE-topping multi-national chief executive. Early indications of his money-making skills included spending all his holiday pocket money at Gatwick before we had left for the West Indies on a reduced-price Inter Milan shirt, a team which he did not support but suddenly had an insatiable passion for. Hilary argued that adult XXL, the only size they had left, was definitely not his size (he was ten at the time) and I pointed out that Ronaldo, the name printed on the back of the shirt, was a player who had left the club that summer for pastures new.* We also reasoned with him that he might want to save his money and buy something in Barbados. It hadn't, of course, occurred to him that it would be boiling hot and not an ideal location for an oversized football shirt. But, no, he HAD to have it. So obsessed with this impulse buy was he that he caused us to be late for the flight and we had to suffer the indignity of walking down the aircraft aisle to our rear seats past the rest of the tutting passengers, who had been strapped in for hours awaiting our arrival. At least Jack was able to make this walk of shame in his newly acquired shirt, which came down to just above his knees.**

Sensing a possible profit one day, Jack and his brother, Barnaby, once set up a table outside our house selling Pokémon cards***, way after the craze for these things had died a slow and terminal death. Surprisingly, however, there was some early business from children returning from the local primary school. Unfortunately the initiative was closed down very abruptly a few days later when several irate mothers arrived at our front door, demanding refunds and accusing Jack of grossly overpricing the cards and demanding money with menaces. He had even persuaded a boy who lived down the road, who was on the mild end of the autistic spectrum, to go home and find his father's wallet to enable him to buy a 'very rare' shiny Pikachu that Jack had valued somewhat steeply at thirty pounds. When the father got home he was round immediately for a refund and, as a gesture of neighbourly goodwill, I said that the boy could keep the card, which Jack was very pissed off about.

*I'm pretty sure this was pointed out to me by the man in the shop, as my dad has at no point in his life been particularly up on the transfer ins and outs of Serie A clubs.

**Irony is, that's the only shirt size the real Ronaldo could fit into now.

***We used the tag-line, 'Pokémon: gotta sell 'em all.'

A year or so later he and his friend Ollie decided to go into the car-valeting business. And although they printed off some business cards on the computer, they failed to invest in any plant or equipment. They would ring doorbells, offer to clean cars and, on the rare occasions that the owners agreed to let them loose on their vehicles, would request buckets, cleaning materials, sponges, chamois leathers, rubber gloves, water and the use of the household's Hoover for the full interior valet service. After they had been cleaned and polished, the cars invariably looked considerably worse than they had beforehand and the boys had great difficulty in securing any return business. They were banned from going anywhere near my car and as they spent most of their time chatting to each other or pissing around on their phones, the business quickly ran out of steam. Their last client, Richard Timpson, who was a neighbour of mine and never an easy man at the best of times, came round to the house one evening and demanded that I paid for his car to be valeted at the local carwash, as Jack and Ollie had smeared the paintwork by washing it with cold, dirty water and in the process had written off the squeegee mop that he had lent them. As a result of this out of court settlement the car-washing business went into voluntary liquidation.

* * *

Oh for God's sake! By eighteen Jack appeared to be sexually active* and thought it appropriate to start using our family home as a knocking shop. I therefore thought it appropriate to start charging him rent, so he needed to find some work. A job in the local pub followed, but he was so busy talking to the customers, telling them jokes and trying out his material, that he was on the slow side at actually serving them drinks. On one occasion I found it very difficult to sympathize with Jack, who arrived back home on the verge of tears after a shift, having served a local connoisseur of fine malt whisky a glass of Glenmorangie with ice and a slice.

'He called me a tosser, Daddy,' said Jack. I held back from telling him that he clearly had been.

As a result of this incident, Jack lost his waiting job and was sent to the sluice to do the washing-up, a development that he failed to share with us. Hilary and I decided to make a surprise visit to the pub shortly after this as we thought it would be fun to be served by Jack.

Our order was in fact taken by a young Colombian man and when I asked him where Jack was he garbled, 'He and me swap job. Me waiter, he washer-up.'

We peered through to the back to see Jack, his sleeves rolled up to the elbow, with a pair of yellow rubber gloves, wrestling with a large stained sauté pan that the chef was hollering for him to hurry up and clean. He wasn't even allowed to come out and say hello as the kitchen was so manic. Although the waiter's English was not very good, he explained that he was working in the pub to improve it as he had the opportunity of an internship with KPMG, having finished top of his year in his finals in Economics at Bogotá University.

'Your parents must be very proud of you,' I said through gritted teeth as I caught a glimpse of Jack dropping a glass salad bowl on the tiled floor of the kitchen. *

*Why have I suddenly become Manuel from Fawlty Towers?

* * *

For his next job Jack signed up to work for a catering company along with his sister Molly. Molly sailed through the day's training, managing to perfect silver service in a very short time; Jack struggled to even get the basics under his belt, just about making it to the end of the day being able to serve a bread roll with a fork and a spoon one-handed.**

**Not basic, that is an extremely difficult skill to master.

Their first jobs were both by coincidence over the same weekend. Molly was sent off to a London hotel to waitress for a charity gala at which one of the guests was Arsène Wenger, who, she said, was incredibly charming. Jack, still a lifelong Arsenal fan to an almost obsessive degree, was furious. He had been assigned a fortieth birthday party in Rickmansworth where he had been put in charge of the children's catering, which meant serving burgers and chips to thirty noisy and generally unappreciative under-tens. The catering company were clearly still worried about whether he had mastered the art of silver service, so thought best not to challenge him too far on his inaugural job.

'I'm never having kids,' he came home grumbling. 'I spent most of the afternoon getting bloody ketchup stains out of the carpet!'

Their second jobs were both sporting events. Jack was off to the newly built Wembley Stadium to work in one of the large restaurants there and Molly was having to get on a six a.m. bus to Windsor Great Park to work at a horse show.

'This is more like it,' said Jack. 'Serve them lunch, then get to watch a football match for free, sounds like a doddle.' Nothing could have been further from the truth. His afternoon was spent serving hordes of drunken, loud and bullish 'corporate wankers', who clicked their fingers at him and said amusing things like 'More wine, *garçon!*' and 'Chop, chop, matey, get these plates cleared.'

The restaurant didn't even have a view of the pitch.

Molly, on the other hand, fared better. On arrival in Windsor she was assigned to the governors' marquee, which was a smallish off-shoot of the main marquee that accommodated twelve guests. The weather was terrible that day and due to the noise of the rain hitting the marquee roof, Molly could hardly hear her manager's instructions as to what she was meant to be doing. He disappeared into the kitchen area, leaving Molly on her own to set the tables for lunch. Just as she was folding the napkins, she looked up to see the door opening and two raincoated men and a woman wearing a headscarf coming in. The two men waited by the door at the far end of the marquee as the woman walked over towards Molly. As she approached her Molly thought to herself how like the Queen she looked. She put down the napkins and looked up again to speak to the woman, who was now standing in front of her. She didn't just look like the Queen, she was the Queen!

'Ghastly weather out there this morning,' she said, shaking the rain off her coat. 'We thought we would come and shelter in here for a minute.'

'Um, yes indeed, Your Majesty,' Molly blurted out as she struggled to remember how to address one's monarch.* There then followed what Molly later described as the most surreal four or five minutes of her life, making more small talk about the weather and what was on the menu for lunch.

*Queenie?

'Right, better go and brave the elements again,' said the Queen as she opened her handbag. She took out her lipstick, skilfully applied a coat with the aid of a little compact mirror, popped them back into the bag, snapped it shut and with that was gone, her two detectives behind her.

On her return home, she and Jack compared notes.

'Mine was awful,' said Jack. 'They treated me like shit. How did you get on?'

'I was put in the governors' marquee,' said Molly.

'Oh, very posh,' said Jack. 'You'll be telling me next that you met the Queen.'*

Jack decided it was time to investigate pastures new. Next up was temporary employment at Clinton Cards, a job that proved to be even more temporary than he'd expected. Although his enthusiasm for the work lasted through the morning and lunch break, by mid-afternoon he was flagging and took to ushering customers out of the shop any time from four o'clock onwards with the advice to go on to moonpig.com as it was a lot easier. Needless to say the manager didn't see the joke and sacked him, telling him to avoid the retail sector in future – advice that he followed enthusiastically.

So it looked as if it was going to have to be comedy. On the minus side, it was a desperately hard industry to get into. On the plus side, he was passionate about it, worked really hard and, by this time, had won through to the finals of three national comedy competitions, one of which would take him back to Edinburgh, but this time as a performer. He was on his way!

1. I totally dispute this Pokémon autistic-boy story. It was not a shiny Pikachu card — for starters you can't even get a shiny Pikachu card, it was a shiny Raichu card, which is actually very rare and I'd say was priced accordingly.

2. I have on occasion shown business acumen. For example, very early on in my career, when it was suggested that you should handle all of my finances I was quick to decline that offer and have therefore avoided becoming the next Macaulay Culkin.

3. I put ice in the whisky, not ice and a slice. I'm not that stupid.

4. OK, I have to come clean and admit that perhaps I was banished to the washing-up sluice because I might have retaliated a bit to the man who called me a tosser. I can't remember exactly what words were said but I may have suggested he stick the bottle of Glenmorangie somewhere inappropriate.

CHAPTER 27

Art

– JACK WHITEHALL –

*Cheap joke, Jack.

**What an
unpleasant expression.

***I said no such thing.

'Gyles Brandreth wants you to paint his wife's pussy,' my father announced to me over breakfast. He was trying to shock me, of course, but it didn't work – I already knew that Gyles was, despite all appearances, heterosexual.* Michèle, Gyles's wife, loved her cat, and had suggested the commission after my mother had told her I was a keen artist. It was true – I'd done some portraits at school – but I'd never had a cat gig before.

'She says she'll pay you a hundred pounds,' my dad went on. Kerching. A hundred quid to paint a cat? Piece of piss. Plus, it was a black cat. I'm not being racist, but black cats do all look the same. This would be the easiest money I'd ever made.

'Just get her to ping me over a photo of it and I'll bang it out this weekend,'** I told my mum, so confident that I used the word 'ping' as a verb for the first and (I promise you) last time in my life. Of course, I had no intention of even looking at the photo. A black cat's a black cat.

Unfortunately my patron thought differently. My father told me that Michèle insisted I travel to her house in Barnes 'to properly see her pussy'.*** I just thought the trip was a bit of a ball ache. Still, a hundred pounds is a hundred pounds. I was eighteen and unemployed at the time.[*] If Michèle had wanted me to come round and massage the cat's paws I would have.

As Michèle showed me into their lavishly decorated house she indicated a small cluster of pictures hanging in the hall: a few paintings and a framed photograph of Gyles in a woolly jumper and women's fishnet stockings and suspenders straddling a man that I think was Tony Blackburn.

'I thought this might give you a little inspiration,' she said. I prayed she wasn't referring to the picture of her husband, and my tears were allayed when she indicated one of the paintings. 'That's the portrait we had done of Maggie by our friend Lowry.' This cat had been painted by L. S. Lowry! That must have set them back a bit. Also, if you've already got a black cat painted by one of the great British artists of the twentieth century, why get me to paint it too? I was pretty cocky, but even I found this a bit daunting. I was honoured, but I was also beginning to wonder if Michèle might not be a little nuts.

Maggie was a nice-looking cat (as cats go, which is not very far) but she wasn't particularly disciplined. Getting her to sit for me proved to be a nightmare.

'Why don't we bind its feet?' I joked, misjudging my audience.

'I would not dream of doing that to her,' said Michèle. I realized I'd found the no-go zone in her sense of humour. Everyone's got one. Turns out cats being treated like Geishas was Michèle's.

I was locked into the room with Maggie the cat for an hour. She spent that time wandering around doing what she pleased. And, as she had no interest in posing for a portrait, this did not involve sitting still in a cute position, making it impossible to paint her. Michèle, meanwhile, didn't check on me once, as she didn't want to disturb 'the artist at work'. This left the artist at work free to spend the hour on the phone to his friends. Lowry had requested such isolation too, apparently. It seems unlikely, though, that he was gossiping about who had fingered[**] who in whose parents' bed.

I told my dad about my first day at the Brandreths' that evening. 'The bar's been set pretty high, Dad. She has a portrait of Maggie done by Lowry!'

'Lowry?' replied my father. 'He died in the mid-seventies. How

* At least when
consulting Who's Who
one is not constantly
asked if one wants to
play online poker or get
a bigger dick!

old is this cat?' On inspection of his *Who's Who* (*Who's Who* is a book which old people who can't work Google have to use to find out things. It's fucking archaic, worse than using Lycos*), Dad worked out that for Lowry to have painted Michèle's cat it would now have to be in its late forties.

'God knows what a pussy looks like at that age,' he said, before I asked him to finally drop the whole 'pussy' thing because he sounded like Mrs Slocombe in *Are You Being Served?*

'Maybe it was someone fleecing her,' I said, preventing him from launching into any showbiz anecdotes about Mollie Sugden. 'You know, posing as Lowry to get more money out of her.'

Michèle loved that cat so much I think she'd have been more than willing to believe a genius wanted to paint it. Damn, I thought, I bet the fake Lowry got paid more than a hundred pounds. I've missed a trick here. Maybe I should tell her I'm Banksy and see if she'll double the fee. I could spray it on the wall outside the Brandreths' house, and put Maggie's face over a full-body picture of Maggie Thatcher drinking milk out of a miner's skull to make it all political. Michèle would definitely buy that.**

** I very much doubt
that; Gyles was a very
close friend of Mrs
Thatcher's. That was
probably why the cat
was called Maggie in
the first place.

I had to do three more sessions with Maggie, one on one, to collect enough sketches to create the portrait. After the first session, I looked on the Internet to see if there were any cat sedatives I could buy in order to knock her out. One man in America was selling some stuff for big cats kept in zoos. But I thought that could be a little heavy-duty, especially as it suggested administering it with a dart gun. If Michèle'd got L. S. Lowry to paint the animal, God knows what she'd do if I made it OD. It would get around Putney pretty quickly and I'd be ostracized, like a middle-class Bobby Brown.***

*** I don't know
who this is but I hope
he's not related to
that odious Scottish
socialist who played at
being prime minister?

On our final meeting, having refused to sit still for the previous two hours, Maggie seemed to have a sudden change of heart. It's almost as though she wanted to call my bluff. Too late. I'd decided these sessions were a waste of time and that I'd finish my portrait as originally intended, using photographic references rather than anything acquired from sittings. Still, it made for an awkward final hour as I chatted away on my mobile with Maggie sat motionless on her chair, staring at me in the judgemental way only a cat can have.

'Shouldn't you be working?' her eyes said like a patronizing teacher. 'And get your hands out of your trousers. Do all teenage boys sit there fondling their balls as they talk to other teenage boys? Bit weird if you ask me.'

'It looks just like her,' gushed Michèle a few weeks later as I unveiled the finished portrait in her kitchen. 'You've really caught the glint in her little eyes, and she's even got that thing she does with her nose. Such a wonderful likeness,' she continued, pressing two crisp fifty-pound notes into my hand.

Odd, I thought, that I've got such a likeness, given that my main reference point had been a picture I'd pulled off Google Images of Salem the talking cat from *Sabrina, the Teenage Witch*. But I felt it best if I didn't shatter the illusion by sharing this information.

'Yeah, I felt like I really got to know Maggie. Hopefully I've conveyed some of her rich and complex personality on the canvas,' I bullshitted. I felt a little guilty but as Michèle took down the picture of Gyles and Tony Blackburn and put it face down on the sideboard I figured at least I'd done some good. My painting was placed on the wall next to Lowry's colourful pastel drawing. Lowry must have been very old when he painted it. He probably had the shakes, too, because the signature at the bottom looked nothing like his.*

After this triumph my career as an artist came to rather an abrupt end. An ill-fated term at the Chelsea School of Art was the death of it. Chelsea School of Art was not an institution I enjoyed belonging to. The student body seemed to be made up of two sorts of people. These were either pretentious hipsters (angular haircuts, glasses with no prescription) who all thought they were the next Damien Hirst, or public-school girls called Panettone or Taramasalata, who'd been travelling through India and now wanted to live the life of a bohemian but who were only really at art school because (despite having had a very expensive education) they were simply too stupid to get into an actual university and study a proper subject. Oh, and me, who, I guess, if anything, probably fell into the latter category.

'I don't want you fucking off to Thailand to inject yourself with skunk, or end up in some poppers den,' my dad told me when he first broached the subject of me attending art school rather than

*We subsequently learnt that Jack had misheard Michèle and she had in fact said that Maggie had been painted by a local artist and friend of theirs called Larry.

having a gap year. 'You can go to art school like your grandmother did.' My grandmother Nora had attended Glasgow School of Art in the 1930s, but Chelsea School of Art in 2006 was a different kettle of fish.*

I'd struggled through the first three months at Chelsea, and just about made it to the final assessment of the term without doing a Van Gogh – not that the tutors would have noticed if I had. They probably would have thought it was some dramatic piece of performance art. Trust me, never have a heart attack in an art school. As you lie frothing on the ground, a dozen scenesters in thick glasses will stand around you, stroking their chins as they admire your commitment to disrupting the normito-mechanical hermeneutics of society. Don't ask me what that means. I learnt it at Chelsea.

And here lay the problem: I'd picked the wrong art school. While I enjoyed figurative drawing, cartoons, portraits and graphic design, Chelsea was heavily geared towards the conceptual. They loved anything with shock factor, especially if the 'artist' accompanied the piece with a blizzard of bullshit about why they felt it was relevant and 'spoke to them'.

The end-of-term assessment was a chance for the tutors to appraise the students' work, and for the bullshitters and haircuts to metaphorically tug each other off over their minimalist films, conceptual installations and deconstructive anti-photographic retrohensivactivisavatardadaism. Again, I have no idea what that means.

It was also a chance to invite friends and family to the gallery, to see what we'd been getting up to. So I invited my father, a man who – for the past forty years – has assembled an impressive collection of twentieth-century British representational art or, to you and me, watercolours of men in fields.**

*I wouldn't be that sniffy about them. They're your inheritance.

***I have my moments.

'This all looks very Tracey Vermin,' he said (quite pleased with his pun)*** as I showed him through the first gallery space. Shock and fury danced across his face: imagine showing Ann Widdecombe an episode of *Geordie Shore*. 'I mean, what's the point of that?' he said, pointing at someone's photography project. 'This is an art school, not Snappy Snaps.'

We arrived at my display area, where I was exhibiting a series of figurative sketches, a few life drawings in charcoal and an oil portrait of Edward Fox, who'd kindly agreed to let me paint him. He's easier to drug than Maggie the cat.

Two tutors sidled over. There was the head of our year, a bald-headed man with thick black-framed glasses and a stupid little beard that looked like Tinker Bell's fanny. His name was Sven, though I suspect this was a made-up name as he had a Midlands accent, and there aren't that many Svens from Dudley, right? With Sven came his sidekick, a wild-eyed lady whose name I forget. Despite being in her late fifties, and in the twenty-first century, she was wearing dungarees. All in all, she looked very much like she'd had the choice of two career paths: art teacher or bag lady. Sadly for me, she chose Chelsea over rootling through bins.

The tutors disliked my work as much as my father disliked them. Neither party made any attempt to hide their displeasure .

'How a woman dressed like that is allowed to make any comment on aesthetics is beyond me,' my father said, probably in her earshot. Sven, meanwhile, appeared quite horrified by my efforts. To judge from his slackened jaw, it was as though I'd framed child pornography. Come to think of it, that may have got me better grades.

After a little chorus of tuts and sighs, Sven gave his damning critique. He decided to serve it up with no sugar-coating, despite my father's presence.

'It's very trad,' he drawled. 'I mean, sure, it's nicely painted, but what do we actually know about the old man? He's still a stranger.'

My dad raised his eyebrows. 'That "old man" is not a stranger. He is Edward Fox, one of the finest actors of his generation!' Sven wasn't expecting this. '*Edward & Mrs Simpson*, *The Day of the Jackal*, do they mean anything to you?' my dad went on. 'Did you never see his General Horrooks in *A Bridge Too Far*? He stole the film!'

Sven clearly had not. Maybe he was more of a James Fox fan.

'Maybe you should cut the picture up and put it in formaldehyde,' my dad said, trying to console me as the tutors gave a glowing assessment to a woman who'd made a sculpture out of horse manure and chicken wire.

The final straw for both me and my dad, though, came as we observed their critique of a mature student called Kybor. Kybor was in his mid-thirties but, other than his age, was typical Chelsea School of Art fare. He cultivated an 'alternative' dress sense, spoke nonsense and made the kind of art that my dad has nightmares about.

Kybor's installation was certainly a piece that stuck with you. He'd suspended a large black dildo from the ceiling. Why a black dildo? We'll never know. This appendage had been hollowed out to form a sort of telescope. The viewer was encouraged to peer through it at a wall plastered with graphic images of men engaging in sexual acts all splattered with white paint.

'You must be fucking joking,' my dad said as he watched Sven take hold of the plastic penis, draw it towards his eye socket and get a closer look at a photograph of two men in vicars collars and nothing else getting to know each other a little better. (I don't think they were actual men of the cloth, vicars don't tend to wear leather cuffs.')*

I wouldn't have put it beyond the Reverend Lindy!

'It represents my repression as a homosexual in this hateful homophobic metropolis,' Kybor explained. It took all of Sven's self-control not to add to the conceptual semen on the wall with some of his own, more literal, stuff.

I was surprised. Kybor didn't seem that repressed, and as a Londoner I've heard a lot of criticisms levelled at my 'hateful' metropolis, its congested tube carriages, unfriendly commuters and expensive bars and restaurants, but never that it's 'not gay-friendly enough'. It's hardly Bible Belt America or Saudi Arabia.

'Vauxhall's just across the bridge,' I felt like saying to Kybor. 'The Royal Vauxhall Tavern? Horsemeat Disco? The Hoist? All good for a great night out.' But I didn't, because I was still a bit cut up, and also because I didn't want my father to hear how much I knew about these rather fruity nightspots.**

**'Shutting the stable door after the horse has bolted' springs to mind here.*

'I'm just glad we didn't bring your mother,' whispered my dad as he beheld Kybor's 'installation' in all its glory. 'It's ridiculous. Apart from anything else, where would you put it? Above the man-telpiece? Maybe in the kitchen? Oh, Hilary, I bought a piece of art today. If you just get plastering this magazine over on that wall in the hallway, I'll string the rubber phallus up from the chandelier.'

'Kybor, it's beautiful. It really speaks to me. So powerful, so relevant,' Sven panted, before excusing himself for a post-coital menthol. Dungaree woman, meanwhile, looked daunted by the prospect of holding the dildo. I doubt she'd had such close contact with a penis, plastic or real, for a very long time. But no sooner was it in her mitt than she became quite breathless.

Kybor's work won best in show and my portrait of Edward Fox was marked somewhere near the bottom of the class. I did not return to the Chelsea School of Art the next term, a decision that, after his visit, was fully supported by my father. I don't know what's happened to Kybor – he's probably won the Turner Prize. I wouldn't know, though, as my experience at Chelsea has meant I've kept a great distance from the art world ever since.

'It's a post-modern proto-minimalist conceptual retro-dada piece of homo-erotic-expressionism.'

If this comedy stuff dries up, though, and anyone wants me to paint their cat or any actor friends they've got, I'll listen to offers of a hundred pounds upwards. And if you're into the modern stuff I don't mind throwing in a dildo telescope for you to look at it through as well.

1. I find that a lot of people, not just Michèle, have no-go zones in their senses of humour. This has been well illustrated since you embarked on a comedy career. I think that your comedy is very funny but appreciate that not all sections of the population agree. Examples being the Rev. Lindy, who pounced on me by the fish counter in Waitrose with the line 'You have a very rude son!', Mr Brien (obviously), Uncle Billy and your mother's chiropodist.

2. I once bumped into Mollie Sugden at the Chichester Festival Theatre. We were both queuing at the same bar and the mix-up of our orders meant that the waiter accidentally handed her my drinks, two large glasses of Pinot Grigio. Once we realized what had happened, she gave me them back and said, 'Someone's thirsty.' It was very amusing and we all laughed heartily. But that was Mollie.
That's the worst anecdote I have ever heard!

3. Gyles and Michèle are very dear friends of mine and it was very kind of them to be your patrons and commission you to paint their cat. And very stupid of you to think that it had been painted by Lowry.

Part XI

All Growed Up

CHAPTER 28

Voting Rights

− JACK WHITEHALL −

My father can get quite agitated watching modern TV. He'll rarely get through a programme without shouting something at the screen. And what he shouts can be entertaining – I reckon he'd make a great addition to the BBC's online output: 'Press the red button now for Michael Whitehall's commentary!'

Say you were watching the *Antiques Roadshow* when you pressed the button. Michael's voice would come booming through your speakers, questioning each valuation and muttering 'tart' every time Fiona Bruce had the temerity to open her Michael Aspel-usurping mouth. Any entertainment show you might be watching, including the ones I appear in,* would end with my dad reminding you that 'Comedy died with Morecambe & Wise'. The Olympics or any World Cup, meanwhile, would prompt a quick-fire blizzard of 'facts' (usually to do with the banana republic in question being little more than a conveyor belt of drug dealers, thieves and 'good runners'),** topped off with warm memories of the British Empire; and if I had a pound for every time I was reminded that Jeremy Isaacs set up Channel 4 to broadcast ballet and opera, and not gypsy weddings and Noel Edmonds opening boxes, I would be a rich man.

I have never called Fiona Bruce a tart. She is a much respected and very competent journalist . . . she's not a patch on Michael Aspel, but that's by the by.

*Especially the ones you appear in.

**What are 'good runners'?

A ghastly show. that, had it not been for my impeccable judgement and strength of conviction, might have featured your sister and 'Roy'.

The only problem with my red-button idea being live is those moments where my father takes things that one step too far. For example, the occasion when we were watching the BBC news one night when a report from Harare was broadcast. Its subject was vote-rigging in the forthcoming Zimbabwean elections.

As they relayed pictures of the prime minister, Robert Mugabe, the veins on my father's forehead began to gently throb and the 'Michael mist' descended over the dinner table.

'He's the most odious little toad,' said my father. 'What a horrible Rhodesian pimp!'

I should point out that I've got to the stage now where I don't bother to correct him on the use of colonial place names. Rhodesia, British East Africa, Ceylon*. He knows they aren't called this any more. He's just saying them to get a rise, so I don't give him the satisfaction.

*Basutoland, Nyasaland, British Somaliland.

'I don't know why the SAS don't just fly over and put a bullet in his head,' added my dad, looking at another shot of a waving Mugabe.

This is his solution to most problems regarding international diplomacy.

In fact, come to think of it, quite a lot of his home politics centre round the 'bullet in the head' method. He suggested the most recent London mayoral elections would have been over a lot quicker if the SAS had shot Ken Livingstone. And if my dad had his way, Peter Mandelson, Ed Balls, Harriet Harman and both Milibands** would even now be piled on top of each other in a lime pit.

On this occasion, though, my dad was getting especially hot under the collar, and his Mugabe rant was getting ugly. His face had puffed up, his eyes seemed more bloodshot than usual, and he was gesturing at the TV with hands in the shape of pistols.

'He's a cretinous, vile, ghastly, evil little –' he paused to choose his next word for maximum impact, before bellowing – 'cunt!'

Yes, in front of my mother, Dad had dropped the C-bomb. My mother (who until now had been washing some wine glasses in the sink in an attempt to ignore her husband's rant) swung round, her Marigolds on, fluffy soap suds up her arms – a picture of outraged domestic bliss. Her eyes blazed with a deathly intensity.

'Michael! How dare you? How dare you use that disgusting word in this house? How dare you use that word in front of my baby!'

**Tony Blair, George Galloway, Bob Crow, Alastair Campbell, Arthur Scargill, Dennis Skinner, Alex Salmond, John Prescott, George W. Bush, the RMT, Nick Griffin, Herman Van Rompuy, Julian Assange, Bob Crow again (just to make sure), Robert Kilroy-Silk, Cristina Fernandez de Kirchner, Sean Penn . . .

... François Hollande,
Jean-Marc Ayrault,
Nicolas Sarkozy,
Jacques Chirac, John
and Sally Bercow,
Robert Mugabe, Sean
Woodward, Yvette Cooper
and Gordon Brown.

*I was certainly not a
fan of Mellor. In fact,
I thought he was rather
repellent and was openly
pleased that he got
chucked out of Putney,
but I couldn't have voted
socialist, even though
when I subsequently met
our new MP I thought he
was quite a decent chap.

she shrieked, pointing at me (eighteen at the time). 'You should be ashamed of yourself, Michael!'

My dad, without hesitation, turned from the TV, faced my mother defiantly and yelled, 'This is typical of you, Hilary. You are always defending Mugabe!'

It's safe to say that – of all the many, many people in the world on my father's hate list – Robert Mugabe is pretty much at the top. Mugabe's like a moustachioed Fiona Bruce or a black Michael Winner (an old *bête noire* of my father). But what my father might not realize is that he and Mr Mugabe may have more in common than meets the eye.

My father has voted Conservative all his life. He would never vote for anyone else, no matter how sleazy or ineffectual the Tory candidate in question. He even voted for David Mellor* when he was our local MP. In my dad's opinion, having sex behind your wife's back (and even doing so in a Chelsea shirt) is a far more forgivable mistake than wanting to bring in a mansion tax.

I have no doubt that – had my father lived in the constituency of that Tory MP found with his pants round his ankles and an orange in his mouth – my father would have voted for his corpse over that of a Labour or Lib Dem candidate. He'd have found some excuse – 'Well, at least he's encouraging people to eat their five a day!'

That's how dedicated a Tory my father is. He has a particular dislike of the Labour Party or, as he calls them, the socialists (see Rhodesia). There was a week, while I was still living at home, when there'd been endless talk in the papers about a possible Cabinet reshuffle. The Labour Party were in power at the time, and some journalists had even speculated that Tony Blair might bring back a few old faces.

I was lying in my bed, sleeping softly, when the door to my bedroom was violently kicked open. I looked through my crusty eyes at my alarm clock. It was seven a.m. In the doorway stood a figure, backlit by the light from the hallway and thus forming a dramatic silhouette. It was my father, wearing his loosely fitting John Lewis silk dressing gown.** In his hand, he held a copy of the *Telegraph*. He didn't say good morning. In fact, there were no pleasantries at all; he just thrust the paper in front of my face and barked, 'Mandelson's back.'***

My first election as a voter was a big moment for me. I remember being very excited about having a say in who would lead my country. A vote was a decision that could help change the world. For me, it was between the Greens and Lib Dems. I hadn't made my mind up which of them I'd vote for, but I'd done lots of research and felt both were viable, admirable parties. I thought that, when I finally saw their names on the ballot paper, I'd instinctively know which box to tick.

Having considered my options in this way, I was proud to be more responsible than my friend Marcus. He was also a first-time voter, who told me he'd gone into the polling station and picked the candidate whose name meant something to him, much like you'd pick a horse in the Grand National.

'I voted for some guy called Derby cos like I'm a Derby County fan, so whatever,' Marcus told me over the phone.

'Did you check what party he represents?'

'Nah, mate, couldn't be arsed. Voting's dry. I'm going down the pub,' came the drongo-like reply.

He'd voted for Simon Darby (not even spelt the same as his beloved Derby), deputy chairman of the BNP. But that was Marcus. Marcus, whose half-Cambodian heritage would doubtless go down a storm with Simon Darby.

Marcus, the same boy who, on hearing that his mother had been awarded an MBE by the Queen for her services to various charities, told us, 'My mum's got an MBE. Isn't that the thing where you're tired all the time?'*

Marcus, who during a history essay on the Second World War had thought that *Arbeit Macht Frei*, the Nazi slogan that adorned the gates of Auschwitz, translated not as 'work will set you free' but 'work hard, play hard'.

Marcus who, in other words, was not the sharpest knife in the box.**

But I wasn't like Marcus, I was a responsible voter. I'd read the literature,*** I'd asked all the right questions, I'd had sleepless nights mulling over my decision. Should it be the Green Party? I cared about the environment and wanted to put an end to global warming. A vote for them was also a vote for future generations.

Or should it be the Liberal Democrats? They played on my social conscience. I knew I'd had a privileged upbringing and this was my

*Yes, the same 'condition' that renders you seemingly unable to make a short trip to the shops to buy tea bags when you have invited guests for tea.

**He is an imbecile.

***I find this very hard to believe.

You can say that again.

first opportunity to atone. I could vote for a party that was fair, that looked after everyone in society and not just the rich. I know, it's hard to believe anyone could ever think those things, but this was way back in 2010.

My decision was made. Yes, I'd have to recycle like hell so as not to feel guilty about turning my back on the Greens, but they were never realistically going to win. Voting Lib Dem was the right call.

I arrived at the polling station with a real sense of purpose, ready to change politics on the local, national and international stage.

'May I ask who you are voting for today, sir?' said a man standing outside the church hall holding a clipboard and wearing a Conservative Party rosette.

'Liberal Democrat,' I said with a haughty disdain for this right-wing lackey. I thought in my angry and ever so slightly conflicted teenage mind that this man wanted single mothers to starve and hospitals to be shut down. Well, not on my watch! I felt like spitting in his face.

At the front of the queue for ballot cards I was confronted by a stern woman with badly dyed hair. She had stacks of paper in front of her.

'Name?' she said.

'Whitehall, Jack Whitehall. Man of the people, defender of the weak.' I might not have said the second bit, but I thought it. She checked down the list, then looked at me with a patronizing sneer.

'Your postal voting form was sent out to you two weeks ago.'

'What?' I exclaimed. 'There must be some kind of mistake.'

'It will have been delivered to your home address.'

'But I never received it!'

'Well, you can't vote here. Next please.'

'Can you just double check?' I bleated, but she wasn't going to budge.

What an outrage! An administrative error was going to deprive me of my right to vote! I was devastated and angry. It was at this moment that I suddenly started to smell a rat. I took out my phone and called home.

'Daddy, it's Jack. I'm just down the –'

'Are you watching that one-eyed Stalin on the TV?' interrupted my dad. 'He called that poor old lady a bigot.'

'Daddy, did you receive a postal voting form for me at home?'

'If thinking that there are far too many scrounging, bone-idle foreigners in this country counts as bigotry, then I, for one, am a card-carrying bigot.'

'Yes, obviously you're a bigot. But have you got my postal vote?'

'Yes,' he replied.

Phew. Crisis over. Panic averted! Fear not, Lib Dem HQ, we're gonna be back on track soon.

'So, I'll come and pick it up,' I said, not realizing how these things work

'That won't be possible,' my father replied. 'I filled it in and returned it for you a week ago.'

'What do you mean, returned it for me? You don't even know how I was going to vote.'

'Don't be ridiculous, Jack. The Whitehall family has voted Conservative for generations.'

'I can't believe you stole my vote!' I shouted. 'I was voting Lib Dem! Lib Dem!'

The phone went dead.

The Conservative Party candidate in Putney won by a landslide. I don't know how many other postal voting forms my father got hold of that year – undoubtedly my mother's and sister's, and I wouldn't be at all surprised if he'd broken into the Royal Mail sorting office and pilfered a few more.*

But stealing your son's postal vote pales into insignificance when compared to what he did during the local council elections.

One day, not being a driver,** I asked my dad to give me a lift to the station. I was staying with a friend and had a big bag with me. Now, of course, I wish I'd carried it all the way to Putney Station.

That morning, the candidates for the upcoming council election had been doing some canvassing in our area. A rather bemused Conservative councillor had been invited in for lunch (and was practically offered a neck rub, just in case the strain of fighting the red tide was getting to him), whereas the Lib Dem lady and a rather tubby Paul Potts look-a-like from Labour had our front door slammed in their faces with the warning that – if they came back – my father would set his hound on them! Our hound being Mabel, the

*While amusing, this entire story is a barefaced lie. I didn't fill in a postal vote for you; you did it yourself. And, as you well know, you voted Conservative and you are too embarrassed to admit it!

**Just imagine the havoc you would cause if you were let loose behind the wheel of a car. In retrospect, thank God you've never taken up my many kind offers of driving lessons.

twelve-year-old terrier with cataracts and a stomach tumour.

I went outside and put my overnight bag in the boot of the car. I was followed by my dad, jangling his keys. It was a hot day and he'd been gardening all morning. In his head, this made it OK to go topless. As he clambered into the car, his grey-hairy chest glistening with sweat, I consoled myself that it was only a very short journey to the station.

We were about five minutes from the house when he suddenly slammed on the brakes. He was peering beadily into his wing mirror.

'Did you hit something?' I asked, checking the road behind us.

'No. Look, it's that tubby little socialist.'

I looked behind us. The Labour Party councillor from earlier was completing his rounds of canvassing, a merry smile across his face as he walked* from one door to the next.

*Waddled.

'Great, Dad. Can we go now? My train leaves in fifteen minutes and I haven't got a ticket yet.'

After a moment, my dad started the car again in the direction of the station. I'd just relaxed when he swerved into a sharp right.

'What are you doing? The station's that way,' I said as he turned round another corner. We'd done a full loop by now and, as we pulled out of another street, I realized he'd taken us to just a few metres behind the canvasser.

'Let's tail the fucker,' whispered my father, grinning like a maniac.

We were now driving at a snail's pace, dribbling along the road a few yards behind the Labour man. As he waved goodbye to the owners of another house he'd canvassed, Paul Potts clocked the Mercedes creeping along behind him. He continued down the street, trying to avoid eye contact with its shirtless driver, but my father was relentless.

'Dad, please can we just go to the station?'

'Shush,' he hissed as he increased our speed so as not to lose Paul, who in turn upped his pace from a waddle to a quickstep, and opted to miss the next house on his route in the vain attempt to escape his predator.

'You do realize what you're doing is intimidation?' I asked my dad.

'Intimidation is knocking on little old ladies' doors and tricking them with propaganda and lies into voting for the socialists. I'm merely playing him at his own low game,' came his reply.

The irony was that, if anyone was acting like a socialist, it was my father. Tailing a political opponent in a car – he would have fitted right in with the Stasi, though I think they were a little stricter when it came to 'tops off' surveillance.

The councillor's quickstep was now a light jog. He began glancing over his shoulder, and had developed quite a sweat (though perhaps not one to rival my father's). Potts looked terrified, which is fair enough: he was being followed by a half-naked man revving his engine like a bull billowing out its nostrils before a charge.

'Here, piggy-piggy-piggy,' Dad muttered under his breath.

'Dad, please can you stop this? The poor guy's shitting himself.' But my plea fell on deaf ears.

We were coming to the end of the road. I looked at the speed dial – we'd hit thirty miles per hour.

'I've got him!' my dad roared. What the fuck was he going to do? He wasn't actually going to mount the pavement and mow him down, was he? I put on my seat belt just in case.

The councillor saw his get-out, a small pedestrian alleyway, which he slid down and out of sight. My dad slammed on his brakes.

'Fuck!' he yelled, hitting the wheel.

'Can we go to the station now?' I asked.

'No! We'll flush the rat out!'

We drove round the block several times, but Potts wisely did not reappear. Come to think of it, he was never seen again in our neighbourhood. No doubt he sat at home, terrified that if he tried any more door-to-door canvassing he'd get run over by the half-naked man in the Mercedes.

I think you can guess the result of the council election as well. Conservative landslide. And I missed my train!

So, whenever I hear my dad ranting and raving about Robert Mugabe, telling me that he's a bully and a thug who only gets into power through underhand tactics and intimidation, I think to myself, 'Kettle and pot!'

1. There is an exaggeration in this chapter, or, to use a more technical term, a lie, regarding my mode of dress. Anyone who is still reading this book will, I'm sure agree, that it is highly unlikely (i.e. a lie) that I would be driving around topless, however hot the weather.

2. And, not wishing in any way to link myself with the former Liberal MP for Eastleigh, I did NOT steal your vote.

3. I only use colonial place names to educate you about the Empire.

4. This Paul Potts comparison is ridiculous. I've no idea who Potts is but I think it's very unfair to compare him to a Liberal Democrat. **Look him up in Who's Who.**

5. A few more names I forgot to add to my list: Sepp Blatter, Silvio Berlusconi, Mohamed Al-Fayed, Jaqui Smith, Fred Goodwin, Quentin Davies, Michael Martin, Bob Crow for a third time just to make really, really sure, Gerry Adams, Bashar Al-Assad, Mahmoud Ahmadinejad and Polly Toynbee.

'Here piggy, piggy!'

CHAPTER 29
Cock Blocking

– JACK WHITEHALL –

'Why don't you go out with that nice girl Hannah? You know, the one who takes our dog for walks,' my dad asked me a few years ago.

'I don't know, Dad,' I replied. 'Maybe because she's twelve.'

'Is she? Well, what about Hattie? She's sweet,' Dad continued. I sensed my mother's hand in this excruciating man-to-man stuff.

'She may be sweet, but she is also technically a cousin.'*

My father's no Paddy McGuiness, and his matchmaking skills leave a lot to be desired. It's mainly because he's very old-fashioned (ideally any wife of mine should come with a dowry) and also that he is very, very judgemental.

For Barnaby and me, bringing a girlfriend back to meet him was a nervy affair. He could mess things up even before he'd met her. I'll always remember Barnaby coming home from his first term at boarding school and telling my mum and dad that he was going out with a girl called Boadicea Money-Coutts.

'Boadicea, what a lovely name,' said my mum.

'Coutts,' added my dad, 'as in the bank Coutts?' He paused for thought. 'Barnaby, whatever you do, don't fuck this up!'

'Daddy, we've been going out for a week,' said Barnaby.

'I want you over this Money-Coutts girl like a cheap suit – one thing you'll never have to endure if you can lock her into a marriage.'

*Only a second cousin.

Marriage?! This seemed a little unlikely as they were barely at the 'holding hands' stage. Unfortunately the pressure got to Barnaby and the relationship was over by the end of the holidays.*

My sister, meanwhile, has had to endure all manner of awkward scenarios with my father. Even leaving Roy from the campsite aside, hers is a somewhat complicated love life. This is not what a man of my father's generation wishes for his only daughter. As a consequence, my father can be a little over-protective.

When Molly was nineteen, she spent a brief time stepping out with the singer Johnny Borrell from the band Razorlight. She was very excited to be dating a rock star, even though, as I pointed out, Johnny Borrell wasn't really a rock star. He was a pop star with a rock star's haircut. He was marketed as 'rock' due to the chronic state of his teeth, which would have been unforgivable seen anywhere except behind a Stratocaster in Camden. Plus the songs he wrote could have been written by a child with severe head injuries; Razorlight tried to break America with a song called 'America' in which the chorus went 'Ooh, ooh, ooh America'. All I know is that Borrell's charms only worked on Molly. America just thought he was a dick, along with the rest of the world.

One evening, Borrell arrived to collect Molly from home. This was the only time he ever encountered my father.

'You must be Razor-rash,' said my dad as he opened the door. Nice one, Dad.

Much to my pleasure, it was not a relationship that lasted long. I must take some blame/credit for this as well. Molly came back one night from his Camden bachelor pad and dreamily told me that her poet boyfriend had written a song about her. She played it to me on her iPod and while nodding along pretending not to hate it my brain began to whirl. My sister had only been seeing this douche-bag for about a week, so how on earth had he managed to conceive, pen and record a song about her in that time? I mean, I know his songs were remedial, but even 'America' must have taken a couple of weekends. I smelt a rat.

After some digging around on the Internet I discovered that the song in question had in fact been written two years prior to his meeting Molly. How many innocent young girls had this man tried to get into bed with this bullshit? Well, I knew one thing for sure, he wasn't going to get away with it with my sister! I presented her with printed documentation to verify the provenance of my claim and suggested she confront Borrell. When challenged with the facts he backtracked and attempted to wriggle out of the situation by claiming the song had been written about a girl 'like' my sister. His days where numbered after that and the relationship was soon over. Yeah, Borrell, that 'I wrote a song about you' shit may have worked with other naive young fan-girls, but you didn't take into account your latest target having a pedantic older brother who had a lot of time on his hands. Whitehall one, Borrell nil. Actually he slept with my sister. Let's call it a draw.*

So, as I say, it's my father who's the overprotective one, I'm cool.

I have always felt the odd pang of guilt for sabotaging this relationship, though, and recently I was afforded the opportunity to make amends. I was doing a charity gig with a mixed bill of music and comedy, and one of the acts was Molly's favourite singer, Olly Murs. (I was far more supportive of this choice of musician, Razorlight are rubbish but Olly Murs is the greatest living singer-songwriter of our times; he invented Reggae music for Chrissakes). I'd never met Olly before, but I waited till he was on stage, broke into his dressing room, wrote 'Call me' with Molly's number on a piece of paper and pinned it to his mirror. Good, I thought, I'm redeemed.

As I left the dressing room, I saw a tuxedo with a bow tie hanging on the back of the door. Unusual, I thought, Olly Murs was more of a T-shirt and waistcoat kind of guy. But, hey, it was a charity night – he was making an effort, maybe he was gonna leave the bow tie undone, rock the open shirt, Bublé style. (OK, I take it back, Michael Bublé is the greatest living musician.)

I went back out front, did my set and then stood in the wings to watch the rest of the show. I got a bit of a shock when I saw the same tuxedo from earlier, now containing *Britain's Got Talent*'s opera singer (and Labour Party Councillor lookalike), Paul Potts.**

I'd got the wrong dressing room. Potts never called Molly but that's fine, as he's not really her type. But – in the unlikely event that Olly Murs is reading this book – can I just make it clear that the offer is still open?

*What?!?! She didn't listen to Uncle Billy?

**It's this bloody Potts man again!

My siblings have suffered at the hands of my dad's social skills, but he always seems to keep his biggest faux pas for me. My parents recently moved house and when I went over to look round the new place my father showed me a wine cellar he'd had installed beneath the kitchen floor.

'Look, isn't it great?' he said, swelling with pride.

'Do you think you might be able to give me a few bottles of wine for my new flat?' I asked him, keen to increase my wine collection from the one lonely box of Franzia that was sitting in my fridge at home.

'Of course, I'll put together a case for you', replied my dad, opening up the door to the cellar. 'Look how easy it is. You just lift up the hatch and down you go.'

'It's like your Fritzl cellar,' I joked. A joke that I don't expect many people to approve of – apart from my father, who decided to claim it as his own. Stealing jokes is a pretty devious thing to do. In his defence it was his wine cellar and he'd always been a fan of bad-taste, off-the-cuff remarks, but I didn't expect him to deploy such a dark quip on my girlfriend Gemma when she met him for the first time. We were round at my parents' house for a boat race party, (yes, we really are that posh) and to put Gemma at ease my father had been making a few light-hearted remarks about my track record with women and how his son was clearly punching above his weight. Jokes that had gone down well, and which had clearly eased him into a sort of comfort zone.

'Now, can I get you a drink?' offered my father.

'I'll have a glass of red wine, please,' Gemma replied.

My dad lifted up the hatch to his wine cellar. 'Oh, tell Gemma what you said the other day', I said, thinking she'd be pleased to hear that it wasn't going to be boxed-wine forever.

He turned to her, smiling. 'Oh, yes, This is the cellar I take Molly into when I need to rape her.'

I wanted the ground to swallow him up. Which, ironically, it did as he disappeared into the cellar without a backwards glance. Gemma looked perplexed.

Taking girls home has always been a nightmare, though. As soon as I became able to inveigle girls back to my bed (aged approximately twenty-three), my mother did every underhand trick she knew of to deter me from having sex in the family home.

My bedroom was desexualized. Old children's toys were littered across the floor. Polly Pockets, My Little Ponies, Barbies – I mean, those are *girls'* toys! They weren't even my Barbies, though I'd thought my dad threw out my Polly Pockets and Ponies years ago, so actually that was a silver lining; even Pocahontas made a reappearance.

Effeminate toys weren't enough, though. Mum brought out the big guns. Family pictures adorned every shelf, a large framed picture of Uncle Billy's bearded grinning face placed prominently on my mantelpiece.

On the bed itself Mum had installed a huge tower of cushions that you'd have to hack your way through by yourself or, if with a lady guest, work through like pre-hose firemen with buckets of feathery embarrassment. Each cushion was embroidered with a little choice phrase that would kill any kind of sexual mood: home sweet home, Mummy knows best,[*] Daddy's under the bed.

*She does.

She also insisted on giving me children's bedlinen. Every duvet cover I had was still *Thunderbirds* or *Postman Pat*. Again, very hard imagery to get aroused around. If you're having sex with a girl and you catch Jess the Cat's innocent eye or – worse – find yourself being waved to by the cheery Mrs Goggins, it really puts you off your stride (in the unsexy stakes, it's right up there with Leslie Grantham telling you that Dean Gaffney never puts the seat down).

One day, I decided I'd had enough. I told my mum I was going to buy myself some new linen. Mum told me not to be silly – she'd buy it for me. I wouldn't get the right measurements, material and so on.

When she came back from John Lewis, though, she hadn't bought me new bedlinen. She'd bought me a new bed!

'Thanks, Mum, that's really nice of you,' I said to her, thinking I'd save her blushes and not ask about the linen.

I soon found out why this bed had been purchased. It was the loudest bed I've ever slept on in my life. This bed would creak in space. If I was ever 'on the job'[**] in my mum and dad's house, I would have to be extremely gentle. The slightest movement would let out a piercing creak that could be heard throughout not only the house, but the whole of Putney.

**A gross thought.

For months, I had to have what I used to refer to as 'stealth sex'. My bedroom was a passion-free zone.

'Jack, do you want to do any role play?' a girl would whisper in my ear.

'Could you just play dead?' came my response.

I'd have sex so quietly I'd be doing it like we were Anne Frank's parents. All this meant that I'd prefer not to take a girl to my house. Although it was my mum who'd put everything in place to deter me from such behaviour, it was my dad who inadvertently put me off bringing back girls forever.

I brought a girl back one night who, for the purposes of this story, and to protect her modesty, and also because I'm ashamed to say I don't remember it, shall remain nameless.*

How ungentlemanly!

We'd met at a party. And I might have told her that I was a multi-millionaire rock star from a band and that I'd written a song about her. What? If you can't beat 'em . . .

Perhaps the deal-clincher was my boast of owning a 'mansion' in Putney, in which I lived alone. As I let her into said 'mansion', she tripped over five muddy sets of Wellington boots, including Molly's Cath Kidson ones, which had been worn the day before when we walked Charlie in Richmond Park.

'That's just how rich I am,' I said to her, slightly slurring my words. 'I have five sets of Wellington boobs – boots. That's just the way I roll. Yeah,' I said, expanding on the theme, 'they're all for different types of terrain. Those are mountain, those are mud, those are –' pointing at the Cath Kidson boots – 'pretentious festivals.'

We crept upstairs, my amour looking around at the decidedly odd décor for a young man to have on display in his millionaire bachelor shag pad. I've never been to the house of any of the Foo Fighters, but I suspect none of them have a collection of Winston Churchill toby jugs on their mantelpieces or leather-bound first editions of Churchill's books in the hall.**

**Not that you would have ever noticed them, let alone read them.*

We went past my mum and dad's room and reached my own. Why this particular millionaire had opted out of sleeping in the master bedroom (in favour of the tiny crooked attic room instead) was a question I thought I'd pre-empt. 'It's got more character. Anyway, the master bedroom's being redecorated . . . along with every other

HIM & ME

room in the house,' I said as I sat on the bed and remembered how drunk I was.

She started getting undressed, but by the time she'd turned round, her rock star millionaire, the self-styled five-wellied poet of Putney, had passed out, still fully clothed.

In my drunken stupor I'd completely forgotten to set an alarm early enough to get her out before my dad rose for breakfast. Me and my mum had a little system in place for situations like this: I would go down, tell her I had company, she'd distract my father and then I'd creep out with the girl. Maybe she couldn't stop her son sleeping with girls, but Hilary Whitehall was damned if she was going to have her breakfast ruined by any of them colliding with her husband.

I give up!

We'd got it down to a fine art. It was like an SAS hostage extraction. Though, in retrospect, I probably shouldn't refer to ladies I took home as hostages. It doesn't sound great.

That particular morning, though, I woke up as a beam of light hit my face. It was my dad opening the door in his dressing gown, holding the morning papers. I saw a sleeping stranger and with lightning speed (given my profoundly hungover state) managed to hurl my *Fireman Sam* duvet over her.

'Morning, Jack. Good to see you up and dressed this early,' my father said, luckily forgetting that I was wearing exactly what I'd left the house in at seven o'clock the previous evening. I should also point out that the party the night before had been a black-tie event. I don't usually wear a dickey bow and cummerbund around the house, but maybe Dad thought I was turning over a new leaf.
'I just wanted to read you this article in the *Telegraph*,' he said, remembering his mission.

As I've already touched upon, my dad had a habit of bursting into my room in the morning with articles from the morning papers, but he'd never yet done it when I had company. Still, at least on this occasion he seemed unusually chipper and it crossed my mind that he might be about to read me a story about Peter Mandelson being arrested or Ken Livingstone getting hit by a bendy bus (his fondest dream). If that were the case, at least he would be brief.

He continued, 'It's by Simon Heffer and it's about the Lisbon Treaty and those bloody socialists lying to us about the Euro.'

He'd opened the paper to a very long-looking comment section. My heart sank. I had to get him out, pronto.

'Really, Daddy, why don't you just leave it on my desk and I promise I'll look at it later?,' I said, but it was too late. He'd already launched into it at the top of his voice.

'"During the current crisis, we have several times heard invoked the wisdom of American economist Milton Friedman . . ."'

Fireman Sam's face was shifting from a beaming smile to a frown as, beneath it, my bedfellow stirred. Shit, my dad's gonna see her, I thought. He'll go ape, plus what's she going to think of my dad? She'll know this isn't my house and that I'm not a millionaire playboy. Maybe I could tell her this man was my butler? Just a slightly over-friendly old butler who liked reading me the paper every morning, like John Gielgud* in *Arthur* or Michael Caine in *Batman*.

She won't believe that, I told myself. She's not an idiot.

Still drunk, I decided the best thing to do was clamp down her side of the duvet to keep her under it. I half hoped that if I cut off her air supply she might pass out and then I could resuscitate her when my dad had left.

'Barnaby, Molly, come in here. You should listen to this. It's your future the socialists are trying to fuck up!' my dad bellowed, loud enough to wake up people in neighbouring houses, let alone in the bed he had now perched on.

A squeak told me he'd perched on her feet.

Molly and Barnaby came in sleepily, followed by my mum, brandishing cups of tea for everyone. I now had my entire family in the bedroom.

'"The truth is that Europe has never had so dire a crisis since the Treaty of Rome was signed in 1957."'

I don't know if you've ever read Simon Heffer, but he is not a journalist who abides by the idiom 'less is more'. His articles are bumbling pieces of right-wing Euro-scepticism that last longer than *War and Peace*. I had to let the girl out. Not 'let her out' – we're back in hostage territory.

'Dad, I'm gonna have to stop you for a moment as I'd like to introduce you to my girlfriend,' I said, whipping back the duvet like I was a minor royal unveiling a plaque at a hospital.

Where has this ridiculous Americanism come from?

*My old friend, Sir John Gielgud, please!

I don't know why I said girlfriend. I guess I thought I'd be judged less harshly if I had serious intentions. But from her point of view, she must have thought I was fucking mental.

I started to introduce her to my bewildered family, but had – even by then – forgotten her name. As I cast around for inspiration, I looked over to the mantelpiece.

'This is Billy,' I said. 'Billy as in . . . Billie Piper.'

There was an awkward pause, one of the most awkward pauses I've ever had to experience. I prayed that Bella Lasagne from my *Fireman Sam* duvet would come to life and entertain my family with her Italian voice and silly pet cat Rosa while I sneaked 'Billie' out of the house.

'I suppose I'll finish this, then,' said my dad to break the long silence. 'Unless you didn't hear the beginning. From under the duvet, I mean. I could always start again?'

'Go from where you were, Dad,' I said in agony. The ordeal ended only fifteen paragraphs later. The *Telegraph* really should employ a more disciplined editor to deal with Simon Heffer's verbosity.

My parents left the room. Surprisingly Billie did not ask for my number, nor did I get a kiss goodbye, but I'll always be indebted to her for playing along. I never had my way with the ladies in my parents' house. On the plus side, I don't think Simon Heffer got his way either.

1. I would like to disassociate myself from the title of this chapter. It is vulgar and coarse and would certainly not appeal to the kind of readership that I hope this book will attract.

2. You criticize Simon Heffer but I might usher you towards his recently published book, Strictly English: The Correct Way to Write . . . and Why it Matters: A Guide to English Grammar and Usage. It might come in handy for a boy who just wrote a chapter containing two 'gonnas'.

3. And was I right to warn you and your bedfellow about the dangers of the Euro? It would appear that if it wasn't for me she would have left our house with nothing.

Glossary of names dropped by Michael Whitehall

(as explained by Jack Whitehall for younger readers)

Dame Eileen Atkins
Distinguished British actress most recently of *Cranford*. Very good sense of humour, she once told me someone had said to her that she looks like Donald Sutherland.

Sir Alan Bates
British film star most famous for nakedly wrestling Oliver Reed in the film *Women in Love*. Like a British version of Russell Crowe.

Simon Russell Beale
Son of Peter Beale. Classically trained and much-respected Shakespearean actor.

Sir John Betjeman
Poet. Went to my school. They were obsessed with him; every surface of every wall had a portrait of him on it. He's good but when you've been made to study him for five years, it eventually begins to lose its appeal. What's so bad about Slough anyway?

Hugh Bonneville
Lord Grantham. Nuff said.

Peter Bowles
One of the big guns of my father's client list in the 1980s. Famous for appearing in the sitcom *To the Manor Born* alongside Penelope Keith. Once turned up at my father's office in a brand-new Rolls-Royce and told him to look out the window because he had a surprise for him. When my father saw the car he embraced Peter, and thanked him for his generosity, only to be told that he'd bought the car for himself and was just showing it to my father. Sports an impressive moustache.

Gyles Brandreth
Jumper-wearing ex-MP, novelist, comedian, personality and *Dictionary Corner* regular. Old friend of my father's. Gyles is also the only person I've ever appeared on a show with and felt butch.

Martin Clunes
Rubber-faced funny man. One of the Men who Behaved Badly.

Judi Dench

Or as my dad always calls her, 'Judi Darling'. My father's desk is still decorated with a set of shark's teeth that she gave him for his birthday once. He's very proud of them, even though they were clearly her way of hinting that she held agents, as a breed, in pretty low regard.

Julian Fellowes

Now Lord Fellowes, creator of *Downton Abbey*.

James Fox

British actor whose credits include *The Servant*, *Performance* and *The Remains of the Day*. Part of the Fox acting dynasty. Your go-to guy for posh, dashing older men.

Edward Fox

If he wasn't available, though, you could always go for . . . James's brother. Quirky stage veteran. Your man for any British Army officer or colonial shit. Old-fashioned English eccentric but utterly brilliant. The kind of man who still writes letters.

Lady Antonia Fraser

Nobel Prize-winning novelist and widow of Harold Pinter. Once fell asleep at the dinner table while sitting next to my father, when he was mid-anecdote.

Sir John Gielgud

Camp old theatrical legend, lots of Shakespeare and was in *Arthur* (not the Russell Brand one). I imagine if you looked up the word 'queen' in the dictionary, he would be next to it.

Walter Gotell

German-born actor, played General Gogol in Bond films and a lot of Nazi officers. Not an actor who feared being 'typecast'.

Richard E. Grant

Withnail actor who sacked my dad and broke his heart. But he's not bitter about it, honest.

Leslie Grantham

Dirty Den from *EastEnders*. My father represented him. He is also my dad's only working-class friend.

Richard Griffiths

Richard, who sadly passed away earlier this year, played Uncle Monty in *Withnail and I* and Uncle Vernon in *Harry Potter,* though to me he will always be Uncle Richard. My godfather and one of my father's closest friends and clients.

Nigel Havers

The charmer and perennial housewives' favourite. Nigel, now famous for playing devious cad Lewis Archer in *Coronation Street*, starred in a string of movies in the 80s and 90s including Oscar-winning *Chariots of Fire*. Nigel is my godfather and was my dad's best man. He is mentioned a lot in this book and if this is ever made into a film (which is very unlikely) my dad has already said that he wants Nigel to play him . . . though this is mainly because he is still his agent.

Nick Hewer

The man who sits beside and a little bit below Lord Sugar on *The Apprentice*. The only person with a more disdainful sneer in his locker than my father.

Sir Anthony Hopkins

Or, as my dad always calls him, 'Tony' (they barely know each other, so this is a little odd). A Welsh Oscar-winner with a penchant for human flesh.

David Irving
Holocaust denier and historian.

Martin Jarvis
Actor best known for his work on radio. He narrates *Just William*.

Stratford Johns
Generously proportioned South African-born character actor. Was in *Z Cars*.

Jeremy King and Chris Corbin
Restaurant impresarios who started the Caprice and the Ivy and now run, among others, the Wolseley, my dad's favourite restaurant. The two men my father sucks up to more than anyone else in the world.

Michael Kitchen
My other father . . . on screen in the ITV comedy drama *The Good Guys*. Best known for *Foyle's War*.

Robert Lindsay
Played the dad in *My Family*. Member of my father's club, the Garrick.

Sir Trevor McDonald
Dong! dong! Reads the *News at Ten*. His son Jack was a friend of mine at school. Surprisingly good tennis player.

Gina McKee
Geordie actress from *Our Friends in the North* and *Notting Hill*. Murdered by Nigel Havers (in my dad's TV film *Element of Doubt*).

Patrick Macnee
John Steed in *The Avengers*.

Peter Mandelson
Camp Labour Party politician and my father's all-time *bête noire*.

Sir Roger Moore
The name's Bond, James Bond. Friend of Joan Collins.

Sir Kenneth More
Major film star of the 1950s and 60s. Best known for *Reach for the Sky* and *Genevieve*. My father's first star client.

Sir John Mortimer
Writer of *Rumpole of the Bailey* and *A Voyage Round My Father*, an auto-biographical book/play about his relationship with his father. I wanted to call this book *A Voyage Away from My Father,* but the publishers said my demographic wouldn't know who Sir John Mortimer was. So now anyone who didn't know does, and we can all read this book knowing what the true title is. And, incidentally, he was a great friend of *my* father's.

Richard Pasco
Leading actor at the RSC in the 1960s and 70s and at the National Theatre in the 80s. The kind of straight man who would get away with greeting you with six kisses.

Anthony Perkins
Famously played Norman Bates in *Psycho*.

Leslie Phillips
Ding Dong Leslie, a stalwart of the *Carry On* films and best known for playing upper-class pervs. Was briefly a client of my father's on two separate occasions and therefore sacked him twice.

Nigel Rees
Oxford-educated Radio 4 broadcaster.

Christopher Reeve

Actor famous for playing Superman in the 1970s, when Superman was fun and wore pants over his clothes, rather than now, when he just pouts and looks moody.

Alan Rickman

The greatest actor in the world ever. The best ever Sheriff of Nottingham and he was even good in *Love Actually.* My dad never represented him and this is something I have never forgiven him for.

Anton Rodgers

Client and friend of my father's. Mr Sitcom – he starred in two series at the same time on different channels in the 90s, *Fresh/French Fields* on ITV and *May to December* on the BBC.

Peter Sallis

In old-codger sitcom *Last of the Summer Wine.* The voice of Wallace from *Wallace and Gromit*, ironically doesn't like cheese. I made that last bit up – I've met him once and the topic of cheese didn't come up.

Sir Donald Sinden

Ex-client of my father's, distin-guished actor, who has a room named after him at the Garrick Club, which my father regards as the greatest accolade any member could ever have bestowed upon them. The Whitehall Room, he thinks, would have a certain ring to it.

Neil Stacy

One of my father's closest friends. An academic turned actor, best known for appearing in 80s sitcom *Duty Free.* Likes cheese, but only at room temperature.

David Suchet

Poirot. Was in my father's production of Terence Rattigan's *Man and Boy.* I was briefly a runner on this and in charge of getting David's coffee – he takes it black, one sugar.

Mollie Sugden

Mrs Slocombe from *Are You Being Served?* The queen of the double entendre.

Angela Thorne

Actress who also appeared in *To the Manor Born,* as well as numerous shows my father produced. She's my brother Barnaby's godmother and, even more importantly, Rupert Penry Jones's mother.

Dame Dorothy Tutin

Another distinguished actress of stage and screen, known to my father as 'Dotty Darling'. Lived on Putney Common, owned a dog, but not one that looked like her.

Simon Ward

Once played Winston Churchill in the film *Young Winston,* which for my dad is enough to afford him a legendary status. Starred in my father's stage production of *The Winslow Boy.*

Michael Winner

Deceased film producer and an old adversary of my father's.

Afterword

So there you have it. We didn't actually remember 1988 to 2007 all that differently and I assure you that any major inaccuracies are entirely due to Jack's constant search for a cheap laugh, or maybe very occasionally due to my fading memory. But they were good times – well, mostly – and we've loved remembering them together and sharing them with you.

Michael Whitehall

Photographs by Hilary Whitehall

Ten Things I Wish to Correct in This Book

1. Much as I love Nigel Havers, he is not my type and definitely not your father. Serge is not my type and definitely not your father either.

2. I can't believe you have shoe-horned the word 'barren' into this book. It is a horrible word and you should both know better than to use it. Ditto the 'c-word'.

3. Your father is certainly very eccentric and I am absolutely not mad.

4. Your father does not wear pyjamas in bed but he does use earplugs, as we live close to a noisy road. The earplugs have nothing to do with my snoring. I only snore on very rare occasions

5. I do not have a drink problem, although once this book has been published and my friends and family have read it, I may lurch into one!

6. Edwin's aunt was not just bristly, she had a full growth of beard and was also wearing trousers!

7. I have never had or considered having an AGA.

8. I can't believe that Michael thinks we went to the Caribbean for our honeymoon. We went to the Seychelles. Perhaps he went to the Caribbean on honeymoon with his first wife.

9. I had a very warm and close relationship with all of our neighbours despite Michael completely ignoring them.

10. I did not go to the enormous lengths to make you look like Harry Potter as: a) I am not a pushy showbiz mother; b) I have a life and c) you needed very little help to look like Harry Potter. You were Harry Potter.

Hilary Whitehall

Acknowledgements

Special thanks to Nick Hewer, Ben Cavey,
Neil Stacy, Jeremy Austin, Freddy Syborn, Jonathan Hackford,
Neil Forsyth, Anthony Horowitz, Gemma Chan,
Nigel Foster, Janie Hextall, Christopher Matthew, Jo Williams
and family, Antonia Wainman and family, Woose,
Molly Whitehall and Barnaby Whitehall.

And our thanks to Hannah Chambers and her team at
Chambers Management and Katy Follain, Beatrix McIntyre,
Steve Boggs, Katya Shipster, Viviane Basset and
Anna Derkacz and the Penguin sales team.

The night that never was.